JEWELRY&GEMS
THE BUYING GUIDE

Books by Antoinette Matlins
(all GemStone Press)

COLORED GEMSTONES: THE ANTOINETTE MATLINS BUYING GUIDE
*How to Select, Buy, Care for & Enjoy Sapphires, Emeralds, Rubies
and Other Colored Gems with Confidence and Knowledge*
2nd edition

DIAMONDS: THE ANTOINETTE MATLINS BUYING GUIDE
*How to Select, Buy, Care for & Enjoy Diamonds
with Confidence and Knowledge*

ENGAGEMENT & WEDDING RINGS
The Definitive Buying Guide for People in Love
3rd edition

GEM IDENTIFICATION MADE EASY
A Hands-On Guide to More Confident Buying & Selling
3rd edition

JEWELRY & GEMS AT AUCTION
*The Definitive Guide to Buying & Selling at the Auction House
& on Internet Auction Sites*

THE PEARL BOOK: THE DEFINITIVE BUYING GUIDE
How to Select, Buy, Care for & Enjoy Pearls
3rd edition

JEWELRY & GEMS
THE BUYING GUIDE
6th Edition

How to Buy Diamonds, Pearls,
Colored Gemstones, Gold & Jewelry
with Confidence and Knowledge

Antoinette Matlins, P.G.
& Antonio C. Bonanno, F.G.A., P.G., A.S.A.

GEMSTONE PRESS
Woodstock, Vermont

Jewely & Gems: The Buying Guide

2006 Sixth Edition, Paperback, Second Printing
© 2005 Sixth Edition by Antoinette Matlins

2005 Sixth Edition, Hardcover and Paperback, First Printing, Revised, Updated, Expanded
2005 Fifth Edition, Paperback, Fifth Printing
2005 Fifth Edition, Paperback, Fourth Printing
2003 Fifth Edition, Paperback, Third Printing
2002 Fifth Edition, Paperback, Second Printing
2001 Fifth Edition, Hardcover and Paperback, First Printing, Revised, Updated, Expanded
2001 Fourth Edition, Paperback, Third Printing
2000 Fourth Edition, Paperback, Second Printing
1998 Fourth Edition, Hardcover and Paperback, Revised, Updated, Expanded
1998 Third Edition, Paperback, Fifth Printing
1997 Third Edition, Paperback, Fourth Printing
1995 Third Edition, Paperback, Third Printing
1994 Third Edition, Paperback, Second Printing
1993 Third Edition, Hardcover and Paperback, Revised, Updated, Expanded
1992 Second Edition, Paperback, Sixth Printing
1990 Second Edition, Paperback, Fifth Printing
1989 Second Edition, Paperback, Fourth Printing
1989 Second Edition, Paperback, Third Printing
1988 Second Edition, Paperback, Second Printing
1987 Second Edition, Paperback, Revised, Updated, Expanded, Published by GemStone Press,
    Woodstock, Vermont, as *Jewelry & Gems: The Buying Guide*
1985 First Edition, Hardcover, Second Printing
1984 First Edition, Hardcover, Published by Crown Publishers, Inc., New York, as
    The Complete Guide to Buying Gems

For information regarding permission to reprint material from this book, please mail or fax your request in writing to GemStone Press, Permissions Department, at the address / fax number listed below, or e-mail your request to permissions@gemstonepress.com.

The Library of Congress has cataloged the earlier edition as follows:

Matlins, Antoinette Leonard.
    Jewelry & gems, the buying guide : how to buy diamonds, pearls, colored
        gemstones, gold & jewelry with confidence and knowledge / Antoinette L.
        Matlins & Antonio C. Bonanno.— 5th ed.
                p.   cm.
    Includes bibliographical references and index.
    ISBN-13: 978-0-943763-31-6
    ISBN-10: 0-943763-30-4 (hardcover) — ISBN-10: 0-943763-31-2 (paperback)
        1. Jewelry—Purchasing. 2. Precious stones—Purchasing. I. Bonanno, Antonio C.
II. Title.
TS756 .M28 2001
736'.2'0297—dc21   2001002527
Sixth edition hardcover ISBN-13: 978-0-943763-47-7
                         ISBN-10: 0-943763-47-9
Sixth edition paperback ISBN-13: 978-0-943763-44-6
                         ISBN-10: 0-943763-44-4

10 9 8 7 6 5 4 3 2
Manufactured in Canada

Cover Photograph: Sky Hall, Long Beach, Calif.
Cover Design: Rachel Kahn

GemStone Press
A Division of LongHill Partners, Inc.
Sunset Farm Offices, Route 4, P.O. Box 237
Woodstock, VT 05091
Tel: (802) 457-4000   Fax: (802) 457-4004
www.gemstonepress.com

To Ruth Bonanno,
who had nothing—and everything—
to do with it

Contents

PART ONE Getting to Know Gems

PART TWO Diamonds

PART THREE Colored Gemstones

PART FOUR
Design & Style: Getting the Look You Want

PART FIVE Important Advice Before You Buy

PART SIX Important Advice After You Buy

Appendix

Index 294

Price Guides

Special Charts and Tables

Color Photograph Sections

Gemstones
(first color section)

Rare and Distinctive—Fancy Natural-Color Diamonds
Red and Pink Gemstones to Warm Any Heart
Blue Gemstones Offer Heavenly Choices
Yellow and Orange Gems to Brighten the Day
Green Gems That Everyone Will Envy
Opals—A Fiery World of Color
Ornamental Stones and Decorative Art
Popular Diamond Shapes ... Old & New

Jewelry
(second color section)

Platinum—Rarest and Purest of Precious Metals
Gold—A Favorite from Ancient Times ... to the Present
  (two pages)
Pearls—Lustrous Beauty for Every Mood (two pages)
Fine Jewelry Design—Art You Can Wear / New Metals—
  New Looks (two pages)
Popular Ring Styles

Acknowledgments

A lthough we are closely related (father and daughter), my coauthor and I found that in many cases we had different people to thank and different reasons for thanking them. For this reason, we have decided to express our gratitude separately.

I first thank my father, who shared with me in this task, who inspired me as a child and filled me with awe and wonder, and who gave so generously of his knowledge. In addition, I want to thank my husband, Stuart Matlins, for his support, encouragement, and willingness to suffer many hours of loneliness as I labored through the days and nights; and my wonderful daughter, Dawn Leonard-Huxoll, for her love, support, and independence, without which I would never have found the time or focus to attempt this undertaking.

Antoinette Matlins, P.G.

I thank Dr. William F. Foshag, Edward P. Henderson, and James H. Benn, all of the United States National Museum, whose generosity and patience started me as a young teenager in this field; Miss Jewel Glass, Dr. Hugh Miser, Dr. Clarence Ross, and Joseph Fahey, all of the United States Geological Survey; Dr. Frank Hess, of the United States Bureau of Mines; and Dr. Hatton Yoder, of the Geophysical Laboratory of the Carnegie Institution, for their interest and help as my interest and thirst for knowledge grew.

Antonio C. Bonanno, F.G.A., P.G., A.S.A.

Together, we would like to express our appreciation to the following for their help:

Karen Bonanno Ford DeHaas, F.G.A., P.G.
Kathryn Bonanno Patrizzi, F.G.A., P.G.
Kenneth E. Bonanno, F.G.A., P.G.

Preface to the Sixth Edition

It is a great pleasure to know that hundreds of thousands of people have benefited from this book. But whatever the gem or jewel you are seeking, with each passing year it seems there is more to know in order to ensure that you make wise choices. Thus, this latest edition!

Whether seeking a sparkling diamond, lustrous pearls, or an exotic colored gem, there are new shapes with greater brilliance and scintillation, gems discovered in sensuous new colors, and stunning new designs in which to set them. Today we even find gemstones that sing (see chapter 3)! But there are also more things to look *out* for, and more reasons *not* to base your choice on price alone. Now more than ever, understanding as much as possible about what you are buying is the key to getting what you really want, paying the right price, and enjoying your gem and jewelry purchases for years to come.

Jewelry & Gems: The Buying Guide was the first book ever written to help consumers understand what they are really buying, and provide step-by-step guidance to make the purchase of gems and jewelry safer, less confusing, and more pleasurable. Now, almost twenty years, five editions, and over 300,000 copies later, in English, Spanish, Arabic, Greek, Hungarian, and Russian, the information it provides is even more indispensable.

- *Diamonds are being treated in new ways*—in addition to high-pressure/high-temperature (HPHT) methods that transform common tinted diamonds into highly prized colorless and "fancy"-color diamonds, today by using HPHT in combination with other treatment techniques, a wider range of "fancy" colors can be produced, including nature's rarest, *red and pink* (see chapters 5, 6, and 8).
- *Jewelry store counters are filled with colored gemstones that have been artificially treated* to look better than they really are (see chapters 12 and 13).

- *There are more synthetic gems,* many so good they are sometimes erroneously identified and sold as natural gems (see chapters 12 and 13).

One area of special focus in this edition covers the latest enhancement
techniques used to alter the appearance of colored gemstones. This has
been addressed in national media in recent years, but prior to his death
in 1996, my father and co-author was very vocal about the prevalence
of *treated* gems being sold as "natural," and the first edition of this book
was the first to candidly address gemstone treatments. Today, treatments
are even more widespread and are used for an increasing number of gemstones, so it is more important than ever before to understand the marketplace in order to be sure you get what you really want, and pay the
right price for what you get. While this situation is covered in chapter
12, it is such an important issue that I would like to comment on it here.

Exceptionally fine *natural* gemstones are rarer and more costly than
ever before. This scarcity has affected what is available in jewelry stores,
and the choices available to consumers. *Natural* emeralds, rubies, and
sapphires—that is, gems not subjected to any type of artificial treatment
or enhancement—have never been rarer than they are today. While they can
still be found, locating a natural gem in a particular size and quality can
take months of intensive searching, and when one is found, it can command
a price prohibitive to all but the most serious collector or connoisseur.

As the beauty and overall quality of natural gemstones available in the
marketplace began to decline over the past few decades, more and more
enhanced gems were introduced in an effort to meet an ever-increasing
demand for beautiful ruby, emerald, sapphire, and other gemstone jewelry.
Given a choice, most people seeking a lovely piece of jewelry would rather
have a treated gem, at an affordable price, than spend the time and money
necessary to find a natural gem and obtain proper documentation of its
authenticity. As a result, virtually all colored gemstones sold routinely in jewelry stores—including the most important salons worldwide—are treated.

There is nothing wrong with buying an enhanced gem as long as you
know the gem is enhanced, pay a fair price for it, and have been advised
as to whether or not its appearance could change at some future time
(see chapters 12 and 14). Anyone buying any colored gemstone sold in
jewelry stores today should assume it has been treated in some way and

should make sure it has been priced appropriately for what it is. Keep in mind that, unfortunately, many salespeople do not know about treatments and, as a result, fail to disclose this information. In some cases, salespeople really believe that the stones they sell are "natural" and sell them as such, even when this is not the case.

The extensive use of treatments has led to greater reliance on reports from respected gem-testing laboratories, and we encourage anyone buying a fine, rare, "natural" colored gemstone to make sure it has accompanying documentation from a respected laboratory. However, the presence of a laboratory report accompanying a gem is not a guarantee, and you must understand what should be included and how to read a colored gemstone report (see chapter 11). It is also important to know that the increased use of lab reports has resulted in an increase in reports from laboratories that are not reliable and fraudulent reports attributed to respected laboratories, so you must also be sure to verify the laboratory and the report attributed to it, and make sure the report relates to the gem you are buying.

For those who prefer only natural stones, some jewelers now offer sapphire, ruby, and emerald in a wider quality range to provide options at a more affordable price, recognizing that some people prefer a natural stone—even if the color is not optimum or if it has visible flaws—to a treated stone. Even more exciting, however, is the increasing interest in—and respect for—lesser-known gemstone varieties that are *not* routinely treated. Some wonderful choices are now available in a wide range of colors, including ruby red spinel, emerald green tsavorite (a green variety of garnet discovered in the 1970s), blue spinel, and fiery orange "Mandarin" garnet. A full list is provided in chapter 15. These gemstones offer beautiful, affordable, *natural* alternatives to treated gems and can usually be found at fine jewelry stores. If you have difficulty finding what you want, a gemologist or independent jeweler may be able to help you.

On the subject of gemstone investment, we want once again to underscore the need for extreme caution. When we wrote the chapter on gem investment, "A Word about Gemstone Investment," for the first edition of this book, we did not recommend gems for the average investor. However, at that time we discussed some investment pros and cons because, whether or not we thought it wise, "investment" was a word the public was applying all too frequently to gem and jewelry purchases.

Subsequent developments—including major fraudulent international

gemstone investment schemes—necessitate continued caution, so we still
do not recommend gems as an investment for the average buyer.

Gemstone investment can be profitable, and investing in fine *natural-*
colored gemstones is especially alluring at this time because prices have
been held artificially low for several decades, but we cannot emphasize
too strongly the need to exercise extreme caution.

Another important development discussed in this new edition is how
the cutting of a diamond is evaluated. New technology and software
that measures the actual performance of light in a diamond—that measures its brilliance, fire, and sparkle—have led to changes in the definition
of what constitutes an "ideal-cut" diamond and overturned long-held
attitudes. This research has led the Gemological Institute of America to
develop a system for grading the cut of a diamond, and cut grades will
soon be appearing on all GIA diamond grading reports. It has also led
to changes in the cut-grading systems of laboratories that have already
been assigning a cut grade on diamond reports. The term "ideal" may
soon be obsolete (see chapter 4).

In short, today there are more alternatives—natural gems, treated
gems, synthetic gems, and imitation gems—in more colors and more interesting designs than ever before. But the marketplace is also more complicated, and this, combined with changes in the nature of retailing itself
and the increase in the number of jewelry salespeople who lack the knowledge necessary to provide reliable information and answer questions accurately, makes the situation for consumers more confusing than ever.

To help you deal with misleading or fraudulent practices, chapters
that cover some of the most frequently encountered types of fraud and
misrepresentation are included in this book. We want to stress, however,
that the purpose is not to give you false confidence, nor is it to frighten
or discourage you from buying gems and jewelry with confidence. Our
primary purpose in covering this material is to make you less vulnerable
to the allure of fake bargains and to make you aware of the importance
of buying only from knowledgeable, reputable jewelers.

Furthermore, please understand that, while information provided here
may enable you to spot some fakes or detect some treatments, no book can
make you an expert. Be sure to follow the advice we offer regarding what
questions to ask, what to get in writing, and how to check it out to be
sure of your purchase. To further pursue the field of gem identification,
treatment, and enhancement, see our book *Gem Identification Made Easy,*

which is a nontechnical book for the lay person (GemStone Press, P.O. Box 237, Woodstock, VT 05091, 800-962-4544, www.gemstonepress.com, $36.95 plus $3.95 shipping/handling).

Whatever your interest in gems, we hope they give you the pleasure and joy they have given us throughout the years. And we hope that *Jewelry & Gems: The Buying Guide* will bring greater clarity to the experience for you, and help make your gem and jewelry buying experience all that it should be: an experience filled with excitement, anticipation, romance, and pleasure.

Antoinette Matlins

Introduction

Throughout history, gems have been a much sought-after commodity. Their beauty, rarity, and inherent "magical powers" have made them the symbol of kings, the symbol of power, the symbol of wealth, and in more recent history the symbol of love. Every civilization, every society, grandly exhibits mankind's fascination with and desire to possess these beautiful gifts of nature.

As the growth of the American jewelry business attests, we are no different from our ancestors. We too share the fascination, appreciation, and desire to possess beautiful gems. If history serves as a sound indicator of taste, we can rest assured that the lure of gems will be just as great in future generations. At least once in a lifetime, nearly every American has an occasion to buy or receive a gem.

The experience of purchasing a gem can be a magical one. It can be filled with excitement, anticipation, and pleasure—and it is to that end that this book is dedicated. The purpose of this book is to provide a basic but complete consumer's guide to buying a gem, whether it be for one's own personal pleasure, for a gift, or for investment. It is designed and written for a wide market—husbands, wives, or parents buying gems as gifts for loved ones for some special occasion; young couples looking for an engagement ring to last a lifetime; tourists, business travelers, and service men and women traveling throughout the world hoping to pick up real bargain gems while they are near the mines; investors looking for a hedge against inflation; or those who are simply interested in gems, perhaps as a hobby. It will explain the variables that affect cost, provide information regarding fraudulent practices, and provide lists of relevant questions that should be asked of a jeweler. It will not make you a gemologist, but it will make you a smart shopper who will be able to derive pleasure from what can become a truly exciting, interesting, and safe experience.

From the time I was a small child, I had the pleasure of being surrounded by beautiful gems and had a unique opportunity to learn the gem business. Having a father who was a well-known gemologist, appraiser, and collector, I was able to spend hours marveling at stones—those in his own private collection as well as those brought to him to be professionally appraised.

Dinner conversation usually centered on the day's events at my father's office. Sometimes he would thrill us with an account of a particularly fine or rare gem he had had the pleasure of identifying or verifying. But too often the subject would turn to some poor, unknowing consumer who had been victimized. It might have been a soldier who thought he had purchased genuine sapphires in Asia, and learned sadly that they were either glass or synthetic; or a housewife who bought a "diamond" ring at an estate sale, only to learn that the stone was a white sapphire or zircon. It might have been a doctor who thought he had purchased a fine, natural "canary" diamond as a gift for his wife, who learned to his dismay that the beautiful bright yellow color was not natural at all but the result of special treatment, so the stone was not worth anywhere near what he had paid for it. But occasionally, my father would have a wonderful story to share. One in particular illustrates especially well how complex the gem business can be. One day an average-looking elderly woman came into my father's office with a green stone she wanted identified and appraised. She had already taken the stone to a well-known jeweler, who also had an excellent reputation as a gemologist-appraiser. The jeweler told her that the stone was a tourmaline worth only a few hundred dollars. She was very disappointed, since it was a family heirloom that she had believed for many years was a fine emerald. Her own mother had assured her of the fact. When she questioned the jeweler about its being an emerald, he laughed and told her that was impossible. He was the expert, so she accepted his appraisal, as most people would.

Many months later, at the insistence of a friend who knew of my father's reputation from the curator of the Smithsonian's gem collection, she sought my father's opinion. In fact, her stone was a genuine emerald, one of the finest my father had ever seen. He could barely contain his excitement about the stone. It was worth about $60,000 even then, over 40 years ago. Fortunately, the woman learned its true identity and value before it was too late.

My first response upon hearing the story was anger at the "dishonest" jeweler, but, as my father explained, he was not dishonest. Dad actually went to see this man, because he knew his reputation was good.

The jeweler discussed the stone with my father, and it became clear that he genuinely believed it to have been a tourmaline. On the basis of the woman's "ordinary" appearance and the absence of any eye-visible characteristics so typical of an emerald, he drew the immediate conclusion that the stone could only be a green tourmaline. His experience with emeralds was limited to those of lesser quality, with their telltale inclusions. His limited experience, combined with his impression of the woman, led him to make an assumption regarding the identity of the stone without even performing any definitive test. He made an incorrect identification of this unusually fine stone, but certainly he was not acting dishonestly in the hope of picking up a steal.

This anecdote illustrates the danger consumers frequently face when they come to buy gems. They are vulnerable not only to intentional fraud but also to unintentional misrepresentation resulting from a jeweler's lack of experience and knowledge. The very person on whom one would naturally rely—the jeweler—sometimes lacks sufficient knowledge about the gems he is selling. Fortunately, such educational institutions as the Gemological Institute of America (GIA), in New York and Los Angeles; our school, the Columbia School of Gemology, near Washington, D.C.; and an increasing number of colleges, universities, and associations across the country that offer gemology courses are helping to rectify this situation. More and more, reputable jewelers are concerned with increasing their own knowledge and that of their salespeople, not only to protect their valued customers but also to protect themselves!

Another incident proves how rewarding education can be. A former student of my father's was visiting in a midwestern city. She decided to go to some pawnshops to kill time, and in one shop she discovered a beautiful diamond-and-emerald ring. The pawnbroker told her that the diamonds were of an unusually fine quality, which her examination confirmed. The ring was also beautifully designed, with outstanding workmanship. Her question was whether the emerald was genuine or synthetic. As she examined the stone she began to suspect it was genuine. But she didn't have the right equipment with her to be sure. The $500 price was appropriate for the diamonds and the gold setting alone, indicating that the pawnbroker believed the emerald was synthetic. But since the visitor liked the ring, and the price was fair, she was willing to take a chance that it might in fact be genuine. Upon her return to Washington she brought the ring to my father's lab, where they proceeded immediately to examine the emerald. It was genuine. Its value was many times what she had paid; it could easily have sold for over $30,000 at a retail jewelry store. She sold it for a very handsome profit. The student profited because of her knowledge; the pawnbroker lost an opportunity because of his lack of it.

As the result of my father's long experience in the gem business, and my own professional experience, I felt that a book about gems—written just for the consumer—was desperately needed. The original edition of *Jewelry & Gems: The Buying Guide* was the first book ever written for the average gemstone consumer. This new edition remains the most comprehensive and accessible gemstone buying guide on the market today, and it is just as needed as the first edition was twenty years ago. The cost of gems is greater than ever before, and projections indicate that prices will continue to rise. Thus, in a market where jewelers and gem dealers are often not as knowledgeable as they should be, where the price of gems continues to rise, and where consumers consider ever more frequently buying gems for investment, the gem buyer must become more informed. A consumer cannot learn to be an expert in gems through reading a single book; a gemologist is, after all, a highly trained, skilled professional. What we can provide here is some basic information that can make buying gems a more pleasurable, less vulnerable experience.

Jewelry & Gems: The Buying Guide covers everything you, the consumer, need to know before buying any of the most popular gems. I hope you will find as much pleasure as I have found in getting to know gems, and that your future purchases will be happy ones.

Antoinette Matlins

PART ONE

Getting to Know Gems

1

Becoming Intimate
with Gems

Gems should never be bought as a gamble—the uneducated consumer will always lose. This is a basic rule of thumb. The best way to take the gamble out of buying a particular gem is to familiarize yourself with the gem. While the average consumer can't hope to make the same precise judgments as a qualified gemologist, whose scientific training and wealth of practical experience provide a far greater database from which to operate, the consumer can learn to judge a stone as a "total personality" and learn what the critical factors are—color, clarity (also referred to in the trade as "perfection"), cut, brilliance, and weight—and how to balance them in judging the gem's value. Learning about these factors and spending time in the marketplace looking, listening, and asking questions before making the purchase will prepare you to be a wise buyer more likely to get what you really want, at a fair price.

Try to learn as much as you can about the gem you want to buy. Examine stones owned by your family and friends, and compare stones at several different jewelry stores, noting differences in shades of color, brilliance, and cut. Go to a good, established jewelry store and ask to see fine stones. If the prices vary, ask why. Let the jeweler point out differences in color, cut, or brilliance, and if he can't, go to another jeweler with greater expertise. Begin to develop an eye for what constitutes a fine stone by looking, listening, and asking good questions.

Here are five key questions to ask yourself initially before you consider buying any stone:

1. Is the color what you desire?
2. Is the shape what you want?
3. Does it have liveliness, or "zip"?

3

4. Do you like it and feel excited by it?

5. Can you afford it?

If you answer yes to all five questions, you are ready to examine the specific stone more carefully.

The Six Key Steps in Examining a Stone

1. *Whenever possible, examine stones unmounted.* They can be examined more thoroughly out of their settings, and defects cannot be hidden by the mounting or side stones.

2. *Make sure the gem is clean.* If you are buying a stone from a retail jeweler, ask that it be cleaned for you. If you are not in a place where it can be cleaned professionally, breathe on the stone in a huffing manner in order to steam it with your breath, and then wipe it with a clean handkerchief. This will at least remove the superficial film of grease.

3. *Hold the unmounted stone so that your fingers touch only the girdle* (the edge where top and bottom meet). Putting your fingers on the table (top) and/or pavilion (bottom) will leave traces of oil, which will affect color and brilliance.

   The *careful* use of tweezers instead of fingers is recommended only if you feel comfortable using them. Make sure you know how to use them, and get the permission of the owner before picking up the stone. It is easy for the stone to pop out of the tweezers and to become damaged or lost, and you could be held responsible.

4. *View the gem under proper lighting.* Many jewelers use numerous incandescent spotlights, usually recessed in dropped ceilings. Some use special spotlights that can make any gemstone—even glass imitations—look fantastic.

   Fluorescent lights are what professionals use for grading, but they may also adversely affect the appearance of some gems. Diamonds will not show as much fire under fluorescent lighting, and some colored gems, such as rubies, look much better under incandescent light. We recommend looking at stones in several types of light.

   The light source should come from above or behind you, shining down and through the stone, so that the light traveling through the stone is reflected back up to your eye.

5. **Rotate the stone in order to view it from different angles.**
6. **If you are using a loupe, focus it both on the surface and into the interior.** To focus into the interior, shift the stone slowly, raising or lowering it, until you focus clearly on all depths within it. This is important because if you focus on the top only, you won't see what is in the interior of the stone.

How to Use a Loupe

A loupe (pronounced *loop*) is a special type of magnifying glass. The loupe can be very helpful in many situations, even for the beginner. With a loupe you can check a stone for chips or scratches or examine certain types of noticeable inclusions more closely. Remember, however, that even with a loupe, you will not have the knowledge or skill to see or understand the many telltale indicators that an experienced jeweler or gemologist could spot. No book can provide you with that knowledge or skill. Do not allow yourself to be deluded, or let a little knowledge give you a false confidence. Nothing will more quickly alienate a reputable jeweler or mark you faster as easy prey for the disreputable dealer.

The loupe is a very practical tool to use once you master it, and with practice it will become more and more valuable. The correct type is a 10x, or ten-power, "triplet," which can be obtained from any optical supply house. The triplet type is recommended because it corrects two problems other types of magnifiers have: traces of color normally found at the outer edge of the lens, and visual distortion, also usually at the outer edge of the lens. In addition, the loupe must have a black housing around the lens, not chrome or gold, either of which might affect the color you see in the stone.

The loupe *must* be 10x because the United States Federal Trade Commission requires grading to be done under ten-power magnification. Any flaw that does not show up under 10x magnification is considered nonexistent for grading purposes.

With a few minutes' practice you can easily learn to use the loupe. Here's how:

1. Hold the loupe between the thumb and forefinger of either hand.
2. Hold the stone or jewelry similarly in the other hand.
3. Bring both hands together so that the fleshy parts just below the

thumbs are pushed together and braced by the lower portion of each hand just above the wrists (the wrist portion is actually a pivot point).

4. Now move both hands up to your nose or cheek, with the loupe as close to your eye as possible. If you wear eyeglasses, you do not have to remove them.

5. Get a steady hand. With gems it's very important to have steady hands for careful examination. With your hands still together and braced against your face, put your elbows on a table. (If a table isn't available, brace your arms against your chest or rib cage.) If you do this properly you will have a steady hand.

A 10x Triplet Loupe

How to hold a loupe
when examining a stone

Practice with the loupe, keeping it approximately one inch (more or less) from your eye, and about an inch from the object being examined. Learn to see through it clearly. A 10x loupe is difficult to focus initially, but with a little practice it will become easy. You can practice on any object that is difficult to see—the pores in your skin, a strand of hair, a pinhead, or your own jewelry.

Play with the item being examined. Rotate it slowly, tilt it back and forth while rotating it, and look at it from different angles and different directions. It won't take long before you are able to focus easily on anything you wish to examine. If you aren't sure about your technique, a knowledgeable jeweler will be happy to help you learn to use the loupe correctly.

What the Loupe Can Tell You

With practice and experience (and further education if you're really serious), a loupe can tell even the amateur a great deal. For a gemologist it can help determine whether the stone is natural, synthetic, glass, or a doublet (a composite stone, to be discussed later) and reveal characteristic flaws, blemishes, or cracks. In other words, the loupe can provide the necessary information to help you know whether the stone is in fact what it is supposed to be.

For the beginner, the loupe is useful in seeing these features:

1. *The workmanship that went into the cutting.* For example, is the symmetry of the stone balanced? Does it have the proper number of facets for its cut? Is the proportion good? Few cutters put the same time and care into cutting glass as they do into a diamond.

2. *Chips, cracks, or scratches on the facet edges, planes, or table.* While zircon, for example, looks very much like diamond because of its pronounced brilliance and relative hardness, it chips easily. Therefore, careful examination of a zircon will often show chipping, especially on the top and around the edges. Glass, which is very soft, will often show scratches. Normal wear can cause it to chip or become scratched. Also, if you check around the prongs, the setter may even have scratched it while bending the prongs to hold the stone.

    In such stones as emeralds, the loupe can also help you determine whether or not any natural cracks are really serious, how close they are to the surface, how deep they run, or how many are readily visible.

3. *The sharpness of the facet edges.* Harder stones will have a sharp edge, or sharper boundaries between adjoining planes or facets, whereas many imitations are softer, so that under the loupe the edges between the facets are less sharp and have a more rounded appearance.

4. *Bubbles, inclusions, and flaws.* Many flaws and inclusions that cannot be seen with the naked eye are easily seen with the loupe. But remember, many are not easily seen unless you are very experienced. The presence of inclusions is not as serious in colored stones as in diamonds, and they don't usually significantly reduce

the value of the stone. However, the *kind* of inclusions seen in colored stones can be important. They often provide the necessary key to positive identification, determine whether a stone is natural or synthetic, and possibly locate the origin of the stone, which may significantly affect the value. With minimal experience, the amateur can also learn to spot the characteristic bubbles and swirl lines associated with glass.

The loupe can tell you a great deal about the workmanship that went into cutting a gem. It can help a professional decide whether a gem is natural, synthetic, a doublet, or glass. It can provide the clues about the gem's authenticity, its durability, and its point of origin. But spotting these clues takes lots of practice and experience.

When you use a loupe, remember that you won't see what the experienced professional will see, but with a little practice, it can still be a valuable tool and might save you from a costly mistake.

2

Looking for a Gem
That's a "Cut Above"

One of the most important things to learn is how to look at a gem, even if you won't see all that a gemologist will. Let's begin by making sure you understand the terms you will be hearing and using to describe what you want—especially terms pertaining to the stone's "cut" and the names for the parts of a cut stone.

It's important to be familiar with a few general terms that are commonly used in reference to faceted stones. The parts of a stone can vary in proportion and thus affect its brilliance, beauty, and desirability. This will be discussed later in greater detail.

- *Girdle.* The girdle is the edge or border of the stone that forms its perimeter; it is the edge formed where the top portion of the stone meets the bottom portion—its "dividing line." This is the part usually grasped by the prongs of a setting.
- *Crown.* The crown is also called the *top* of the stone. This is simply the upper portion of the stone: the part above the girdle.
- *Pavilion.* The pavilion is the bottom portion of the stone, the part from the girdle to the "point" at the bottom.
- *Culet.* The culet is the lowest part or point of the stone. It may be missing in some stones, which can indicate damage, or, particularly with colored stones, it may not be part of the original cut.
- *Table.* The table is the flat top of the stone and is the

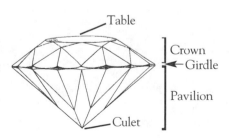

Parts of a faceted stone

9

stone's largest facet, often called the face. The term *table spread* is used to describe the width of the table facet, often expressed as a percentage of the total width of the stone.

The Cut of the Stone

The most important—and least understood—factor that must be evaluated when one considers any gem is the *cutting*. When we talk about cut, we are not referring to the shape but to the care and precision used in creating a finished gem from the rough. There are many popular shapes for gemstones. Each shape affects the overall look of the stone, but if the stone is cut well its brilliance and value endure no matter what shape it is. For the average consumer, choosing a shape is simply a matter of personal taste. Some of the most popular shapes are pictured. New shapes are discussed in chapter 4.

Classic Shapes

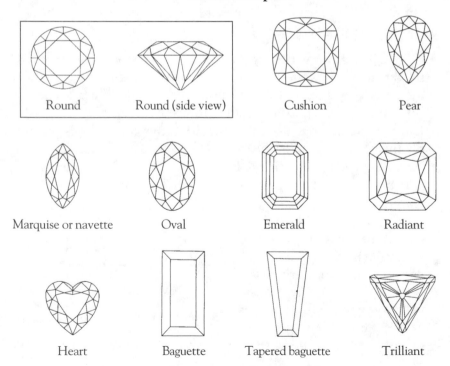

Round   Round (side view)   Cushion   Pear

Marquise or navette   Oval   Emerald   Radiant

Heart   Baguette   Tapered baguette   Trilliant

Make Makes a Big Difference

The shape of the stone may affect the personality it displays, but it is the overall cutting that releases its full beauty. A term used by professionals to describe the overall quality of the cutting is *make*. This term pertains to the overall precision of the cutting, especially the proportioning and finish (polish and symmetry). Having a "good make" is especially important in diamonds. A diamond with an "excellent make" will sell for much more than one with a "fair make." The difference in price between a well-cut diamond and one that is poorly cut can be as much as 50 percent or more. Even more important, careless cutting, or cutting to get the largest possible stone from the rough, can sometimes result in faults that may make a stone more fragile and vulnerable to breakage. Such stones should sell for much less, although the fault may not be visible without careful examination by an expert. Here we will discuss cutting in a general way. It will be discussed in greater detail later.

How to Know If a Stone Is Well Cut

The precision of the cutting dramatically affects the beauty and value of any stone. This is especially true in *faceted* stones, those on which a series of tiny flat planes (facets or faces) have been cut and polished. (Nonfaceted stones are called *cabochons;* these are discussed in part 3.) You should also keep in mind that there are several cutting styles used for faceted stones: brilliant cut, as seen in round diamonds (using many triangular and kite-shaped facets); step cut, as seen in emerald-cut stones (using trapezoid or rectangular facets); and mixed cut, which combines both styles.

Whichever faceting style is used, by following some general guidelines for looking at faceted gemstones, you can better determine both the quality of the stone and the quality of the cut. The first thing to keep in mind is that if the basic material is of good quality, the way it is cut will make the difference between a dull, lifeless stone and a beautiful, brilliant one. In diamonds, the cutting and proportioning have the greatest influence on the stone's brilliance and fire. In colored gems, the perfection of the cut is not as important as with diamonds, but proportioning remains critical because it significantly affects the depth of color as well as the stone's brilliance and liveliness.

Look at the stone face up, through the top (table). This is the most critical area to view, since this is the one most often noticed. If you are looking at a diamond, does it seem to sparkle and dance across the whole stone, or are there dead spots? In a colored gem, does the color look good from this direction? Is the table centered and symmetrical?

A quick way to check the symmetry of a round diamond is to look at the table edges. The lines should be straight, regular, and parallel to one another. The table edges should form a regular octagon, with the edges meeting in sharp points. If the lines of the table are wavy, the overall symmetry is not good, and the symmetry of the adjoining facets will also be affected.

Table centered
but not symmetrical

Table off-center
and asymmetrical

Table centered and
symmetrical—the ideal

Next, look at the stone from the side. Note the proportion of the stone both above and below the girdle.

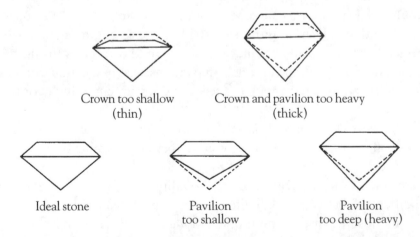

Crown too shallow
(thin)

Crown and pavilion too heavy
(thick)

Ideal stone

Pavilion
too shallow

Pavilion
too deep (heavy)

The stone's proportion—whether it is too thin or too thick—will have a marked effect on its overall beauty. With colored stones, the relative terms of thickness or thinness vary greatly because of the inherent optical properties of different gems. As a general guide when you are considering colored stones, keep in mind these three points:

1. If the stone appears lively and exhibits an appealing color when viewed through the table, no matter how the proportion appears (thick or thin), it is usually correct and acceptable proportioning for that particular stone.
2. The depth of color (tone) will become darker as the stone is cut thicker, particularly if the bottom portion (pavilion) is deep and broad.
3. A stone's depth of color will become lighter as the stone is cut thinner. This is especially important when you are considering a pastel-colored stone. A pastel stone should always have fairly deep proportioning.

The effects of cut and proportioning will be discussed in greater detail in parts 2 and 3, as the factors affecting cut and proportioning are somewhat different for diamonds and colored gems. It is an important first step, however, to become aware of general views and to begin to have a feeling about what looks "right."

Before Beginning

As you shop for any fine gem or piece of jewelry, keep in mind the importance of visiting fine jewelry stores to look at stones and compare them. Many of the factors discussed in the following chapters will become clearer when you have actual stones before you to examine, and you will gain a deeper understanding and appreciation for the gem you are considering. Knowledgeable jewelers will also be happy to take time to help you understand differences in quality and cost.

Also keep in mind the importance of buying only from a well-trained, reputable jeweler. Remember, you are not an expert. The information provided here should help you begin your search more confidently and gain insights that will make the experience more fun, more challenging, and more fulfilling. But perhaps just as important, we hope it will help you make a wiser decision about the jeweler with whom you decide to do business, and about his or her knowledge, professionalism, and integrity. If so, this book will have provided a valuable service and perhaps saved you from a costly mistake.

PART TWO

Diamonds

3

The Magic of Diamonds

The diamond has been one of the most coveted gems in history. Uncut diamonds adorned the suits of armor of the great knights; cut diamonds have adorned the crowns of kings and queens throughout the ages. Today the diamond is internationally recognized as a symbol of love and betrothal and is the recipient of increasing interest as a means of investment.

The diamond has been credited with many magical powers. At one time it was considered the emblem of fearlessness and invincibility; the mere possession of a diamond would endow the wearer with superior strength, bravery, and courage. It was also believed that a diamond could drive away the devil and all spirits of the night.

During the 1500s, diamonds were looked upon as talismans that could enhance the love of a husband for his wife. In the Talmud, a gem that from its description was probably a diamond was worn by the high priest and served to prove innocence or guilt. If an accused person was guilty, the stone grew dim; if the person was innocent, it shone more brilliantly than ever.

Besides being colorless, diamonds occur in every color of the rainbow. The Hindus classed diamonds according to the four castes. The Brahmin diamond (colorless) gave power, friends, riches, and good luck; the Kshatriya (brown/champagne) prevented old age; Vaisya (the color of a kodali flower) brought success; and the Sudra (a diamond with the sheen of a polished blade—probably gray or black) brought all types of good fortune. Red and yellow diamonds were exclusively royal gems, for kings alone.

Diamonds have been associated with almost everything from producing sleepwalking to producing invincibility and spiritual ecstasy. Even sexual prowess has been strongly attributed to the diamond. There is a catch, however, to all the mythical powers associated with this remarkable gem. One must find the diamond "naturally" in order to experience its magic, for it loses its powers if acquired by purchase. However, when a diamond is offered as a pledge of love or friendship, its potency may return—another good reason for its presence in the engagement ring!

What Is Diamond?

Chemically speaking, a diamond is the simplest of all gemstones. It is plain, crystallized carbon—the same substance, chemically, as the soot left on the inside of a glass globe after the burning of a candle; it is the same substance used in "lead" pencils.

The diamond differs from these in its crystal form, which gives it the desirable properties that have made it so highly prized—its hardness, which gives it unsurpassed wearability; its brilliance; and its fire. (But note that while diamond is the hardest natural substance known, it *can* be chipped or broken if hit hard from certain angles, and if the "girdle"—the edge of the diamond that forms the perimeter—has been cut too thin, it can be chipped with even a modest blow.)

The transparent white (or, more correctly, *colorless*) diamond is the most popular variety, but diamond also occurs in colors. When the color is prominent it is called a *fancy* diamond. Diamond is frequently found in nice yellow and brown shades. Colors such as pink, light blue, light green, and lavender occur much more rarely. In diamonds, the colors seen are usually pastel. Deep colors in hues of red, green, and blue are extremely rare. Historically, most colored diamonds have sold for more than their colorless counterparts, except for light yellow or brown varieties. Yellow or brown in *very* pale shades may not be fancy diamonds but *off-color* stones that are very common and sell for much less than colorless diamonds or those with a true "fancy" color.

India was one of the earliest known sources of diamond, and the most important, until the eighteenth-century discovery of diamonds in Brazil. In the nineteenth century, a major diamond discovery was made in South Africa, and the twentieth century saw diamond discoveries in other African nations such as Botswana and Angola, and in Russia, Australia, and most recently Canada. Commercial diamond mining is also taking place in the United States.

Many diamonds mined today have no "jewelry" value because they are too tinted and heavily flawed, but they are used for many industrial purposes. Colorless and fancy-color diamonds remain rare, with red diamond being the rarest and most valuable of all gems.

The Four Factors That Determine Diamond Value

Diamond quality and value are determined by four factors, which are called the "four Cs." They are often listed as follows:

1. Color (body color or *absence* of color)
2. Clarity (degree of flawlessness)
3. Cutting and proportioning (often referred to as the *make*)
4. Carat weight (which affects the size)

In terms of determining beauty, however, we would rank them in a different order:

1. Cutting and proportioning
2. Color
3. Clarity
4. Carat weight

Finding the Right Combination

Keep in mind, however, that the key to being happy with your diamond purchase is understanding how each of these four Cs affects beauty and durability, cost, and the stone *as a whole*. It may sound complicated at first, but when you begin looking at stones you'll see it really isn't. With a little experience, you'll decide which Cs are most important to you, and you'll know what to look for to get the right combination—one that meets your emotional *and* financial needs.

Because each factor is a lesson in itself, we have devoted a chapter to each. We will begin with a discussion of diamond cutting and proportioning because it is the least understood and because we think it's the most important factor in terms of the stone's beauty. Equally important, as we mentioned earlier, the cutting of a diamond has a significant effect on cost and can even affect the stone's durability.

4

The Importance of
Cut & Proportion

It is important to distinguish exactly what "cut" means in reference to diamonds and other stones. *Cut* does not mean *shape*. Shape pertains to the outline of the diamond's perimeter. The selection of shape is a matter of individual preference. No matter which shape is selected, its *cutting* must be evaluated.

There are several different cutting styles: *brilliant* cut, *step* cut, or *mixed* cut. A brilliant cut uses many facets, usually triangular and kite-shaped, arranged in a particular way to create maximum brilliance. A step cut uses fewer facets, usually rectangular or trapezoid in shape, arranged in a more linear pattern (as you see in the emerald cut). Although usually less brilliant than those cut in a brilliant style, step-cut diamonds can produce a lively, fiery stone with a very elegant and under-stated personality. You often see step-cut triangle, square, and trapezoid shapes in Art Deco period jewelry (1920s). A mixed-cut style incorporates elements from both the step-cut and brilliant-cut styles.

The term "cut"—also referred to as a stone's "*make*"—is especially important because of its effect on the beauty and personality of a diamond. When we evaluate the cut, we are really judging the stone's proportioning and finish, the two factors that are most directly related to producing the *fire* (the lovely rainbow colors that flash from within) and *brilliance* (the liveliness, the sparkle) that sets diamond apart from all other gems. Regardless of the shape or cutting style, a stone with an excellent make will be exciting, while a stone with a poor make will look lifeless; it will lack the sparkle and personality we identify with diamond. In addition, diamonds are often cut to make them *appear* larger. But a stone that looks much larger than another of the same weight will not be as beautiful as a smaller stone that is properly cut.

Differences in cutting can also affect the *durability* of a diamond. Some cutting faults weaken the stone and make it more susceptible to breaking or chipping.

Fine cutting requires skill and experience, takes more time, and results in greater loss of the "rough" from which the stone is being cut, resulting in a stone that yields less weight when finished. For all these reasons, a well-cut diamond commands a premium and will cost much more than one that is cut poorly.

There are many popular shapes for diamonds. Each shape affects the overall look of the stone, but if the stone is cut well, beauty and value endure no matter which shape you choose. We will begin our discussion of diamond cutting with the round brilliant cut, since this is the most popular shape. (57 + culet)

A modern round brilliant-cut diamond has fifty-eight facets. There are thirty-three on the top, twenty-four on the bottom, plus the culet—the "point" at the bottom, which normally is another tiny facet (although many diamonds today are cut without a culet). Round brilliant-cut stones that are small in size are referred to as "full-cut" to distinguish them from "single-cut" stones that have only seventeen facets or "Swiss-cut" with only thirty-three facets. Older pieces of jewelry such as heirloom diamond bands, or inexpensive pieces containing numerous stones, often contain these cuts instead of full-cut stones. They have less brilliance and liveliness than full-cuts, but with fewer facets they are easier and less expensive to cut. Jewelry containing single- or Swiss-cut stones should sell for less than jewelry with full-cut stones.

When a round brilliant-cut diamond is cut well, its shape displays the most liveliness because it enables the most light to be reflected back up through the top. This means that round brilliant-cut diamonds will have greater brilliance, overall, than other shapes, but other shapes can also be very lively. New shapes are also appearing, some of which compare very favorably to round stones for overall brilliance and liveliness.

As a rule of thumb, if the top portion of the stone (the crown) appears to be roughly one-third of the pavilion depth (distance from girdle to culet), the proportioning is probably acceptable (see diagram on the following page).

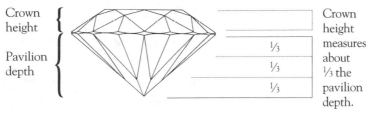

Crown height {

Pavilion depth {

Crown height measures about ⅓ the pavilion depth.

⅓

⅓

⅓

A well-proportioned stone

Types of Diamond Proportioning

The proportioning—especially the height of the crown in relation to the depth of the pavilion, and the width of the table facet in relation to the width of the stone—is what determines how much brilliance and fire the stone will have. Several formulas for correct proportioning have been developed for round diamonds. Stones that adhere to these very precise formulas are considered to have an "ideal" make and will cost more than other diamonds because of the extra time and skill required to cut them, and because more diamond "rough" is lost in the cutting.

How Cutting Affects Brilliance

Light Reflection in an Ideally Proportioned Diamond
Ideal proportions ensure the maximum brilliance.
When light enters a properly cut diamond, it is reflected from facet to facet, and then back up through the top, exhibiting maximum fire and sparkle.

Light Reflection in a Diamond Cut Too Deep
In a diamond that is cut too deep, much of the light is reflected to opposite facets at the wrong angle and is lost through the sides. The diamond appears dark in the center.

Light Reflection in a Diamond Cut Too Shallow
A diamond cut too shallow (to make it look larger) loses brilliance. The eye sees a ring of dull reflection instead of the great brilliance of a well-cut diamond.

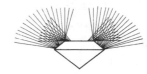

What Is Ideal?

Diamond cutting is an art form that is still evolving, and technological advances continue to shed new insights on how cutting affects the way light travels through diamond to create a scintillating stone. Today there are several slightly differing formulas for cutting an "ideal" stone, and there is no consensus as to what is "best," but each results in an exceptionally beautiful stone. Generally speaking, diamonds that are cut with smaller tables exhibit more fire; those with larger tables exhibit more brilliance. Larger tables seem to be more in fashion today. But, as common sense may tell you here, both can't excel in the same stone. A larger table can create greater brilliance but may cause some reduction in fire; a smaller table area can increase fire but may reduce brilliance. The ideal would be a compromise that would allow the greatest brilliance and fire simultaneously. No one has come to agreement, however, on what the percentages should be, since some people prefer fire to brilliance, and vice versa. This is one reason why there are several different types of proportioning found in diamonds, and "best" is usually a matter of personal preference.

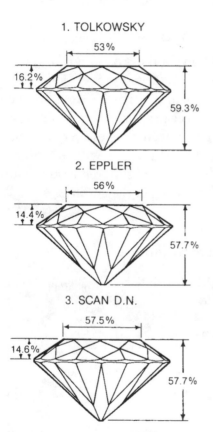

1. TOLKOWSKY
53%
16.2%
59.3%

2. EPPLER
56%
14.4%
57.7%

3. SCAN D.N.
57.5%
14.6%
57.7%

Three standards for "ideal" diamond proportioning

In 1919, Marcel Tolkowsky developed what he thought would be the best combination of angles to allow light to enter the stone and be reflected back in such a way as to create the most vivid fire combined with intense brilliance. The Tolkowsky cut provided the basis for the modern American ideal make, but today there are several variations of Tolkowsky's formula, some with "brand" names such as the *Lazare Kaplan Ideal®*, the *EightStar®* (which exhibits eight perfectly aligned arrows that can be seen with a special viewer), and the *Hearts on Fire®* (which produces a hearts-and-arrows pattern that can be seen with a special viewer). Whatever "ideal" you choose, each results in a very beautiful diamond, but you must compare them for yourself to discover which "ideal" you prefer.

EightStar® Diamond

The "Ideal" May Not Always Be Ideal

We should also caution you against diamonds that are described as "ideal" but really are not. Such diamonds are graded "ideal" because they have a depth percentage and a table percentage that are in the "ideal" range, but the *particular* table percentage is not correct for the *particular* depth percentage. These stones may sell for a premium because of their "ideal" grade, but will lack the beauty of other "ideal" cut stones, and are often less beautiful than stones that have been cut with proportions and percentages not currently considered "ideal." We've seen diamonds cut to "ideal" proportions that are not as brilliant and fiery as diamonds cut to non-ideal proportions and vice versa. And to compound matters further, some people simply like the look of diamonds that have tables that are wider than what is currently considered "ideal." We've even seen diamonds with tables exceeding 64 percent that were surprisingly beautiful and very desirable.

What Is "Ideal" Today May Not Be Called "Ideal" Tomorrow

While no one questions the importance of cutting on the beauty of a diamond, the term "ideal" may soon become obsolete. Years of research by major laboratories, and the development of advanced technology, has changed our prior understanding of the factors affecting brilliance, fire, and scintillation in diamonds. Using new instrumentation that actually measures the performance of light within the stone—how much brilliance and fire is produced—researchers have learned that proportioning is only *one* of *numerous* factors that can affect the stone's beauty and liveliness. For example, altering the length of certain facets on the top and bottom of a diamond can result in a stone with a table or depth percentage outside of today's "ideal" parameters but in which there is even greater brilliance and fire than one cut *within* the "ideal" parameters.

The most important outcome of the research is that we are seeing changes that allow for a broader range of proportioning for top grades. Cut grades at the American Gem Society Laboratory (AGSL) will soon be "performance-based" rather than "proportion-based" because they will be using state-of-the-art ray tracing software to measure the light *performance*—the quality and quantity of light being returned to the viewer—in addition to proportions, symmetry, polish, and other factors. In addition, the Gemological Institute of America, which has never included a cut grade on diamond grading reports, has developed new software based on years of research that also incorporates light performance with other important factors, and with which they will soon begin to evaluate and assign cut grades on reports.

As a result of these changes, even the term "ideal" itself has come under scrutiny. Labs such as the AGSL do not use this term, nor will the GIA when it adds cut grades to its reports; GIA will use the terms "Excellent," "Very Good," "Good," "Fair," and "Poor" to indicate the quality of the cutting.

Beauty Is in the Eye of the Beholder

Despite the debate over what is really "ideal," or what terminology will be used in the future to communicate the quality of the cutting, no one will argue that a diamond that is really beautiful, one that exhibits a brilliant, fiery character, *is* well cut, regardless of what it is called.

But what you might consider the most beautiful stone may not be the choice of another. Diamonds exhibit different personalities depending on the make. What we currently call an "ideal" make will exhibit one personality, while another diamond with different proportioning will exhibit a different personality. Some stones throw out much more white light than others, while some seem more fiery because of the way they break up the white light into pinpoint flashes of its component rainbow colors. Some seem to have more contrast within the stone, and exhibit an interesting pattern within the stone, while others do not. Today a diamond cut with an "ideal" make may cost more, but that doesn't mean everyone will prefer the appearance of that stone to another that is cut to different proportions. *You* must decide what you really like the best, not the salesperson.

Experienced professionals know when they look at a diamond, regardless of its proportioning, whether or not it has a fine make. If you take the time to focus on a stone's personality and overall character, to focus on how it really looks to your unaided eye, you can also learn to see differences and recognize whether or not a stone is well cut. Let your eye be responsible for making the final determination. In general, when you look at a diamond that has a lot of brilliance and fire, the cutting and proportioning will be good. A stone that appears lifeless or dead, or seems dark across the center, probably suffers from poor cutting and proportioning. The more time you take to look at and compare diamonds of different qualities and prices, the better trained your eye will become to detect differences in brilliance and fire, lifelessness and dullness.

When purchasing a diamond, ask about its "make." Ask the seller how they would describe it: Excellent or Exceptional ("ideal"), Very Good, Good, Fair, or Poor. This is an important question because a diamond with a "poor" or "fair" make should sell for less, often much less, than a diamond with a "good" make. A diamond with a "very good" or "excellent" make will sell for more.

Gem Testing Laboratories that Provide Diamond Cut Grades or Information on the Cut of a Diamond

Despite the effect of cutting on a diamond's beauty, durability, and cost, only a few laboratories currently assign a cut "grade" on reports or provide any information indicating how well or poorly cut the stone may be. None of the European laboratories provide cut grades on diamond reports because they think research findings still do not reflect the whole story, and that cut-grading systems still omit important factors that affect the overall appearance of any diamond. This is also the case among laboratories in most other parts of the world, including South America, Asia, the Middle East, and Africa.

For those who want to have more information about the cut of a particular diamond or a cut "grade," American laboratories that currently provide this information include: American Gem Society Laboratory (AGSL) in Las Vegas; American Gemological Laboratories (AGL) and Gemworld International Laboratories, both in New York City; and Professional Gem Sciences Laboratory (PGS) in Chicago. In addition, the Gem Certification and Appraisal Lab (GCAL) in New York City provides reports on cutting to supplement information provided on other diamond reports that lack cutting information, such as those issued at this time by GIA.

Whether or not your diamond has a diamond grading report or a "cut grade," no matter what the proportions are, before making a final decision on a particular stone, ask yourself whether or not you think it is beautiful. If you like it, don't allow yourself to be overly influenced by formulas, terms, or numbers on a report.

Faulty Cuts

Many errors that affect the appearance and value of a diamond can occur in the cutting. Remember that some cutting faults will make a stone more vulnerable to breakage. We recommend avoiding such stones unless they can be protected by the setting.

There are several cutting faults to watch for in round diamonds. First, look carefully for a *sloping table* or a table that is not almost perfectly perpendicular to the point of the culet.

Second, the culet can frequently be the source of a problem. It can be chipped or broken, open or large (almost all modern cut stones have culets that come nearly to a point), or it can be missing altogether.

Third, repairs to chipped areas can result in *misaligned facets,* which affect the stone's symmetry.

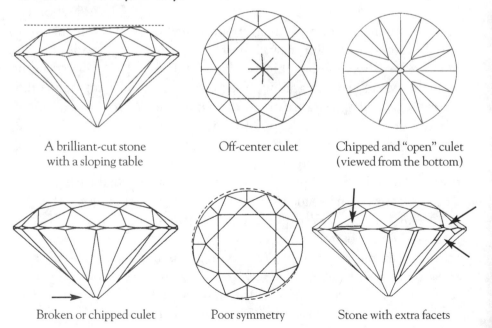

A brilliant-cut stone
with a sloping table

Off-center culet

Chipped and "open" culet
(viewed from the bottom)

Broken or chipped culet

Poor symmetry

Stone with extra facets

Sometimes, too, as a result of repair, an *extra facet* will be formed, often in the crown facets, but also on or just below the girdle. These extra facets may slightly affect the stone's brilliance.

Girdle Faults

The girdle is often the source of faults. *Bearded* or *fringed girdles* are common. A fringed girdle exhibits small radial cracks penetrating into the stone; these can result from a careless or inexperienced cutter. A bearded girdle is similar but not as pronounced a fault and can be easily repaired by repolishing, with minor loss in diamond weight.

The relative thickness of the girdle is very important because it can affect the durability as well as the beauty of the stone. Any girdle can be nicked or chipped in the course of wear, or by careless handling, but if the girdle is too thin it will chip more easily. Some chips can be easily removed by repolishing, with minimal diamond weight loss. If there are numerous chips, the entire girdle can be repolished. Chips or nicks in the girdle are often hidden under the prongs or concealed by the setting.

If the girdle is too thick, the stone may look smaller because a disproportionate amount of its weight will be in the girdle itself; such stones,

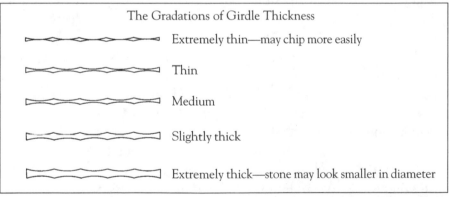

The Gradations of Girdle Thickness

Extremely thin—may chip more easily

Thin

Medium

Slightly thick

Extremely thick—stone may look smaller in diameter

Wavy girdle

Out-of-round girdle

for their weight, will be smaller in diameter than other stones of compara-ble weight. The girdle can also be *wavy, rough,* or *entirely out-of-round.*

A *natural* may be present on the girdle and may, or may not, be a "fault." A natural is actually a piece of the natural surface of the dia-mond crystal. In cutting, a cutter may decide to leave part of the "natural" rough surface in order to get as large a diamond as possible from the rough stone. If this natural is no thicker than the thickness of the girdle and does not distort the circumference of the stone, most dealers consider it a minor defect at worst; if it extends into the crown or pavilion of the stone, it is a more seri-ous fault.

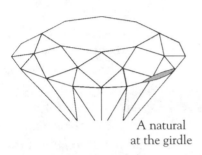

A natural
at the girdle

Sometimes if the natural is somewhat large but slightly below the girdle, it will be polished off. This produces an extra facet.

Other Popular Shapes

Unlike round diamonds, set formulas have never been developed for "fancy" shapes—all shapes other than round—so evaluating the cutting of fancy cuts has always been more subjective. Table and depth percent-age can vary widely among individual stones of the same shape, each pro-ducing a beautiful stone. Personal taste also varies with regard to what constitutes the "ideal" for shapes other than round. Nonetheless, there are certain visual indicators of good or poor proportioning—such as the bow tie effect—which even the amateur can learn to spot. There are rec-ommended ratios for overall shape and symmetry, but a preferred shape is largely a personal matter. Ranges for what is acceptable or unacceptable have been developed. As you gain experience looking at specific shapes, you will be able to spot faults, and begin to determine what is within an acceptable range. Moderate deviations will not significantly affect the beauty or value of a stone; however, extreme deviations can seriously reduce a stone's beauty and value.

While cut "grades" for round, brilliant-cut diamonds are currently available from several gem testing laboratories, the only laboratory grad-ing the cutting of fancy shapes at this time is the AGS lab (see appen-dix). Applying the advanced technology currently used by labs to measure light performance in round diamonds, AGS has expanded its application and research to include fancy shapes. They are now providing cut grades for princess-cut diamonds (see page 32) and have announced plans to introduce cut grades on other fancy shapes in the near future.

Cutting Faults in Popular Fancy Shapes

One of the most obvious indicators of poor proportioning in fancy shapes is the *bow tie* or *butterfly* effect: a darkened area across the center or widest part of the stone, depending on the cut. The bow tie is most commonly seen in the pear shape or marquise, but it may exist in any fancy shape. Virtually all fancy shapes cut today will exhibit some minimal bow tie effect. Nonetheless, the presence or absence of a bow tie is an indicator of proper proportioning. In poorly proportioned stones there is a pronounced bow tie; the more pronounced, the poorer the proportioning. The less pronounced the bow tie, the better the proportioning. The degree to which the bow tie is evident is the first indicator of a good or a poor make. A diamond with a pronounced bow tie should sell for much less than one without.

Marquise with a pronounced bow tie, or butterfly

As with the brilliant-cut diamond, fancy shapes can also be cut too *broad* or too *narrow*, and the pavilion can be too *deep* or too *shallow*.

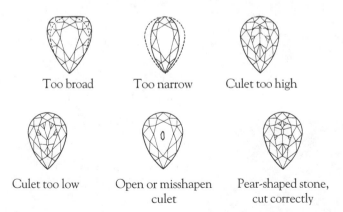

| Too broad | Too narrow | Culet too high |

| Culet too low | Open or misshapen culet | Pear-shaped stone, cut correctly |

Personal taste will always play a role in fancy shapes—some prefer a narrow pear shape, for example, while others might prefer a fatter pear. Whatever the shape you are considering, you must ask yourself whether or not you find the stone exciting. Does it have a pleasing personality? Does it exhibit good brilliance and fire? Is the entire stone brilliant, or are there "dead" spots? Are there any cutting faults that might make it more susceptible to chipping? Then you must make the choice.

New Shapes Create Excitement

Today we can choose from many shapes and cuts, ranging from the classics—round, oval, pear, marquise, emerald cut, and heart shape—to new shapes that appear as cutters continue to experiment with novel looks. Here are some of the most popular:

Radiant   Crisscut®

The *radiant cut* is perfect for the person who likes the shape of an emerald cut—square or rectangular—but wants more sparkle and brilliance, a personality closer to a round diamond. The *Crisscut®* is a wonderful blend between the two, more understated than the radiant but livelier than an emerald cut.

Standard   Quadrillion™
princess

The *princess cut,* a square brilliant cut, is ideal for bezel and channel settings (see chapter 18) or any setting in which you want the stone to be flush with the mounting. The *Quadrillion™* was the first trademarked "princess," cut to unique specifications for maximum brilliance and fire.

Gabrielle®   Spirit Sun®

The *Gabrielle®* cut has 105 facets uniquely arranged to create more scintillation, more sparkle, than is seen in traditional cuts. The Gabrielle® comes in all the classic shapes. The *Spirit Sun®*, a revolutionary new cut with only 16 facets and a pointed crown, represents an entirely new cutting approach. It achieves exceptional brilliance and reflectivity.

A new cut patented by Tiffany, the *Lucida*™ blends a modern, square brilliant cut with the high crown and small tables of an antique old-mine cut (cushion). This cut is available only from Tiffany, but similar cuts are available. Another of the new "square" cuts, the *Context*®, creates a wholly new look with amazing luminosity. The epitome of simplicity, it can be fashioned only from rare, perfectly formed diamond crystals—one in one hundred thousand—and maintains the inherent shape of the natural crystal.

Lucida™   Context®

The *trilliant cut* is a popular shape for use as a center stone or as side stones. This brilliant cut is also a thin cut, giving a large appearance for its weight. Extra facets and precision cutting produce high brilliance. The *Lily Cut*® is a brilliant new cut shaped like a four-leaf clover, and is great in pendants and earrings.

Trilliant   Lily Cut®

As we learn more and more about diamond cutting and how various facet arrangements and angles affect the way light performs in a diamond, new cuts continue to emerge. These include the *New Century*®, a patented 102-facet, round, super brilliant cut; the Zoë, a scintillating 100-facet cut; the extra fiery 82-facet *Royal 82;* the 80-facet *Spirit of Flanders*™; the 66-facet *Leo Diamond*™; and the new 97-facet, 12-sided *Escada*® that was created exclusively for the great fashion house.

In addition to the new cuts above, we are also seeing cutting innovations in baguettes, with new brilliant-cut baguettes, such as the *Princette*™ and the *Bagillion*™. They occur in straight and tapered shapes. There are also Crisscut® baguettes and tapered baguettes. These are gaining in popularity because they have greater brilliance than traditional baguettes. They can be used to flank diamonds or other stones in traditional settings, or are used in very contemporary jewelry design with straight, clean lines.

Early Cuts Enjoy Renewed Popularity

Interest in antique and period jewelry is growing rapidly. As it does, the diamonds that adorn them are arousing renewed attention and gaining new respect. The way a diamond is cut is often one of the clues to the age of a piece. Older diamonds can be replaced or recut to modern proportions, but replacing or recutting stones mounted in antique or period pieces could adversely affect the value of the jewelry. To preserve the integrity of the piece, antique and period jewelry connoisseurs want original stones, or, if stones have been replaced, at least stones cut in the manner typical of the period. The market is becoming increasingly strong for diamonds with older cuts, and prices are also strengthening.

As these early cut diamonds receive more and more attention, a growing number of people are beginning to appreciate them for their distinctive beauty and personality and for the romance that accompanies them. The romantic element—combined with a cost that is more attractive than that of new diamonds—is also making them an increasingly popular choice for engagement rings.

Some of the earliest cuts are the *table cut,* the *rose cut,* the *old-mine cut,* and the *old-European cut.* (Before 1919, when America began to emerge as an important diamond cutting center, most diamonds were cut in Europe. Thus, most "old European" diamonds were cut before the first quarter of the twentieth century.)

The *table cut* illustrates history's earliest cutting effort. By placing the point of a diamond crystal against a turning wheel that held another diamond, the point could be worn down, creating a squarish, flat surface that resembled a *tabletop.* Today we still call the flat facet on the very top of the stone the table facet.

The *rose cut* is a sixteenth-century cut, usually with a flat base and facets radiating from the center in multiples of

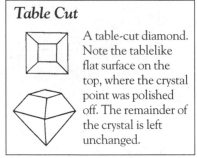

Table Cut

A table-cut diamond. Note the tablelike flat surface on the top, where the crystal point was polished off. The remainder of the crystal is left unchanged.

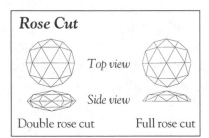

Rose Cut

Top view

Side view

Double rose cut   Full rose cut

six, creating the appearance of an opening rosebud. The rose cut appears in round, pear, and oval shapes.

The *old-mine* is a precursor to the modern round. This cut has a squarish or "cushion" shape (a rounded square). Proportions follow the diamond crystal, so the crown is higher and the pavilion is deeper than in modern stones. The table is very small, and the culet is very large and is easily seen from the top (resembling a "hole" in the diamond). These lack the brilliance of modern stones but often exhibit tremendous fire. The old-mine is enjoying a resurgence in popularity today.

Appearing in the mid-1800s, the *old-European* is similar to the old-mine cut but is *round* rather than squarish, with fifty-eight facets. The crown is higher than in modern cuts but not as high as in the old-mine cut; it has a deep pavilion, but not as deep as in old-mines. The culet is still "open" but smaller than in old-mines.

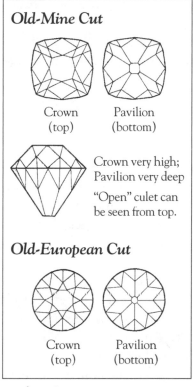

Old-Mine Cut

Crown   Pavilion
(top)   (bottom)

Crown very high;
Pavilion very deep

"Open" culet can
be seen from top.

Old-European Cut

Crown   Pavilion
(top)   (bottom)

Rectangular and square cuts were introduced in the late 1800s. By the turn of the century, the Asscher had become very popular, and it is enjoying a

Contemporary
Royal Asscher®

revival today. Its unique proportions and angles—characterized by large angular corners, small table, high crown, and open *square* culet—produced greater liveliness and fire than seen in other emerald-cut diamonds at the time. The 74-facet *Royal Asscher®* is a contemporary version of the original, with slight modifications that result in an elegant, classic, and extremely beautiful stone.

Old cuts can be very beautiful. The intense "fire" exhibited by some old-mine and old-European cuts can have tremendous allure. By today's standards, however, they have less brilliance, and a very large culet may detract from the stone's beauty.

Are Diamonds with Old Cuts Valuable?

Old-mine cut and old-European cut diamonds are normally evaluated by comparison with modern-cut stones. Value is usually determined by estimating the color, the clarity, and the weight the stone would *retain* if it were recut to modern proportions. However, this practice is now changing because of the increasing demand for old cuts, as mentioned earlier.

We don't suggest recutting old diamonds if they are in their original mountings. The overall integrity of the piece—and its value—would be adversely affected.

If the setting has no special merit, the decision must be an individual one, based on whether or not the stone appeals to you. As we have said, some older cuts are very lovely, while others may look heavy, dull, or lifeless. An unattractive older cut may benefit from recutting, and although it will lose weight, it may have equal or greater value because of the improved make. In addition, recutting can sometimes improve the clarity grade of an older stone. Finally, before deciding whether or not to recut, you should note that the increasing popularity of older cuts is driving prices higher since they are difficult to find. In addition to their unique personalities, old cuts can have a distinctive character that sets them apart from more modern cuts. For more on cutting, and for pricing guidelines on old cuts, see *Diamonds: The Antoinette Matlins Buying Guide*.

A Word about Recutting Diamonds

There are many fine diamond cutters in the United States—New York City is one of the most important diamond cutting centers in the world for top-quality diamonds—and many diamonds can be greatly improved by recutting. The cost is surprisingly low when one considers the benefit to the stone and the effect of recutting on the diamond's beauty and value. Sometimes the clarity grade is also improved.

If you have an old-cut diamond that you don't care for, or a damaged diamond, your jeweler can consult with a diamond cutter—or refer you to one—to determine whether or not your stone can be improved by recutting and, if so, what risks and costs might be involved.

Normally, the cost to recut a diamond ranges from approximately $350 *per carat* to as much as $500 *per carat,* depending on the skill required and the labor involved. In rare instances, the cost might be more. Thus, if the labor estimate to recut a stone is $350 per carat, recutting a two-carat diamond will cost $700.

A knowledgeable jeweler can help you decide whether or not a diamond should be recut, make arrangements for you, and help assure you that you've received the same stone back. For your own comfort and security, as well as the cutter's, we always recommend that before having a stone recut you obtain a diamond grading report or a thorough appraisal so that you have a point of reference when the stone is returned.

5

Body Color

Color is one of the most important factors to consider when select-ing a diamond because one of the first things most people notice is whether or not the diamond is white, or, more accurately, *colorless* (there actually are *white* diamonds, but they are extremely rare and not very attractive). It is also one of the most significant factors affecting value.

Color refers to the natural body color of a diamond. The finest and most expensive "white" diamonds are absolutely colorless, as in pure springwater. Most diamonds show some trace of yellowish or brownish tint. Diamonds also occur in every color of the rainbow. Natural-colored diamonds are called *fancy-color* diamonds. Fancy colors include red, pink, blue, green, yellow, and brown.

How to Look at a Diamond
to Evaluate Color

In white diamonds, color differences from one grade to the next can be very subtle, and a difference of several grades is difficult to see when a diamond is mounted. Keep in mind that it is impossible to accurately grade color in a mounted diamond. When looking at an unmounted stone, however, even an amateur can learn to see color differences if the stone is viewed properly.

Because of the diamond's high brilliance and dispersion (fire), the color grade cannot be accurately determined by looking at the stone from the top, or face-up, position. It is best to observe color by examining the stone through the pavilion, with the table down. Use a flat white surface such as a folded white business card, or a *grading trough,* which can be purchased from a jewelry supplier.

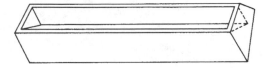

A grading trough, available in plastic or in handy disposable folding white cardboard stand-up packs. Be sure to use a *clean* trough.

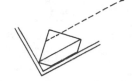

Examine the stone through the pavilion, with the table down.

What Is Body Color?

When we discuss body color in white (colorless) diamonds, we mean how much yellow or brown tint can be seen. We are not referring to the rare natural-color diamonds that occur in such shades as blue, green, yellow, and red, which are designated in the trade as fancy-color diamonds.

Today, most white diamonds in the United States and other countries are graded on an alphabetical scale beginning with the letter D. This letter designation is part of a color-grading system introduced by the Gemological Institute of America (GIA) and is used extensively in the diamond trade worldwide. The GIA classification progresses from D, the rarest classification on this scale (colorless), through the alphabet to Z, getting progressively more tinted. The grades D, E, and F are exceptionally fine and are the only grades that should be referred to as colorless. (Technically, E and F are not colorless, since they possess a trace of yellow or brown, but the tint is so slight that referring to them as colorless is acceptable.)

A diamond with the color grade D exhibits the most prized color. It is essentially colorless—like crystal-clear springwater—and is considered the most desirable. Diamonds with D-color are becoming very rare, and a significant premium is paid for them. A diamond with the color grade E also possesses an exceptionally fine color and is almost indistinguishable from D except to the very experienced. Nonetheless, diamonds graded E in color cost significantly less per carat than those graded D, despite the difficulty in seeing the difference. The next color grade is F, and it is close to E, but there is more gradation in color than the difference observed between D and E.

What Color Grade Is Most Desirable?

The colors D, E, and F can all be grouped as exceptionally fine, rare colors and may be referred to as *colorless, exceptional white,* or *rare white,* as they are often described by diamond dealers. The colors G and H may be referred to as *fine white* or *rare white.* These grades are all considered very fine. The I and J colors are slightly more tinted than G and H, and sell for less, but diamonds possessing color grades G through J are all fine colors and are classified as *near colorless.* The colors K and L show a stronger tint of yellow or brown, but settings can often mask the tint. Grades M through Z will show progressively more and more tint of yellowish or brownish color. Grades D through J seem to have better resale potential than grades K through Z. This does not mean, however, that diamonds having less rare color grades are less beautiful or desirable. Sometimes a more tinted diamond can exhibit a warmth not shown by other diamonds and create a very beautiful ring with a unique appeal.

Diamond Color Grades		
COLORLESS	D E F	Loose diamonds appear colorless.
NEAR COLORLESS	G H I J	When mounted in a setting, these diamonds may appear colorless to the untrained eye.
FAINT YELLOWISH* TINT	K L M	Smaller diamonds look colorless when mounted. Diamonds of ½ carat or more show traces of color.
VERY LIGHT YELLOWISH* TINT	N O P Q R	These diamonds show increasingly yellow tints to even the untrained eye, and appear very "off-white."
TINTED LIGHT YELLOWISH*	S T U V W X Y Z	

* Usually yellow, but can be brown or gray

To What Extent
Does the Color Grade Affect Value?

To an untrained eye, discerning the difference in color from D down to H in a mounted stone, without direct comparison, is almost impossible. Nevertheless, the difference in color greatly affects the value of the diamond. A one-carat, flawless, excellently proportioned, D-color diamond might retail for $30,000, while the same stone with H-color might sell for only $12,000 and the same stone with K-color might sell for only $7,500. And, of course, if the stone were not flawless, it could sell for much less (see next chapter). This sounds complicated, but the range of color will become clear to you the moment you begin looking at stones. It is our intention to inform you of the variations so that you will be watchful when you go to purchase a stone.

In diamonds over one carat, the whiter the stone, the more critical it becomes to know the exact color grade because of its effect on value. On the other hand, as long as you know for sure what color the stone is and are paying the right price, choosing one that is a grade or two lower than another will reduce the cost per carat, and there will be little, if any, visible difference when the stone is mounted. Therefore, for the difference in cost, you might be able to get a larger diamond, or one with better cutting or a better clarity grade, depending on what is most important to you.

Natural Color or HPHT Processed

Color differences can be subtle, but the difference in cost can be extreme. It is important to know the precise color grade, but it is even more important to know whether the color is natural or the result of some type of treatment. In chapter 8 we discuss several fraudulent techniques that have been used on colorless diamonds for many years, as well as new techniques that are being applied routinely to certain types of diamonds. Where colorless diamonds are concerned, until recently, techniques to alter color produced results that were temporary, and any competent gemologist could detect the treatment. This is no longer true; the latest techniques are difficult to detect and require sophisticated testing.

A new process developed in the 1990s uses high-pressure/high-temperature annealing (often referred to as the HPHT process) to transform very tinted, off-white diamonds into colorless and near-colorless stones, ranging from D through H in color. These stones were originally referred to as GE-POL diamonds but are now called Bellataire™ diamonds. The results are permanent and irreversible. Unlike earlier treatments, detection requires sophisticated testing available only at major gem-testing laboratories (see appendix).

Not all tinted diamonds can be transformed into colorless or near-colorless diamonds. Only very rare diamond types respond to HPHT whitening techniques. Of all diamonds mined, it is estimated that less than 2 percent produce the desired effect. Today the process is also being used to produce fancy-color yellow, pink, blue, and red diamonds (see page 46).

Some retailers charge a small premium because of the rarity of diamonds that can be treated in this manner, while others provide an incentive to customers by pricing them at 15 to 20 percent below their natural-color counterparts. To many, these newcomers are a beautiful and exciting high-tech alternative. Ultimately, however, it will be consumer acceptance and demand that determine their pricing.

Caution: HPHT "Colorless" Diamonds Sold as "Natural"

In addition to GE-POL and its Bellataire™ brand, other companies are producing colorless diamonds that have been whitened by this process. We do not know how many are now being sold, or when they actually began to enter the marketplace, but we do know that some are being sold without any disclosure. Equally important, before being aware of the use of this technology on diamonds, the major gem-testing laboratories were not checking for it, nor did they have the data to understand how to detect it. Today most diamonds treated in this manner can be identified, but caution must be exercised when you buy any fine, colorless diamond to ensure that you know whether or not the color results from this technology. Labs such as the GIA, the Swiss Foundation for the Research of Gemstones (SSEF), and the European Gemological Laboratory (EGL) will grade diamonds treated in this manner, indicating the use of this process on the report, under "Comments" (see appendix for laboratory addresses). See chapter 8 for advice on how to protect yourself from buying an HPHT diamond unknowingly.

Commonly Used Diamond Color Grading Systems

The GIA and American Gem Society (AGS) grading systems are the most commonly used in the United States. The GIA system is the most widely used in the world. Scandinavian diamond nomenclature (Scan D.N.) is often used in Scandinavian countries, as well as a system developed by CIBJO (the International Confederation of Jewelry, Silverware, Diamonds, Pearls, and Stones). Participating member nations include most European nations, Japan, and the United States. Another system, HRD, is applied by the Belgian Diamond High Council.

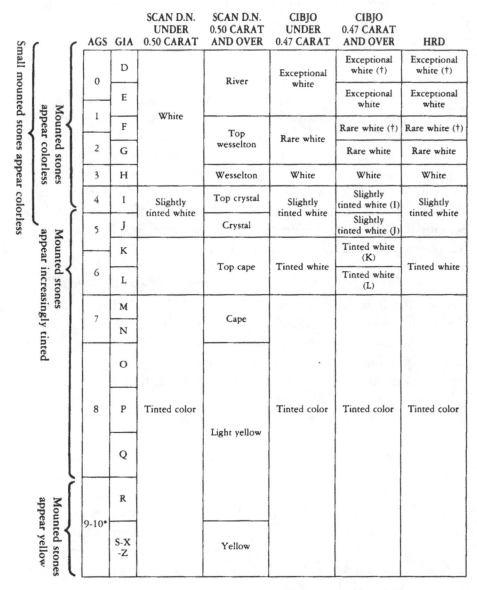

Appearance	AGS	GIA	SCAN D.N. UNDER 0.50 CARAT	SCAN D.N. 0.50 CARAT AND OVER	CIBJO UNDER 0.47 CARAT	CIBJO 0.47 CARAT AND OVER	HRD
Small mounted stones appear colorless / Mounted stones appear colorless	0	D	White	River	Exceptional white	Exceptional white (†)	Exceptional white (†)
	0	E	White	River	Exceptional white	Exceptional white	Exceptional white
	1	F	White	Top wesselton	Rare white	Rare white (†)	Rare white (†)
	2	G	White	Top wesselton	Rare white	Rare white	Rare white
	3	H	White	Wesselton	White	White	White
	4	I	Slightly tinted white	Top crystal	Slightly tinted white	Slightly tinted white (I)	Slightly tinted white
Mounted stones appear increasingly tinted	5	J	Slightly tinted white	Crystal	Slightly tinted white	Slightly tinted white (J)	Slightly tinted white
	6	K	Tinted color	Top cape	Tinted white	Tinted white (K)	Tinted white
	6	L	Tinted color	Top cape	Tinted white	Tinted white (L)	Tinted white
	7	M	Tinted color	Cape	Tinted color	Tinted color	Tinted color
	7	N	Tinted color	Cape	Tinted color	Tinted color	Tinted color
	8	O	Tinted color	Light yellow	Tinted color	Tinted color	Tinted color
	8	P	Tinted color	Light yellow	Tinted color	Tinted color	Tinted color
	8	Q	Tinted color	Light yellow	Tinted color	Tinted color	Tinted color
Mounted stones appear yellow	9-10*	R	Tinted color	Yellow	Tinted color	Tinted color	Tinted color
	9-10*	S-X-Z	Tinted color	Yellow	Tinted color	Tinted color	Tinted color

*AGS grade 9 corresponds to GIA, R–U inclusive. AGS grade 10 corresponds to GIA, V–Z inclusive.

† The use of the term *blue-white* is discouraged today, since it is usually misleading.

What Is Fluorescence?

If the diamond you are considering is accompanied by a diamond grading report issued by the GIA or another respected lab, it will indicate whether or not the diamond has some degree of *fluorescence*. Fluorescence refers to whether or not a stone produces a color reaction when exposed to ultraviolet radiation—a color seen *only* when the stone is exposed to ultraviolet radiation. Whether or not a diamond fluoresces, and the strength of its fluorescence (faint, weak, moderate, strong, very strong) are determined by viewing the diamond with a special lamp called an ultraviolet lamp, which emits only ultraviolet radiation. When we say a white (colorless) diamond fluoresces blue, we mean that its color will appear to be blue when we view it under the pure ultraviolet light produced by the ultraviolet lamp. The stone is really a colorless diamond and will appear colorless in normal light. Some diamonds fluoresce; others do not. A diamond can fluoresce any color, but most diamonds fluoresce blue, white, or yellow.

It is important to note whether or not a diamond fluoresces, and what color it fluoresces, because there are varying wavelengths of ultraviolet radiation all around us. Ultraviolet radiation is present in daylight (that's what causes sunburn) and wherever there are fluorescent light fixtures (those long tube lights you see in the ceilings of many stores and office buildings). This means that, depending upon the strength of a diamond's fluorescence, and the intensity of the ultraviolet radiation in the light source, its color may not appear the same in all lights.

A diamond that fluoresces a strong blue, for example, might appear whiter in daylight, or in an office with fluorescent lights, because the ultraviolet radiation present will cause the diamond to emit some degree of blue, masking any faint yellow or brown tint that might be present. The same stone might appear less white when seen at home in incandescent light—any warm light, such as a household lightbulb—where you see the stone's true body color, without the benefit of any fluorescence stimulated by ultraviolet radiation. A white diamond that fluoresces "strong yellow" can look more yellow in some lights. But remember, whatever color is produced by fluorescence, it occurs *only* in daylight or fluorescent light.

To ensure that the true body color is being graded, a professional always tests a diamond for fluorescence with an ultraviolet lamp before color grading it. Blue fluorescence is more common than white or yellow. Some white diamonds that fluoresce blue may actually look blue-white in the right light. The results of a recent study conducted by the GIA showed that consumers found the presence of blue fluorescence to be a benefit; participants in the study actually preferred diamonds that fluoresced blue to other diamonds because they seemed "whiter," despite the fact that you will not really notice fluorescence with the naked eye.

Does Fluorescence Affect Value?

Generally, the presence or absence of fluorescence has little if any effect on value. However, if the stone has a strong yellow fluorescence it may sell for 10 to 15 percent less, since this will make the stone appear more yellow in some lights than another stone with the same color grade.

Blue fluorescence may be considered an added benefit—a little bonus—because it may make the stone appear whiter in some lights, and yet there may be no difference in cost or the stone may sell at a modest *discount* (although this may change after the results of the GIA study).

You must be careful, however, to look closely at stones with *very strong* fluorescence, whatever color the stone flouresces. Such stones may seem a little less "lively" than they should, or even oily or murky in appearance. If liveliness is only slightly reduced, the stone should sell for 15–20 percent less than another of comparable quality; if it is oily or murky, it may sell for 40–50 percent less.

If a diamond fluoresces, its true body color can be misgraded. This can be costly to the buyer, but the error can be easily avoided. Knowledgeable jewelers or appraisers will always test a diamond to see whether or not it fluoresces, and to what degree, in order to color grade it accurately.

Colorful Choices: Fancy-Color Diamonds

Diamonds occur naturally in almost every color and shade: blue, red, green, yellow, lavender, pink, gunmetal blue, coffee brown, and black. The color can be intense or very pale. Some colors are rarer than others. The most common fancy colors are shades of yellow (a very intense, bright yellow is often called canary), orange, and brown. Such colors as pink, light green, and lavender occur much more rarely. Deep blue, red, and green diamonds are among the rarest—and most valuable—gems on earth. Black diamonds are relatively common. Most fancy-color diamonds found in nature tend to be pastel.

Except for very pale yellow and very pale brown varieties—which are very common and not considered "fancies" but, more properly, off-white—fancy-color diamonds often sell for more than fine colorless diamonds. An extremely rare red diamond that weighed less than one carat and had very poor clarity brought the highest price ever paid for a single gem—almost $1 million "per carat"—at auction in 1987. A fine pink or blue diamond can bring hundreds of thousands of dollars *per carat*.

Fancy-color diamonds occur naturally, but fancy colors can also be produced artificially by exposing very inexpensive brownish or yellowish stones to certain types of radiation and heating techniques. Many unattractive, off-white stones are changed in this manner to beautiful "fancy" colors. Yellow, blue, pink, and green diamonds can be the result of such treatment. If you are considering any natural-color diamond, it should be accompanied by a report from a respected laboratory, or the sale should be contingent on getting proper documentation. For more in-depth information about fancy-color diamonds and how they are graded and evaluated, see the book *Diamonds: The Antoinette Matlins Buying Guide*.

What Is a Chameleon Diamond?

A *chameleon* diamond is one that changes color when exposed to heat! Several diamonds that show this very unusual phenomenon have been sold recently at auction, and they make interesting conversation pieces. Whatever color they exhibit in natural or fluorescent light, or when heated, usually becomes more yellow when they are left in the dark for a time.

Special Tips on the Subject of Color

Keep It Clean If You Want the Color to Look Its Best

A dirty diamond will not look white, nor will it sparkle. An accumulation of dirt, especially greasy dirt, will give a diamond a yellowish cast, so if you want to see and enjoy its full beauty, keep your diamond clean.

This principle applies especially when you are looking at old jewelry for possible purchase. When you are considering old diamond pieces, pay particular attention to whether or not it is impacted with dirt accumulated by years of use. If it is, there is a possibility that the diamond will have a better color grade than it may appear to have at first glance. This is because the dirt may contain varying amounts of fatty deposits (from dishwashing, cosmetics, etc.), which yellow with age. When this type of dirt builds up and is in contact with the diamond, it will also make the diamond appear more yellow.

White or Yellow Gold Setting?

The color of the metal in the setting (see chapter 18) can affect your perception of the color of the stone—sometimes adversely and sometimes beneficially. A very white diamond should be held in a white metal such as white gold, platinum, or palladium. If you prefer yellow gold, it's possible to have just the portion of the setting that holds the diamond itself fashioned in white metal. For example, a diamond ring can be made with a yellow gold shank to go around the finger and a white metal head to hold the diamond. An all-yellow setting may make a very white diamond appear less white because the yellow color of the setting itself is reflected into the diamond.

On the other hand, if the diamond you choose tends to be more yellow than you'd like, mounting it in yellow gold, with yellow surrounding the stone, may make the stone appear whiter in contrast to the strong yellow of the gold.

The yellow gold environment may mask the degree of yellow in a yellow diamond, or it may give a colorless diamond an undesirable yellow tint. The setting can also affect future color grading should you ever need an updated insurance appraisal.

6

Clarifying Clarity

Clarity classification—also called *flaw* clssification—is one of the criteria used to determine the value of a diamond. As with all things in nature, however, there is really no such thing as "flawless." Even though some very rare diamonds are classified "flawless," the term is somewhat misleading, and you must be sure you understand what it really means.

When we talk about this classification, we are referring to the presence of tiny, usually microscopic, characteristics. Today, use of the term *flaw* is discouraged because it suggests something bad when this is not really the case; rather, the flaw grade, or preferably clarity grade, simply provides part of the complete description of the stone. However, it is difficult to ignore the word "flaw" when the rarest clarity grade is "*Flaw*less."

It is important to understand that as diamonds form in nature, *every* diamond develops certain types of internal characteristics. They might be microscopic cracks shaped like feathers—some are quite lovely when viewed with the microscope—or microscopic diamond crystals, or even crystals of some other gemstone! *Every diamond contains distinctive internal characteristics:* when internal they are called *inclusions;* when external they are called *blemishes.*

Each diamond's internal picture—its internal character—is unique. No two are alike, so the clarity picture can be an important factor in identifying a specific diamond.

To What Extent Does Clarity Affect the Beauty of a Diamond?

It is very important to understand that clarity may have little or no effect on the beauty of a diamond if it falls within the first eight clarity grades discussed later in this chapter (FL through SI). Few people can discern any visible difference between stones until they reach the imperfect grades, and even then it is sometimes difficult to see anything in the stone without magnification.

Many people mistakenly believe that the clarity grade affects a diamond's brilliance and sparkle. This is not true; the clarity grade has little effect on a diamond's visible appearance except in the very lowest grades. Many people think that the better the clarity, the more brilliant and sparkling the diamond. Perhaps it is the term itself, *clarity,* that leads to the confusion (and the reason we don't like the term *clarity grade*). Whatever the case, as discussed in chapter 4, it is the precision of the *cutting* that determines how brilliant and sparkling a diamond will be.

To the buyer, the flaw grade, or clarity grade, is important because it indicates, on a relative basis, how "clean" the diamond is, and this ranking has a significant effect on cost. The cleaner the stone, the rarer; the rarer the stone, the costlier.

Diamonds don't have to be flawless to be beautiful and sparkling. As you will see when you shop and compare, you can find very beautiful, sparkling diamonds in a wide range of clarity grades. Juggling the clarity grade can give you tremendous flexibility in getting a whiter or larger diamond for your money. Just keep in mind that you won't see differences with the eye alone, so you must take care to know for sure what the specific clarity grade is.

How Is the Clarity Grade Determined?

Diamonds used in jewelry are usually very clean, and little if anything can be seen without magnification. This is starting to change as an increasing number of diamonds with visible cracks or other inclusions enter the market—stones in the I_1 through I_3 range and below—but for the most part, differences in clarity cannot normally be seen simply by looking at the stone with the naked eye. The clarity grade is based on what can be seen *when the diamond is examined with magnification* under a loupe (see chapter 1) and it is determined by what is seen at *ten-power (10x) magnification.* The clarity grade is based on the number, size, color, and location of inclusions or blemishes in the stone. The flawless grade is given to a stone in which no imperfections can be seen internally (inclusions) or externally (blemishes) when examined with 10x magnification, although at higher powers inclusions will be visible even in a flawless diamond. For clarity grading purposes, if an inclusion can't be seen at 10x, it doesn't exist.

Clarity grading requires extensive training and practice, and proper grading can be done only by an experienced jeweler, dealer, or gemologist. If you want to examine a diamond with the loupe, remember that only in the mid-to-low grades will an inexperienced person be able to see inclusions or blemishes easily, and even with the loupe it will be difficult to see what a professional will see easily. Few amateurs will see anything at all in the highest clarity grades.

Today, a jeweler might use a microscope with a video monitor to help you see what is inside a diamond you are considering. Be sure that the jeweler focuses at different depths into the stone and that the microscope is set at 10x (higher power may actually conceal something in the diamond because of the difficulty in focusing properly at higher powers). And remember: don't panic—what you are seeing is magnified ten times!

We recommend that you first examine the stone carefully with your eyes alone, then with a simple loupe, saving the microscope, when offered, for last. Examining a diamond in this way will help you become familiar with the particular characteristics of the stone you purchase, and may give you information that will enable you to always recognize your diamond should it be necessary at some future time (after having it mounted in the ring, for example). For more information on the specific types of internal and external flaws, see *Diamonds: The Antoinette Matlins Buying Guide*.

Commonly Used Clarity Grading Systems

There are several recognized clarity grading systems in use worldwide, but the system used most widely in the United States and an increasing number of other countries was developed by the GIA. The terms *clarity grade* and *flaw grade* may be used interchangeably, but today the term *clarity* is more commonly used.

The most widely recognized clarity grading scales were introduced by these organizations:

- CIBJO (International Confederation of Jewelry, Silverware, Diamonds, Pearls, and Stones). Participating member nations that use this system include Austria, Belgium, Canada, Denmark, Finland, France, Great Britain, Italy, Japan, Netherlands, Norway, Spain, Sweden, Switzerland, United States, and West Germany
- Scan D.N. (Scandinavian Diamond Nomenclature)
- GIA (Gemological Institute of America)
- AGS (American Gem Society)
- HRD (Hoge Raad voor Diamant, the Diamond High Council of Belgium)

The chart on the following page shows the relationship between the GIA system and others used internationally.

How Does the Clarity Grade Affect Diamond Value?

We will use the GIA system to explain clarity and its effect on value because it is the most widely used in the United States. As you can see from the comparison chart, other systems now use similar classifications. Should you have a diamond with a report from one of these, you can use this chart to find the corresponding GIA grade.

On the GIA scale, *FL* is the grade given to a stone that has no visible flaws, internal or external, when examined under 10x magnification. Only a highly qualified person will be able to determine this grade. If you are using a loupe as you examine diamonds, remember that it is very difficult for the inexperienced viewer to see flaws that may be readily observable to the experienced jeweler, dealer, or gemologist, and you will not have the experience to determine whether or not a diamond is flawless. Often the novice is unable to see any flaws, even in SI grades, even with use of the loupe. A flawless, colorless, correctly proportioned stone, particularly in a one-carat size or larger, is *extremely* rare and is priced proportionately much higher than any other grade. Some jewelers insist there is no such thing available today.

IF is the grade given to a stone with no internal flaws and with only minor external blemishes that could be removed with polishing, such as nicks, small pits not on the table, and/or girdle roughness. These stones,

Commonly Used Diamond Clarity (Flaw) Grading Systems

CIBJO UNDER 0.47 CARAT	CIBJO 0.47 CARAT AND OVER	HRD	SCAN D.N.	GIA	AGS
Loupe clean	Loupe clean	Loupe clean	FL	FL	0
			IF (Internally Flawless	IF	1
VVS	VVS$_1$	VVS$_1$	VVS$_1$	VVS$_1$	
	VVS$_2$	VVS$_2$	VVS$_2$	VVS$_2$	2
VS	VS$_1$	VS$_1$	VS$_1$	VS$_1$	3
	VS$_2$	VS$_2$	VS$_2$	VS$_2$	4
SI	SI$_1$	SI	SI$_1$	SI$_1$	5
	SI$_2$		SI$_2$	SI$_2$	6
Piqué I	Piqué I	P$_1$	1st Piqué	I$_1$ (Included)	7
					8
Piqué II	Piqué II	P$_2$	2nd Piqué	I$_2$	9
Piqué III	Piqué III	P$_3$	3rd Piqué	I$_3$	10

VV = Very, Very   S = Slight or Small
V = Very   I = Inclusion or Included or Imperfect (Imperfection)

For example, VVS may be translated to mean Very, Very Slightly (Included); or Very, Very Small (Inclusion); or Very, Very Slightly (Imperfect). Some jewelers prefer to classify the stone as "very, very small inclusion" rather than "very, very slightly imperfect" because the former description may sound more acceptable to the customer. There is, in fact, no difference.

No difference can be seen between these two diamonds with the unaided eye, but accurate grading is important because it can dramatically affect price.

Flawless   SI$_2$

in colorless, well-proportioned makes, are also rare and are priced proportionately much higher than other grades.

VVS$_1$ and *VVS$_2$* are grades given to stones with internal flaws that are very, very difficult for a qualified observer to see. These grades are also difficult to obtain and are priced at a premium.

VS$_1$ and *VS$_2$* are grades given to stones with very small inclusions, difficult for a qualified observer to see. These stones are more readily available in good color and cut, and their flaws will not be visible except under magnification. These are excellent stones to purchase.

SI$_1$ and *SI$_2$* grades are given to stones with flaws that a qualified observer will see fairly easily under 10x magnification. They are not as rare as the higher grades, so they are less costly; in these grades, flaws may sometimes be visible without magnification when examined from the back side or laterally. These grades are still highly desirable, and since they cannot normally be seen with the naked eye when mounted, they may enable one to select a stone with a higher color, or in a larger size, when working with a limited budget.

The *imperfect* grades are given to stones in which flaws may be seen by a qualified observer without magnification; they are readily available and are much less expensive. They are graded *I$_1$, I$_2$,* and *I$_3$.* (These grades are called *first piqué* (pronounced pee-kay), *second piqué,* and *third piqué* in some classification systems.) I$_1$, I$_2$, and *some* I$_3$ grades may still be desirable if they are brilliant and lively, and if there are no inclusions that might make them more susceptible than normal to breaking. They should not be automatically eliminated by a prospective purchaser who desires lovely diamond jewelry. As a general rule, however, imperfect grades may be difficult to resell should you ever try to do so.

You must also keep in mind that each grade covers a range—some will border the next higher, rarer grade, others the next lower, less rare grade—and this affects the cost. For example, a VS2 grade might be on the high end of the range, bordering a VS1, or it might be on the low end of the range, bordering SI1. Even though two diamonds may have the same grade on a report, this does not mean that they are the same nor that they should sell for the same price.

Exercise Care When Considering a Stone in the Imperfect Range

For those considering a diamond with an I₃ clarity grade, we must issue a word of warning: *some diamonds graded I₃ today are actually industrial quality and not suited for jewelry use.* Some cutters are cutting material that is lower than what is considered acceptable for jewelry. Since there is no grade lower than I₃ at this time, these stones are lumped in with other "better" (jewelry-quality) I₃ stones and are given an I₃ grade as well. But I₃ grade diamonds are *not* all comparable in terms of their clarity, and some should sell for much less than others. Be sure to shop around and compare I₃ diamonds to become familiar with what is acceptable for jewelry use.

Clarity Enhancement

Today, technological advances have made it possible to improve diamond clarity. Several clarity enhancement techniques are available; some are more or less permanent, and others are definitely not permanent. Unfortunately, clarity enhancement frequently is not disclosed, either to jewelers themselves or by jewelers to their customers. It is important to buy diamonds from knowledgeable, reputable jewelers who check for such treatments. In addition, before buying any diamond, you must *ask* whether or not the stone has been clarity enhanced. If the stone has been enhanced, ask what method was used, and be sure this is stated on the bill of sale. In addition, be sure to ask about special care requirements that might be necessitated by the process.

The two most widely used methods of clarity enhancement are lasering and fracture filling.

Lasering

Laser treatment is used today to make flaws less visible and thus improve the stone aesthetically. Laser technology makes it possible to "vaporize" black inclusions so they practically disappear. With the loupe, however, an experienced jeweler or gemologist can usually see the "path" cut into the diamond by the laser beam—this path may look like a fine, white thread starting at the surface of the stone and traveling into it—and other indicators of lasering. The effects of the laser treatment are permanent. If a lasered diamond is accompanied by a diamond grading report issued by a respected lab, the report will state that the stone is lasered.

A lasered stone should cost less than another with the "same" clarity, so it may be an attractive choice for a piece of jewelry—as long as you *know* it's lasered and therefore pay a fair price for it. Depending upon how many lasered inclusions are present, and their placement, lasered stones should sell for 20–30 percent less than stones of the same clarity grade without lasering. GIA and other labs will grade lasered diamonds, but the use of lasering is indicated on the report under "Comments" or "Key to the Symbols." If considering a diamond without a diamond grading report, you must be sure to ask whether or not the diamond is lasered. Some countries don't require disclosure, and for several years the Federal Trade Commission suspended the requirement to disclose lasering in the United States. This position was reversed—disclosure is now required—but it may take several years for compliance to be restored. If a lab report does not accompany the stone, you must be sure to ask explicitly, and verify it with an independent gemologist-appraiser.

Fracture Filling

Fractures—cracks or breaks—that would normally be visible and detract from the beauty of a diamond can often be filled with a nearly colorless, glasslike substance. After filling, these breaks virtually disappear and will no longer be seen, except under magnification. Filling is *not* a permanent treatment, and special precautions are required when cleaning and repairing jewelry containing a filled diamond. With proper care, such stones may remain beautiful for many years. Careless handling, however, can cause the filler to leave the stone or change color, resulting in a much less attractive diamond. Some filling materials are much more stable than others, but at present it is usually not possible to know what filler has been used in a given stone. Should the filler be accidentally removed, your jeweler can have the treatment repeated to restore the stone's original appearance. The GIA will not issue a grading report on a filled diamond, but other labs will (indicating the grade it appears to be after filling).

Filled diamonds cost much less than other diamonds. They can be a very attractive and affordable alternative as long as you know what you are buying, understand the limitations, and pay the right price. Be sure to ask explicitly whether or not the stone has been fracture-filled, and if the stone does not have a report from a respected lab (see appendix), get a statement *on the bill of sale* as to whether or not it is fracture-filled.

7

Weight

What Is a Carat?

Diamonds are sold by the *carat* (ct), not to be confused with *karat* (kt), which in the United States refers to gold purity. Since 1913, most countries have agreed that a carat weighs 200 milligrams, or $\frac{1}{5}$ gram.

Before 1913, the carat weight varied depending on the country of origin—usually weighing *more* than the modern carat. The Indian carat didn't weigh the same as the English carat; the French carat was different from the Indian and the English. This is important if you have, or are thinking of buying, a very old piece that still has the original bill of sale indicating carat weight. Since the old carat usually weighed *more* than the post-1913 *metric carat,* an old three-carat stone will often weigh more than three carats by modern standards. Today the term *carat* means the metric carat, the 200-milligram carat with five carats weighing one gram.

Jewelers often refer to the carat weight of diamonds in terms of *points.* This is particularly true of stones under one carat. There are 100 points to a carat, so if a jeweler says that a stone weighs 75 points, he means it weighs $\frac{75}{100}$ of a carat, or $\frac{3}{4}$ carat. A 25-point stone is $\frac{1}{4}$ carat. A 10-point stone is $\frac{1}{10}$ carat.

The carat is a unit of weight, not size. We wish to stress this point, since most people think that a one-carat stone is a particular size. Most people, therefore, would expect a one-carat diamond and a one-carat emerald, for example, to look the same size or to have the same apparent dimensions. This is not the case.

Comparing a one-carat diamond with a one-carat emerald and a one-carat ruby easily illustrates this point. First, emerald weighs less than

Sizes and Weights of Various Diamond Cuts				
Weight (ct)	Emerald	Marquise	Pear	Brilliant
5				
4				
3				
2½				
2				
1½				
1¼				
1				
¾				
½				

diamond, and ruby weighs more than diamond. This means that a one-carat emerald will look larger than a one-carat diamond, while the ruby will look smaller than a diamond of the same weight. Emerald, with a mineral composition that is lighter, will yield greater mass per carat; ruby, with its heavier composition, will yield less mass per carat.

Let's look at the principle another way. If you compare a one-inch cube of pine wood, a one-inch cube of aluminum, and a one-inch cube of iron, you would easily choose the cube of iron as heaviest, even though it has the same *volume* as the other materials. The iron is like the ruby, while the wood is like the emerald and the aluminum like the diamond. Equal *volumes* of different materials can have very different weights, depending on their density, also called mass or specific gravity.

Equal volumes of materials with the same density, however, should have approximately the same weight, so that in diamond, the carat weight has come to represent particular sizes. These sizes, as we've discussed, are based on diamonds cut to ideal proportions. Consequently, if properly cut, diamonds of the following weights should be approximately the sizes illustrated in the chart on page 62. Remember, however, *that these sizes will not apply to other gems.*

How Does Carat Weight Affect Value in Diamonds?

Diamond prices are usually quoted *per carat*. Diamonds of the finest and rarest quality are sold for the highest price per carat, and diamonds of progressively less rare quality are sold for a progressively lower price per carat. For example, a rare-quality diamond might sell for $20,000 per carat. So, a stone in this quality weighing 1.12 carats would cost $22,400. On the other hand, a stone of exactly the same weight, in a less rare quality, might sell for only $10,000 per carat, or $11,200.

Also, as a rule, the price increases per carat as we go from smaller to larger stones, since the larger stones are more rare and more limited in supply. For example, stones of the same quality weighing ½ carat will sell for more per carat than stones weighing ⅓ carat; stones weighing ¾ carat will sell for more per carat than stones of the same quality weighing ½ carat. For example, the per-carat price of a particular quality ½-carat stone might be $5,000, while the per-carat price for a ⅓-carat stone of the

Diameters and Corresponding Weights of Round Brilliant-Cut Diamonds

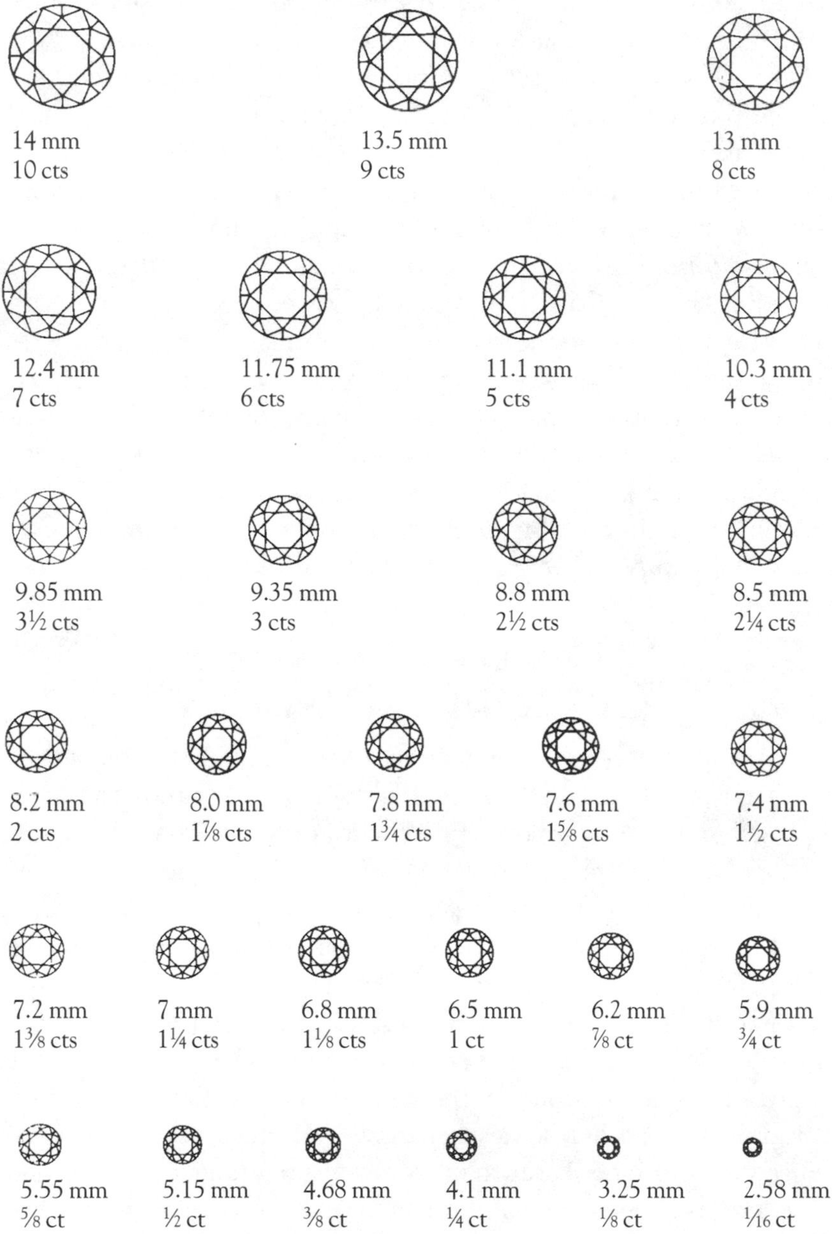
14 mm
10 cts
13.5 mm
9 cts
13 mm
8 cts
12.4 mm
7 cts
11.75 mm
6 cts
11.1 mm
5 cts
10.3 mm
4 cts
9.85 mm
3½ cts
9.35 mm
3 cts
8.8 mm
2½ cts
8.5 mm
2¼ cts
8.2 mm
2 cts
8.0 mm
1⅞ cts
7.8 mm
1¾ cts
7.6 mm
1⅝ cts
7.4 mm
1½ cts
7.2 mm
1⅜ cts
7 mm
1¼ cts
6.8 mm
1⅛ cts
6.5 mm
1 ct
6.2 mm
⅞ ct
5.9 mm
¾ ct
5.55 mm
⅝ ct
5.15 mm
½ ct
4.68 mm
⅜ ct
4.1 mm
¼ ct
3.25 mm
⅛ ct
2.58 mm
1/16 ct

same quality would be $3,000. The stones would cost $2,500 (½ x $5,000) and $1,000 (⅓ x $3,000) respectively.

Furthermore, stones of the same quality weighing exactly one carat will sell for *much* more than stones weighing 90 to 96 points. Thus, if you want a one-carat stone of a particular quality, but you can't afford it, you may find you can afford it in a 95-point stone—and a 95-point stone will give the impression of a full one-carat stone when set. You might be able to get your heart's desire after all.

As you will see, the price of a diamond does not increase proportionately; there are disproportionate jumps. And the larger and finer the stone (all else being equal in terms of overall quality), the more disproportionate the increase in cost per carat may be. A top-quality two-carat stone will not cost twice as much as a one-carat stone; it could easily be *three* times as much. A top-quality five-carat stone would not be five times the cost of a one-carat stone; it could easily be as much as ten times what a one-carat stone might cost.

What Is *Spread?*

The term *spread* may be used in response to the question "How large is this diamond?" But it can be misleading. Spread refers to the size the stone *appears* to be, based on its diameter. For example, if the diameter of the stone measured the same as you see in the diamond sizes chart, which represents the diameter of a perfectly proportioned stone, the jeweler might say it "spreads" one carat. But this does not mean it *weighs* one carat. It means it *looks* the same size as a perfectly cut one-carat stone. It may weigh less or more—usually less.

Diamonds are generally weighed before they are set, so the jeweler can give you the exact carat weight, since you are paying a certain price per carat. Remember, also, that the price per carat for a fine stone weighing 96 points is much less than for one weighing one carat or more. So it is unwise to accept any "approximate" weight, even though the difference seems so slight.

As you can see here, it is also important when buying a diamond to realize that since carat refers to weight, the manner in which a stone is cut can affect its apparent size. A one-carat stone that is cut shallow (see chapter 4) will appear larger in diameter than a stone that is cut thick (heavy). Conversely, a thick stone will appear smaller in diameter.

Furthermore, if the diamond has a thick girdle (see chapter 4), the stone will appear smaller in diameter. If this girdle is faceted, it tends to hide the ugly, frosted look of a thick girdle, but the fact remains that the girdle is thick, and the stone suffers because it will appear smaller in diameter than one would expect at a given carat weight. These stones are therefore somewhat cheaper per carat.

8

False Claims & Costly Bargains:
How to Spot Fraud and
Avoid Misrepresentation

As you have seen, many factors affect quality and value in diamonds. When the average person is looking at a stone already set, it is very difficult, if not impossible, to *see* differences that can dramatically affect cost. For this reason, we recommend buying any important diamond *unmounted,* and mounting it only after all the facts have been verified. But you don't have to be a gemologist or fear buying jewelry. Anyone who follows a few simple steps can buy with confidence.

Four Key Steps to Avoiding
Fraud or Misrepresentation

- *The first step is to buy from someone both accessible and knowledgeable.* Sellers should have the skill to know for sure what they themselves are buying and selling. This is not to say that there aren't bargains to be found in flea markets, estate sales, and so on, but you run a higher risk when purchasing in such places because of possible misinformation, intentional or otherwise. You must weigh the risk versus the potential reward. In addition, before making a final purchasing decision, ask yourself whether or not you will be able to find the seller again if what you bought turns out to be other than represented. This is equally true when you are traveling and are considering a jewelry purchase abroad.

  Keep in mind that unless the jeweler also does business in the

country where you live, it may be cost prohibitive to try to rectify any misrepresentation if it occurs.

- *Second, ask the right questions.* Don't be afraid to ask direct,
even pointed questions. The key to getting complete information
about what you are buying is asking good questions so you can be
sure you are aware of important factors affecting quality and
value. (To help you ask the right questions, we provide a complete
list in chapter 20.)

- *Third, get the facts in writing.* Be sure the seller is willing to put
in writing the answers to the questions you ask, and any representations made about the gem or jewelry you are considering. If
not, we recommend against purchasing from this seller unless
there is an unconditional return policy that allows merchandise to
be returned within a reasonable period of time for a full refund
(not a store credit). In this case, follow the next step to be safe.

- Finally, *verify the facts with a gemologist-appraiser.* It's especially
important to verify whatever has been put in writing with a professional gemologist-appraiser (see chapter 24). Some unscrupulous dealers are willing to put anything in writing to make the sale,
knowing that written assurances or claims about the stone are
often sufficient to satisfy buyers' doubts. So this last step may be
the most important to ensure that you make a wise decision.

In general, you need not worry about fraud or misrepresentation,
whether deliberate or unintentional, if you simply follow these four easy
steps. They may require a little more time and nominal additional
expense, but the end result will be greater knowledge—and assurance—
about your jewelry choice and your jeweler. And, they may save you from
a costly mistake.

Types of Misrepresentation
Beware of Bargains!

Diamonds Represented to Be Better Than They Are

Beware of bargains. Most are not. When a price seems too good to be
true, it usually is, unless the seller doesn't know its true value (which
reflects badly on the seller's expertise).

A large jewelry store in Philadelphia was found guilty of misrepresenting the quality of diamonds it was selling. Sales staff consistently represented their diamonds to be several color grades and/or flaw grades better than they actually were. As a result, their prices seemed much more attractive than those of other jewelers. Customers thought they were getting a much better buy from this firm than from others in the area, which may not have been the case; since customers didn't know the true quality of the stones they were buying, they couldn't make a fair comparison with what other jewelers were offering. Other jewelers in the area were, in fact, giving better value on stones comparable to what was actually being sold by this "bargain" firm.

Such firms can be found in every city. Many are even willing to put everything in writing, often including a full "appraisal." Such dishonest practices often go undetected because most people assume that when a seller is willing to "put it in writing," he or she is properly representing the item. Most buyers never bother to have the facts verified.

Are Wholesale Prices Really Wholesale?

It is natural to be lured by the promise of getting a diamond at a wholesale price: a price significantly below what most retailers charge. We've already discussed some of the pitfalls, but many fall into the trap of believing that even if they don't get exactly what they are told, they will still get it at a price below what they might have paid at a local jewelry store. Yet, this is frequently not the case.

We recently went undercover for one of the TV networks and made a purchase from a diamond dealer touting "wholesale" prices. In addition to misrepresentation of quality, the price we paid for the diamond was *double* the stone's *retail* value. We purchased a stone described by the seller to have a color grade of J–K and a clarity grade of SI_2. He gave us an appraisal with all the representations stated clearly in writing. The diamond was actually X-color, and the clarity was no better than I_2. It was also fracture-filled, despite the fact that he had shown us fracture-filled diamonds, explaining what they were—and supposedly gaining our confidence by so doing—and we had told him explicitly that we did not want a fracture-filled diamond! We paid $3,200 for the stone; the *retail* value was $1,400 to $1,500. We could have purchased this stone from any retail jeweler for less. The moral: don't assume you get a good buy just because you are in a "wholesale" jewelry district.

Scams Involving "Appraisals" Prior to Sale

Beware of jewelers who are not willing to put the facts in writing but who offer to let you take the stone, before the sale, to an appraiser in the neighborhood. This may be a scam. It is often seen in wholesale districts like New York's famous 47th Street.

The first step in this scam is to build you up with all the reasons why you are going to get an exceptional buy because the seller "bought it right" (whatever that means), or wants to "pass the savings on to you," or, isn't greedy ("I don't care who I sell to at wholesale; after all, a sale is a sale"), and so on. When you find something you are seriously interested in buying, the seller then explains, for a variety of seemingly valid reasons, why he or she will not put any information pertaining to the quality of the stone in writing, on the bill of sale. The salesperson offers to permit you to go with one of the firm's "bonded guards" to a local appraiser so that you can verify the facts and learn for yourself what a bargain you are getting. Many people are immediately hooked, and conclude erroneously that since they can get an appraisal if they choose, everything must be in order. So they don't. And they become the victims of intentional misrepresentation.

Those who do wish to get an appraisal usually face another problem. They don't know any appraiser—or certainly not any in the neighborhood. Many visitors to 47th Street, for example, are from out of town and don't know anyone local. Unscrupulous sellers often count on this because it gives them the opportunity to recommend several "reliable" appraisers. Or, rather than be so obvious, they suggest you "choose" your own (some even make a fuss about not wanting to know whom you choose). Many purchasers make a big mistake here because they don't realize that *all appraisers are not the same, nor are all appraisers equally competent or reliable* (see chapter 24). Unfortunately, the "reliable appraiser" in this situation often means that the seller can rely on the appraiser to tell the prospective buyers what the seller wants them to hear.

One must always be careful of recommendations from the seller. While legitimate jewelers usually know better than anyone else who the best gemologist-appraisers are in their communities, and their recommendations should be respected, you must still be sure to check the credentials yourself to avoid such scams. Unfortunately, especially in the jewelry districts of major cities, far too many appraisers are not qualified, and some are in collusion with unscrupulous jewelers.

One of our clients had an experience that provides an excellent example of how this type of scam can work. She went to a 47th Street firm in New York. She was offered a five-plus carat diamond ring at a price that was one-fourth the price most retailers had been quoting for what appeared to be comparable quality. She thought the ring looked very beautiful and became very excited about being able to get such a bargain. But when she asked the seller if he would back up his description of the quality of the diamond in writing, he said it was against his store policy, but he would be happy for her to take the ring to a neighborhood appraiser before she purchased it.

This made her cautious, especially since she didn't know any local appraiser. Luckily, we were in New York at the time and were able to use a colleague's lab to examine the ring carefully (it was awkward for the seller to refuse). Not surprisingly, the quality was not as represented. The flaw grade had been misrepresented by *four* grades, and the color had been enhanced *seven grades* by "painting" (painted diamonds have a coating that doesn't come off with normal cleaning and may take months or years to wear off. We had to clean the stone chemically to determine that it was painted and to reveal its true color)!

In this particular case, given the true value of the diamond, the price being asked for the ring was certainly not the "steal" it appeared to be. It wasn't a bad price, but other retailers were offering comparable stones at comparable prices or less.

Such practices are overtly dishonest, of course, but all too often they leave honest jewelers in a bad light as a result. In such cases, the dishonest jeweler will appear to be offering the best price, while the honest jeweler—who may actually be offering the best value—falsely appears to be charging "too much."

In general, you need to guard against fraud or misrepresentation in one of the following four areas:

- Weight misrepresentation
- Color alteration and misgrading
- Flaw concealment and misgrading
- Certification—alteration and counterfeit certificates

Weight

Giving "total weight" of all stones where more than one is involved, rather than the exact weight of the main stone, is another form of misrepresentation. This is in strict violation of Federal Trade Commission rulings. When the weight is given, particularly on any display card, descriptive tag, or other type of advertising for a particular piece of jewelry, the weight of the main stone or stones should be clearly indicated as well as the total weight of all the stones.

Thus, if you purchase a "three-carat diamond" ring with one large center stone and two small side stones (as found in many engagement rings), the center stone's weight should be clearly stated; for example, "The weight of the center stone is 2.80 carats, with side stones that weigh 0.10 carat each, for a total weight of 3.00 carats." There is a tremendous price difference between a single stone weighing three carats and numerous stones having a total weight of three carats. A single three-carat stone of good quality could sell for $50,000, while three carats consisting of numerous stones (even with some weighing as much as a carat or more) of the same quality could sell anywhere from $5,000 to $20,000, depending on how many there are and the weight of each.

When inquiring about the weight of a diamond, don't ask the wrong question. Usually the jeweler will be asked how *large* the stone is, rather than how much it *weighs*. In any case, the answer should provide the exact carat weight. Beware when the response includes the word spread: "this stone *spreads* one carat." *A stone that spreads one carat does not weigh one carat.* That simply means it *looks* like a one-carat stone in its width.

Color

Enhancing Color Artificially— High-Tech Treatment with Permanent Results

Diamonds can be treated in many ways to improve their color. Some are temporary and others are permanent. Regardless of permanence, any treatment should be disclosed so that you know you are paying an appropriate price.

High-pressure/high-temperature annealing (HPHT). This is a new treatment being used to enhance diamonds. The process can transform very tinted, off-white diamonds (as low as Q–Z colors) into colorless and near-colorless stones—even D, E, F! It can also be used to create fancy colors. Fancy colors include greenish yellow, yellowish green, and even very rare shades of pink and blue. The change is permanent, but detection requires sophisticated equipment that can be found only in major gem-testing laboratories.

In the case of colorless diamonds, this particular treatment process is effective only on very rare diamond types (Type IIa and Type Ia/b). Where consumers are concerned, this is fortunate because a competent gemologist can determine whether or not a diamond is one of these rare types. If a diamond is not, then it could not have been treated in this manner; if it is, only then must it be submitted to a major laboratory such as the GIA to determine whether or not the color has been enhanced by HPHT annealing. The GIA and other labs will issue a diamond grading report on diamonds treated in this manner, indicating the treatment under the "comments" section of the report.

It has been estimated that fewer than 2 percent of all diamonds are Type IIa; Type Ia/b is even rarer. They represent a larger percentage of jewelry-quality diamonds, however, and some are unusually large and clean. Therefore, if a diamond is transformed from a strongly tinted yellow or brown color into a "colorless" stone, the cost difference could be very great. It is more important than ever to have laboratory documentation on any fine diamond purchased today.

A word of caution: Diamonds treated by HPHT annealing entered the marketplace before the gemological community was aware of the use of this technology on diamonds and before they understood how to distinguish them from natural diamonds. *We recommend that any colorless or near-colorless diamond that has a diamond report issued between January 1996 and June 2000 be examined by a gemologist to determine whether or not it is Type IIa or Ia/b, and if so, that it be resubmitted to a major gem-testing lab (see appendix) for verification.*

Fancy-color diamonds produced by the HPHT annealing process, especially pink and blue diamonds, are more difficult to detect and involve not only Type IIa and Ia/b diamonds but other diamond types as well, so merely having a gemologist confirm whether or not the stone is

Type IIa and Ia/b will not necessarily be useful. We highly recommend that fancy-color blue and pink diamonds purchased recently be accompanied by a lab report issued by a major lab, and that if a report already accompanies the stone, that it be resubmitted if the report predates December 2000.

Radiation treatment. Exposing off-color diamonds such as yellowish or brownish tinted stones (and also badly flawed stones in which the flaws would be less noticeable against a colored background) to certain types of radiation can result in the production of fancy-colored stones. This treatment produces rich yellows, greens, and blues, and greatly enhances salability because these colors are very desirable. In and of itself, radiation is not fraud; in fact, it may make a "fancy" color diamond affordable to someone otherwise unable to afford one. But again, just be sure that the stone is properly represented and you know what you are buying, and that you are getting it at the right price—which should be much lower than that of the natural fancy.

Temporary Color Enhancement

Touching the culet with ink. Touching the culet, or side, of a slightly yellow stone with a coating of purple ink, such as found in an indelible pencil, neutralizes the yellow, producing a whiter-looking stone. This can be easily detected by washing the stone in alcohol or water. If you have any questions about the color, tactfully request that the stone be washed (in front of you) for better examination. A reputable jeweler should have no objection to this request.

Improving the color by using a sputtering technique. This technique (also called "painting" the diamond) involves sputtering a very thin coating of a special substance over the stone or part of the stone, usually the back, where it will be harder to detect when mounted. The girdle area can also be "painted" with the substance and create the same effect. The substance, like indelible pencil, also neutralizes the yellow and thereby improves the color by as much as seven color grades, but unlike indelible ink, *the substance will not wash off.* It can be removed in two ways: by rubbing the stone briskly and firmly with a cleanser, or by boiling the stone carefully in sulfuric acid. If the stone is already mounted and is coated on the back, using cleanser is not feasible. The sulfuric acid method is the only way. *But please note:* using sulfuric acid can be extremely dangerous and must be done only by an experienced person. We cannot over-state the hazards of conducting this test.

This technique is not frequently used, but stones treated in this man-ner do appear often enough to be worth mentioning.

Coating the diamond with chemicals and baking it in a small lab-type oven. This technique also tends to neutralize some of the yellow, thereby producing a better color grade. This coating will be removed eventually by repeated hot ultrasonic cleanings, which will gradually erode the coating. A more rapid removal can be accomplished by the more dangerous method of boiling in sulfuric acid.

Treated stones must be represented as "treated stones" and should be priced accordingly. Unfortunately, too often, in their passage through many hands, the fact that they have been treated ("radiated" or "bom-barded") is overlooked or forgotten—intentionally or accidentally. Whether the color is natural or treated can often be determined by spec-troscopic examination, which can be provided by a gem-testing labora-tory (see appendix). Not all gemologists, however, are competent with spectroscopic procedures, and some fancy-color diamonds require exam-ination with very sophisticated equipment not available to most labs. If your gemologist lacks the skill or equipment, stones can be submitted to a laboratory such as the GIA's Gem Trade Laboratory for verification. Most *natural* fancy-colored diamonds sold by jewelers in the United States are accompanied by a GIA report.

Erroneous Color Grading

Mistakes in grading of color may be unintentional (resulting from insufficient training or experience, or simply from carelessness), or they may be deliberate. You're safer considering the purchase of a stone that has had such important data as color described in a diamond grading report (or certificate) issued by one of several different laboratories offer-ing this service. Many jewelry firms now offer diamonds accompanied by grading reports; those issued by the GIA are the most widely used in the United States. Diamonds accompanied by reports usually sell for slightly more per carat, but they provide an element of security for the average consumer as well as credible documentation if you wish to sell this stone at some future time. If the stone you are considering is accom-panied by such a report, be sure to verify that the information on the certificate is accurate by taking the stone to a competent gemologist or lab (see chapter 24).

Clarity Enhancement and Flaw Concealment

Clarity Enhancement

Be especially alert to the possibility that clarity may be enhanced. The two most frequently used techniques are lasering inclusions and filling fractures. In both cases, dark inclusions or cracks that might normally be visible—in some cases, very visible—are concealed or become much less noticeable (these techniques are discussed in chapter 6). Be sure to ask whether or not the stone has been lasered or filled. As long as you know, and pay the right price, a clarity-enhanced diamond may be an attractive choice.

Flaw Concealment

Where possible, flaws are concealed by their settings. The good stone setter will try to set a stone in such a manner that the setting will help to conceal any visible imperfections. For this reason, flaws near or at the girdle will downgrade a stone less than those in the center of a stone; since most settings cover all or part of the girdle, they are simply less visible here. Indeed, a setting can make a flaw "invisible."

There is nothing fraudulent in such uses of settings as long as the stone is properly represented. The only danger is that not only the customer but also the jeweler may not have seen the imperfection concealed by the setting.

Can concealment affect value? In most diamonds other than grade FL or grade IF, the presence of a minor flaw concealed under a prong will not affect the price significantly. However, given the difference in price between diamonds graded FL or IF and VVS_1, a minor blemish or inclusion hidden by the setting that might result in a VVS_1 stone being graded FL could have a significant effect on value, especially if the stone has exceptionally fine color. For this reason, FL or IF stones should be viewed *unmounted*.

Certification of Diamonds

Today, most fine diamonds weighing one carat or more are carefully evaluated by a respected laboratory, such as the GIA or the American Gemological Laboratories (AGL), before being set and are issued a diamond grading report. That report both certifies the diamond as genuine and describes it, providing such important information as color grade, flaw grade, weight, cutting and proportioning, and so on. If you are considering the purchase of a very fine diamond weighing one carat or more and it is *not* accompanied by such a report, we would strongly recommend that you or the seller have the stone evaluated by the GIA or another respected laboratory before purchase. You should do so even if it means having a stone that is already set removed from the setting and reset. Given the significant difference in cost that can result from a grading error in the rarer grades, we believe this procedure is worth the inconvenience and expense.

Unfortunately, the confidence of the public in stones accompanied by certificates has given rise to the practice of altering and counterfeiting them. While you can be relatively sure that "certificated" stones sold by reputable, established jewelry firms are what they claim to be, some suppliers and dealers seize opportunities to prey on the unsuspecting. This is one compelling reason to seek a gemologist-appraiser with respected credentials to examine the diamond and accompanying documentation (see chapter 24).

Altering Certificates

Sometimes information is changed on an otherwise valid certificate; for example, the flaw or color grade may be altered. If you have any question regarding the information on the certificate, a phone call to the lab, giving them the certificate number and date, will enable you to verify the information on the certificate.

Counterfeit GIA Certificates and Certification from Non-Existent Laboratories

Producing a certificate from a nonexistent lab is an increasingly common problem as is the use of counterfeit reports purportedly issued by GIA when they are not. A major New York diamond dealer was recently

arrested for selling diamonds on the Internet with counterfeit GIA diamond grading reports. Stones accompanied by fancy "certificates" from
impressive-sounding labs that don't exist are also appearing more and
more frequently. If the certificate is not from one of the recognized labs
(see appendix), it should be carefully checked. Have reputable jewelers
in the area heard of this lab? Has the Better Business Bureau had any
complaints? If the lab seems legitimate, call to verify the information on
the certificate, and if all seems in order, you can probably rest comfort-
ably. Otherwise, you may need to have the facts verified by another
gemologist or recognized lab.

Some jewelers may not allow verification of an existing certificate by
a little-known lab simply because they've been victims themselves or it
isn't worth the inconvenience to them. In this case, you might ask the jeweler to get the stone certificated by one of the recognized labs. Many
jewelers today are happy to provide this service. If not, then you must
decide how badly you want the stone, how much you feel you can trust
the jeweler, and what degree of monetary risk you can afford.

Switching the Stone Described on a Report

In some cases the report is bona fide but the stone has been switched.
To protect both the consumer and the lab, some labs are taking advantage
of ingenious techniques to ensure against switching. For example, a service called Gemprint utilizes laser technology to display a diamond's unique
pattern of reflection and then records it photographically. The result is an
electronic "fingerprint" of the diamond, which can be used for identification purposes (see chapter 24). In addition, the GIA and other labs can now
actually inscribe its report number, which is visible only under magnification, directly onto the diamond, along the girdle. By so doing, one can
very easily be sure a specific stone matches a specific certificate simply by
matching the numbers. There is an additional fee for this service.

In the absence of such a mark, one clue to a switched stone might be
provided by comparing the carat weight and dimensions given on the
report. If the measurements and weight match exactly, the probability is
slim that the stone has been switched, provided the report hasn't been
altered. But it's always a good idea to contact the lab to confirm the
details of the report, and then double-check all the information. If the
measurements don't match, the type and placement of inclusions or blem-

ishes might enable you to determine if the stone in question is the one described on the report but has been altered; the dimensions might differ if, for example, the stone was nicked or chipped and subsequently recut or repolished. In such a case, ask the jeweler to place the stone under the microscope to enable you to see what should be in the stone.

Unfortunately, if the stone has been mounted, it may be difficult to get precise measurements to compare. In this case, if there is any cause for suspicion, you may be taking a risk to buy the stone unless the seller allows you to have the stone removed from the setting and to have both the report and the stone verified by a qualified gemologist-appraiser. This arrangement requires an understanding in writing that the stone can be returned within a certain time limit if the customer learns it is not as represented.

Always make sure in this situation, for both your protection and the jeweler's, that the jeweler writes down on the bill of sale or memo *all* of the stone's dimensions as best as can be determined: diameter or length and width, depth, and weight. This is to help ensure that you aren't accused of switching the stone after leaving the premises in the event you must return it.

Avoid "Bargains"—And Avoid Costly Mistakes

Take time to do your homework first, to learn what to look for and what questions to ask. Keep our recommended four-step procedure in mind, then shop carefully and compare stones being offered by several fine jewelers in your community. This will give you a chance to get a clearer sense of what something should legitimately sell for, decide whether or not something sounds "too good to be true," and, most important, make sounder decisions about which jeweler is asking a *fair* price.

And remember: No one gives away a valuable gem. There are very few "steals," and even fewer people are qualified to truly know a "steal" when they see one.

Is It a Diamond or a Diamond Imposter?

How can you tell if a stone is really a diamond? As we have said many times, unless you are an expert—or consult one—you cannot be sure about the identification of a stone. Nevertheless, there are a few simple tests you can perform that will show up most diamond imposters quite quickly. Here are a few things to look for.

Is newsprint readable or observable through the stone? If the stone is a round, modern-cut stone and is loose or mounted in such a way as to allow you to place it table-down over some small newsprint, check whether you can see or read any portion of the lettering. If so, it is not a diamond. Refraction of light within a genuine diamond is such you will not be able to see any of the letters in the newsprint.

Is the stone glued into the setting? Diamonds are seldom glued in. Rhinestones often are.

Is the back open or closed? If the stone is a properly set diamond, the back of the setting will usually be open, allowing you to readily see a portion of the pavilion. Some *antique* pieces containing rose-cut or single-cut diamonds may have closed backs, and some of today's finest custom designers may use a closed-back technique. Otherwise, if a piece has a closed back it is probably rhinestone, the back being closed to conceal silver foil applied to the back of the stone to create greater brilliance.

Recently a young woman called and asked if we would examine an antique diamond ring she'd inherited from her great-grandmother. She mentioned that as she was cleaning it, one of its two diamonds had fallen out of the setting, and inside the setting she saw what she described as pieces of "mirror." She added, "Isn't that strange?" Of course our suspicions were immediately aroused, and upon examination of the piece, they were completely confirmed.

When we saw the ring, we could immediately understand why she felt it was a valuable heirloom. It was beautiful, with a classic design. It held two "diamonds" appearing to be approximately one carat each. The ring mounting was finely worked platinum filigree. But the design of the mounting, which had been common in her great-grandmother's day, made viewing the stones from the side of the ring almost impossible. The top of the stone and the beautiful platinum work were visible, but little more. Furthermore, the back was not completely enclosed; a small round hole would easily have led to the assumption that the stones were the real thing, since the setting wasn't completely closed, as were most imitations at that time. The "set" diamond appeared to be a well-proportioned old-mine cut with very good color. The loose stone, however, with some of the "shiny stuff" still clinging to it, lacked brilliance and fire.

This was one of the finest examples of fraud we had seen in a long time. The "stones" were well cut and proportioned; the mounting was beautifully worked in a precious metal; the stones were held by very small prongs, which was typical of good design at that time. But inside the mounting, backing the stones, was silver foil. They were not genuine diamonds but foil-backed glass.

The use of silver foil is an effective method to "create" a diamond. It acts as a mirror to reflect light and makes the stone appear so brilliant and lively that it can pass as a diamond. The foiling seen today consists of making the back facets into true mirrors and then giving the backs of these mirrors a protective coating of gilt paint. These are then set in jewelry so that their backs are hidden.

It's a sad story, but not an altogether uncommon one. We don't know how many more rings as cleverly done exist today, but approximately 5 percent of the antique jewelry we see is set with fake gems. Fine glass imitations (often referred to as "paste") have been with us since the Venetians of the Renaissance period perfected the art of glassmaking. Fraud, unfortunately, has been with us since time immemorial. Don't allow yourself to be deluded into believing that something you possess is "genuine" simply because it is "antique" or has "been in the family" for a long time.

How many facets are visible on the top? In cheaper glass imitations, only nine top facets are usually visible, as opposed to thirty-three visible top facets in a diamond or "good" simulation. Single-cut or Swiss-cut diamonds (see chapter 4) will also show only nine facets on top, but they will be set in open-back mountings, whereas cheap glass imitations are usually set in closed-back mountings.

Does the girdle of the stone appear to be "frosted?" The girdles of most diamonds are unpolished, with a ground-glass–like appearance that suggests frostiness. Some diamond imitations also have a frosted appearance, but of all of these, a diamond has the whitest frostiness—like clean, dry, ground glass. On the other hand, some diamonds do have polished or faceted girdles, and thus no frostiness will be present. You can develop an eye for this by asking a reliable jeweler to point out the differences between a polished girdle, an unpolished girdle, and a faceted girdle.

Is the cut symmetrical? Since diamond is so valuable and symmetry so important to its overall appearance and desirability, the symmetry of

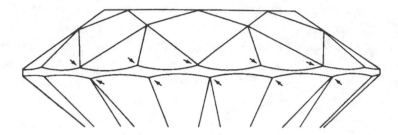

Misalignment of crown and pavilion

the faceting on a diamond will be very carefully executed, whereas in diamond simulations the symmetry of the facets may be sloppy. For example, the eight kite-shaped facets (sometimes called bezel facets) will often be missing one or more points on the side, or on the top or bottom, showing a small straight edge rather than a point. This sloppy faceting can be an important indication that the stone in question is not a diamond, since it indicates that the cutter did not take proper care. It should be noted that some poorer-grade or old-cut diamonds may also show sloppiness.

Are the crown and the pavilion of the stone properly aligned? While occasionally a diamond may show partial misalignment, imitations are frequently and often badly misaligned.

Are the facet edges or faces scratched, chipped, or worn? Diamond imitations include some stones that are very soft and/or brittle, such as zircon, GGG (an artificial simulation), Fabulite (an artificial diamond simulation also known as Wellington Diamond), and glass. Because of their lack of hardness and, in the case of zircon, possible brittleness, these imitations will show wear easily, and one can often detect scratches or chips on the facet edges or faces. The edges are somewhat more vulnerable, and scratches or chips may be more easily seen there, so check the edges first. Then check the flat faces for scratches. Check both the areas that would be most exposed and the areas around the prongs, where a setter might have accidentally scratched the stone while setting it.

Zircon, a stone found in nature that is often confused with cubic zirconia (CZ), an artificial imitation, is relatively hard but very brittle, so it will almost always show chipping at the edges of the facets if the stone has been worn in jewelry for a year or more. Glass and Fabulite will also show scratches after minimal exposure to handling and wear. Fabulite further differs from diamond in its fire; it will show even more fire than diamond, but with a strong bluish cast.

In addition, with a very good eye or the aid of a magnifier, you can examine the lines or edges where the facets come together in these imitation materials. In diamond, these facet edges are very sharp because of the stone's spectacular hardness. In most simulations, however, since the stone is so much softer, the final polishing technique rounds off those edges, and that sharpness is absent.

Some diamond look-alikes, however, are more durable and resistant to noticeable wear. These include colorless synthetic spinel, colorless synthetic sapphire, colorless quartz, YAG (yttrium aluminum garnet; artificial), and CZ. While these may scratch or chip over time with regular wear and daily abuse, scratches or chips are not as numerous and will be less noticeable.

An Important Word about Cubic Zirconia

Cubic zirconia is the best diamond simulation made to date, and even some jewelers have mistaken these stones for diamonds. Shortly after its appearance, several well-known jewelers in Washington, D.C., found themselves stuck with CZ instead of the one-carat diamonds they thought they'd purchased. The crooks were very clever. A well-dressed couple would arrive at the diamond counter and ask to see various one-carat round, brilliant-cut loose diamonds. Because of their fine appearance and educated manner, the jewelers relaxed their guard. The couple would then leave, not making a purchase decision just then, but promising to return. When the jewelers went to replace their merchandise, something didn't seem quite right. Upon close examination, the jewelers discovered that the "nice couple" had pocketed the genuine diamonds and substituted CZ.

Cubic zirconia is almost as brilliant as diamond, has even greater fire (which masks its lesser brilliance), and is relatively hard, giving it good durability and wearability. It is also being produced today in fancy colors—red, green, and yellow—and can provide a nice diamond alternative as a means to offset or dress up colored stones in jewelry if diamonds are unaffordable.

But make sure you *know* what you are buying. For example, if you are shown a lovely amethyst or sapphire ring dressed up with "diamonds," make sure to ask whether the colorless stones are diamonds. And if you are having your own piece of jewelry custom made, you might want to consider using CZ. You can ask your jeweler to order CZ for you. CZ makes attractive jewelry that can be worn every day without worry.

How Can You Tell If You Have a CZ?

Some of the tests already discussed may help you detect a CZ. The following, however, may eliminate any remaining doubt.

If it is a loose stone, have it weighed. If you are familiar with diamond sizes (see pages 60 and 62) or have a spread gauge (which can be purchased for under $10), you can estimate the diamond carat weight by its spread. A loose stone can be weighed on a scale, which most jewelers have handy, and you can determine how much it should weigh if it is truly a diamond. If the weight is much greater than the diamond weight should be, based on its spread, then it is not a diamond. A CZ is approximately 75 percent heavier than a diamond of the same spread. For example, a CZ that looks like a 1-carat diamond size-wise will weigh $1\frac{3}{4}$ carats; a CZ that looks like a $\frac{1}{4}$-carat diamond in terms of size will weigh approximately $\frac{40}{100}$ carat.

Look at the girdle. If the girdle is frosted, a subdued whiteness resembling slightly wet or oiled frosted glass will indicate CZ. Unfortunately, looking at girdles to differentiate between the appearance of frosted CZ and frosted diamond girdles requires considerable experience.

Test the stone with a carbide scriber. CZ can be scratched with a fine-point carbide scriber, also available at most jewelry supply houses for under $15. If the scriber is forcibly pushed perpendicularly to any of the facets (the table being the easiest) and then drawn across this flat surface, you will scratch it. You cannot scratch a diamond except with another diamond. But be sensible and considerate. Don't heedlessly scratch merchandise that doesn't belong to you—particularly if the jeweler or seller doesn't represent the stone as a diamond.

Examine the stone, loose or mounted, for fluorescence. Both CZ and diamond fluoresce, but the colors and intensities will be different.

Use an electronic diamond tester. There are pocket-size diamond testers for under $175 that will tell you whether or not you have a dia-

FALSE CLAIMS & COSTLY BARGAINS   83

mond. If you follow the instructions, they are easy to use and fairly reliable. Most won't tell you what you have if it's *not* diamond; they will only confirm whether or not it *is* diamond.

If after these tests you have some questions, take the stone to a qualified gemologist with lab facilities for positive identification.

Synthetic Moissanite—A Sparkling Newcomer

A new diamond imitation is being sold today under the name *moissanite,* although it should be called *synthetic moissanite,* since what is being sold in jewelry stores is not natural but created in laboratories. It is silicon carbide, named after Dr. Moissan, the French scientist who discovered it. Advertisements describe it as one of nature's rarest gems, but it does not occur in nature as a gemstone, only as a microscopic inclusion.

It made news upon its introduction because it fooled most electronic diamond testers (those measuring thermal conductivity), indicating "diamond" when tested! Many concluded from this that it was indistinguishable from diamond, but this is far from the case. It has several distinctive characteristics that immediately separate it from diamond. Nevertheless, synthetic moissanite is being misrepresented as diamond in new and antique jewelry, and there have been several cases in which jewelers have switched stones substituting synthetic moissanite for the original diamond. Gemologists can quickly and easily separate diamond from synthetic moissanite with simple tests, in most cases using only a 10x loupe. There is also new diamond testing equipment that can instantly distinguish between the two.

Synthetic moissanite is lighter than diamond, so weighing it is a quick way to distinguish it from diamond if the stone is unmounted. While moissanite is not as hard as diamond, it is harder than CZ and even harder than ruby and sapphire, which means it is a very durable material that can take a very high polish. It has even greater brilliance and much more dispersion (fire) than either diamond or CZ. One disadvantage in comparison with CZ is that it is much more expensive, costing approximately a tenth of what a comparable diamond costs.

Synthetic moissanite has a distinctive appearance and may make an attractive choice for those who want something new and different. As a diamond imitation, given its high cost and the fact that CZ actually looks more like diamond, only time will tell whether or not it will replace CZ as the diamond imitation of the twenty-first century. No synthetic gem has ever attained the status of a natural gem, and moissanite is a "new gem" without a natural counterpart, so its success remains an even bigger question.

A Word about Synthetic Diamonds

Synthetic diamonds are diamonds that are made in the laboratory. Unlike CZ, moissanite, and other diamond imitations, all of which differ from diamond physically and chemically, synthetic diamond *duplicates* the natural. That is, it is scientifically produced in a laboratory with virtually the same physical and chemical properties. In essence, it is diamond. But it is not identical. Since it is grown in laboratories, it shows distinctive growth features not seen in natural diamonds, so all synthetic diamonds now being produced can be distinguished from natural diamonds. In many cases, however, identification requires sophisticated scientific instrumentation found only in major gem-testing laboratories. For this reason, we once again stress the importance of having laboratory documentation for any fine diamond. *Note:* Electronic diamond testers have become very popular and are very effective in distinguishing diamond imitations, such as CZ, YAG, Fabulite, and others, from diamond. However, they *cannot* distinguish between synthetic and natural diamonds, and they *will* indicate "diamond" when testing synthetic diamond.

Synthetic gem-quality diamonds are now commercially available in a range of sizes, shapes, and colors. Yellow, red, blue, and pink stones are now being produced in sizes up to two carats and are creating a sensation in the marketplace because they provide very beautiful alternatives to their much rarer, and much costlier, natural counterparts. Where colorless and near-colorless synthetic diamonds are concerned, laboratories have succeeded in producing them, but production costs are still too high for them to be commercially viable at this time.

Comparison of Diamonds and Diamond Look-Alikes

Name of Stone	Hardness (Mohs' Scale 1–10, 1 = Soft, 10 = Hardest)	Read-through*	Degree of Dispersion (Fire, Flashes of Color Observed)	Wearability
Diamond	10 (Hardest natural substance in existence)	None, if properly cut	High; lots of fire and liveliness	Excellent
Strontium titanate (also known as Fabulite or Wellington Diamond)	5–6 (Soft)	None, if properly cut	Extremely high; too high (much more than diamond); shows lots of blue flashes	Poor—scratches and wears badly
Cubic zirconia (CZ)	8.5 (Hard)	Slight	Very high; lots of life	Very good
Gadolinium gallium garnet (GGG; produced very briefly)	6.5 (Somewhat soft)	Moderate	High; almost identical to diamond	Fair—scratches easily; wears badly; sunlight causes brownish discoloration
Yttrium aluminum garnet (YAG; used extensively)	8.5 (Hard)	Strong	Very low; almost no visible display of fire	Good
Synthetic rutile (shows yellowish color)	6.5 (Soft)	None	Extremely high; lots of life—but strong yellowish flashes	Poor; scratches easily and shows excessive wear
Zircon	7.5 (Moderately hard)	Moderate	Good; lively	Fair—hard but brittle, so chips easily and shows wear equivalent to much softer stones
Synthetic sapphire	9 (Very hard)	Very strong	Very low; little life or display of color flashes	Very good
Synthetic spinel	8 (Hard)	Very strong	Low; little "life"	Very good
Glass	5–6.5 (Soft)	Very strong	Variable—low to good depending on quality of glass and cut	Poor; susceptible to scratches, chipping, and excessive wear
Synthetic moissanite	9.25 (Very hard)	None	Extremely high; much too high for diamond; higher than CZ	Excellent

*This technique—the ability and ease with which one can read print while looking through the stone—is reliable only when looking at round, brilliant-cut stones (although it is *sometimes* useful for ovals and some fancy cuts).

9

Comparing Diamond Prices

A ll too often, people look for easy answers to complex problems. Many would like to have a simple list of diamond grades and corresponding prices, by size. Unfortunately, market conditions are constantly changing, and, more important, significant differences in price often result from subtle differences in quality not readily discernible to any but the professional. Therefore, it is not possible to provide a simple answer to this complex question.

But that does not mean we cannot provide you with some general guidelines that will help you understand the *relative* effects of each of the four primary factors used to determine the value of diamonds. The following charts are not intended as hard price lists of what you should be paying in a jewelry store; instead, they should be used as a guideline—a foundation on which you can place more current information that reflects the variations in a constantly fluctuating market. Keep in mind that these prices are for unmounted stones. Fine settings and custom designed one-of-a-kind pieces can add substantially to the price.

Extreme differences between the prices given on the following pages and a price you might be quoted for a diamond should be examined carefully; if the price is *much lower,* be sure to seek a gemologist or gemologist-appraiser to check the quality and verify that the stone is as represented. If the price is *much higher,* do some comparison shopping in your community to be sure the seller is offering good value.

Note that the prices given here are for round, brilliant-cut diamonds with good proportioning; stones with excellent proportioning will sell for more, while stones with poor proportioning can sell for much less. Diamonds having fancy shapes—shapes other than round—normally sell for anywhere from 5 to 15 percent less. However, if a particular shape is in great demand, the price can be higher than for round stones.

Finally, before relying too heavily on the prices listed in this chapter, be sure you read the information on diamond grading reports (for detailed information on how to read a diamond report, read *Diamonds: The Antoinette Matlins Buying Guide*). This knowledge will give you additional input on adjusting diamond prices according to the more subtle factors that affect quality and value. Finally, if you are contemplating the purchase of a particular stone, be sure to have the facts verified by a qualified gemologist-appraiser.

Retail Price Guide for Well-Cut Round Diamonds*

Notice both the tremendous price fluctuation among stones of the same size due to differences in the flaw grades and color grades, and the disproportionate jumps in cost *per carat*, depending upon size.

lightface indicates $\dfrac{\text{PRICE PER CARAT}}{\textbf{PRICE PER STONE}}$ in U.S. Dollars
boldface indicates

½ Carat   COLOR GRADE

		D	E	F	G	H	I	J	K
	IF†	15,650	12,650	11,500	10,125	8,750	7,700	7,200	6,050
		7,825	**6,325**	**5,750**	**5,063**	**4,375**	**3,850**	**3,600**	**3,025**
	VVS₁	12,900	12,200	10,125	9,425	8,275	7,475	6,900	5,750
		6,450	**6,100**	**5,063**	**4,713**	**4,138**	**3,738**	**3,450**	**2,875**
F	VVS₂	12,000	10,350	9,200	8,500	7,825	7,350	6,625	5,475
L		**6,000**	**5,175**	**4,600**	**4,250**	**3,913**	**3,675**	**3,313**	**2,738**
A	VS₁	10,350	8,975	8,275	7,825	7,350	7,200	6,325	5,175
W		**5,175**	**4,488**	**4,138**	**3,913**	**3,675**	**3,600**	**3,163**	**2,588**
(CLARITY)	VS₂	8,525	8,050	7,700	7,475	7,200	6,625	5,750	4,900
GRADE		**4,263**	**4,025**	**3,850**	**3,738**	**3,600**	**3,313**	**2,875**	**2,450**
	SI₁	8,050	7,825	7,625	7,200	6,900	6,050	5,175	4,600
		4,025	**3,913**	**3,813**	**3,600**	**3,450**	**3,025**	**2,588**	**2,300**
	SI₂	6,900	6,625	6,325	6,050	5,750	5,475	4,600	4,025
		3,450	**3,313**	**3,163**	**3,025**	**2,875**	**2,738**	**2,300**	**2,013**
	I₁	5,175	5,000	4,600	4,325	4,025	3,450	3,175	3,025
		2,588	**2,500**	**2,300**	**2,163**	**2,013**	**1,725**	**1,588**	**1,513**

* Prices compiled from *The Guide*, Gemworld International, Inc., and adjusted to retail.
† The price difference between FL and IF stones is approximately 5–8% in D–F colors and 1–2% in G–J colors; there is no cost difference in stones of colors below J.

3/4 Carat

FLAW (CLARITY) GRADE		D	E	F	G	H	I	J	K
	IF†	17,475	14,025	13,350	12,200	9,650	8,750	8,275	7,825
		13,106	10,519	10,013	9,150	7,238	6,563	6,206	5,869
	VVS₁	14,250	13,350	11,725	10,350	9,200	8,275	7,825	7,475
		10,688	10,013	8,794	7,763	6,900	6,206	5,869	5,606
	VVS₂	12,875	11,725	10,575	9,425	8,750	8,050	7,700	7,200
		9,656	8,794	7,931	7,069	6,563	6,038	5,775	5,400
	VS₁	11,275	10,350	9,425	8,750	8,400	7,600	7,475	6,900
		8,456	7,763	7,069	6,563	6,300	5,700	5,606	5,175
	VS₂	9,900	9,425	8,975	8,275	7,925	7,475	7,350	6,625
		7,425	7,069	6,728	6,206	5,944	5,606	5,513	4,969
	SI₁	8,750	8,500	8,050	7,825	7,600	7,350	7,200	6,325
		6,563	6,375	6,031	5,869	5,700	5,513	5,400	4,744
	SI₂	7,825	7,475	7,200	6,900	6,775	6,550	6,200	5,750
		5,869	5,606	5,400	5,175	5,081	4,913	4,650	4,313
	I₁	6,325	6,050	5,750	5,475	5,325	5,175	4,900	4,025
		4,744	4,538	4,313	4,106	3,994	3,881	3,675	3,019

Light Carat

FLAW (CLARITY) GRADE		D	E	F	G	H	I	J	K
	IF†	20,000	15,400	14,025	12,425	11,050	9,650	8,750	8,500
		18,000	13,860	12,623	11,183	9,945	8,685	7,875	7,650
	VVS₁	15,400	14,025	12,875	11,275	10,350	9,200	8,500	8,050
		13,860	12,623	11,588	10,148	9,315	8,280	7,650	7,245
	VVS₂	14,025	13,100	11,725	10,575	9,900	8,975	7,925	7,775
		12,623	11,790	10,553	9,518	8,910	8,078	7,133	6,998
	VS₁	12,875	11,500	10,800	10,350	9,650	8,750	7,700	7,475
		11,588	10,350	9,720	9,315	8,685	7,875	6,930	6,728
	VS₂	11,275	10,575	10,125	9,650	8,975	8,500	7,350	7,200
		10,148	9,518	9,113	8,685	8,078	7,650	6,615	6,480
	SI₁	10,350	9,900	9,425	8,975	8,275	8,050	7,125	6,900
		9,315	8,910	8,483	8,078	7,448	7,245	6,413	6,210
	SI₂	9,425	8,975	8,500	8,050	6,900	7,475	7,025	6,325
		8,483	8,078	7,650	7,245	6,210	6,728	6,323	5,693
	I₁	7,475	7,200	6,900	6,625	6,325	5,750	5,175	4,600
		6,728	6,480	6,210	5,963	5,693	5,175	4,658	4,140

* Prices compiled from *The Guide*, Gemworld International, Inc., and adjusted to retail.
† The price difference between FL and IF stones is approximately 5–8% in D–F colors and 1–2% in G–J colors; there is no cost difference in stones of colors below J.

1 Carat

COLOR GRADE

FLAW (CLARITY) GRADE		D	E	F	G	H	I	J	K
	IF†	32,200	22,075	19,775	15,875	14,025	12,200	10,575	9,425
		32,200	22,075	19,775	15,875	14,025	12,200	10,575	9,425
	VVS$_1$	22,075	19,775	17,025	14,950	13,350	11,500	10,350	8,975
		22,075	19,775	17,025	14,950	13,350	11,500	10,350	8,975
	VVS$_2$	19,550	16,325	14,950	14,025	12,875	11,050	10,125	8,750
		19,550	16,325	14,950	14,025	12,875	11,050	10,125	8,750
	VS$_1$	16,325	15,650	14,725	13,575	12,650	10,575	9,650	8,500
		16,325	15,650	14,725	13,575	12,650	10,575	9,650	8,500
	VS$_2$	14,725	14,025	13,800	12,875	11,950	10,125	8,975	8,050
		14,725	14,025	13,800	12,875	11,950	10,125	8,975	8,050
	SI$_1$	13,100	12,425	12,200	11,500	10,800	9,425	8,500	7,350
		13,100	12,425	12,200	11,500	10,800	9,425	8,500	7,350
	SI$_2$	11,725	11,275	10,800	10,125	9,425	8,275	7,600	7,125
		11,725	11,275	10,800	10,125	9,425	8,275	7,600	7,125
	I$_1$	7,825	7,350	7,125	6,900	6,675	6,200	5,950	5,425
		7,825	7,350	7,125	6,900	6,675	6,200	5,950	5,425

2 Carat

COLOR GRADE

FLAW (CLARITY) GRADE		D	E	F	G	H	I	J	K
	IF†	51,050	38,400	33,575	26,675	23,225	17,700	14,950	12,650
		102,100	76,800	67,150	53,350	46,450	35,400	29,900	25,300
	VVS$_1$	37,725	33,575	27,150	24,375	20,250	17,025	14,500	11,950
		75,450	67,150	54,300	48,750	40,500	34,050	29,000	23,900
	VVS$_2$	33,575	27,600	24,850	22,075	18,850	16,325	14,025	11,500
		67,150	55,200	49,700	44,150	37,700	32,650	28,050	23,000
	VS$_1$	28,300	25,300	22,300	21,150	18,175	16,100	13,100	10,800
		56,600	50,600	44,600	42,300	36,350	32,200	26,200	21,600
	VS$_2$	22,075	21,850	20,700	20,000	16,800	14,950	11,950	10,125
		44,150	43,700	41,400	40,000	33,600	29,900	23,900	20,250
	SI$_1$	19,100	18,625	17,700	17,025	15,400	13,575	11,050	9,425
		38,200	37,250	35,400	34,050	30,800	27,150	22,100	18,850
	SI$_2$	15,175	14,950	14,725	13,800	12,650	10,800	9,900	8,500
		30,350	29,900	29,450	27,600	25,300	21,600	19,800	17,000
	I$_1$	8,975	8,500	8,275	8,050	7,825	7,600	7,125	6,900
		17,950	17,000	16,550	16,100	15,650	15,200	14,250	13,800

* Prices compiled from *The Guide*, Gemworld International, Inc., and adjusted to retail.
† The price difference between FL and IF stones is approximately 5–8% in D–F colors and 1–2% in G–J colors; there is no cost difference in stones of colors below J.

3 Carat

FLAW (CLARITY) GRADE

	D	E	F	G	H	I	J	K
IF†	77,750	54,975	46,925	36,100	28,750	22,775	17,700	16,100
	233,250	164,925	140,775	108,300	86,250	68,325	53,100	48,300
VVS₁	55,200	47,150	36,575	29,675	25,750	20,475	16,800	15,400
	165,600	141,450	109,725	89,025	77,250	61,425	50,400	46,200
VVS₂	47,600	36,575	30,600	26,675	23,700	19,550	16,100	14,250
	142,800	109,725	91,800	80,025	71,100	58,650	48,300	42,750
VS₁	37,025	30,825	27,150	25,525	21,850	17,950	14,725	13,350
	111,075	92,475	81,450	76,575	65,550	53,850	44,175	40,050
VS₂	30,350	27,375	25,750	22,775	19,550	15,875	13,350	11,950
	91,050	82,125	77,250	68,325	58,650	47,625	40,050	35,850
SI₁	24,375	23,225	21,625	19,550	16,325	14,250	12,425	11,050
	73,125	69,675	64,875	58,650	48,975	42,750	37,275	33,150
SI₂	18,625	17,475	16,325	15,400	14,500	12,875	11,275	9,650
	55,875	52,425	48,975	46,200	43,500	38,625	33,825	28,950
I₁	13,575	12,650	11,725	11,050	10,350	9,200	8,750	7,825
	40,725	37,950	35,175	33,150	31,050	27,600	26,250	23,475

* Prices compiled from *The Guide*, Gemworld International, Inc., and adjusted to retail.
† The price difference between FL and IF stones is approximately 5–8% in D–F colors and 1–2% in G–J colors; there is no cost difference in stones of colors below J.

PART THREE

Colored Gemstones

10

The Mystery & Magic
of Colored Gems

The fascination with colored gemstones dates back to the very beginning of civilization. For our ancestors, the blue of sapphire produced visions of the heavens; the red of ruby was a reminder of the very essence of life. By Roman times, rings containing colored gems were prized symbols of power—and the most powerful wore rings on every joint of every finger!

Since ancient times, colored stones have been thought to possess innate magical powers and the ability to endow the wearer with certain attributes. According to legend, emeralds are good for the eyes; yellow stones cure jaundice; red stones stop the flow of blood. At one time it was believed that a ruby worn by a man indicated command, nobility, lordship, and vengeance; worn by a woman, however, it indicated pride, obstinacy, and haughtiness. A blue sapphire worn by a man indicated wisdom, and high and magnanimous thoughts; on a woman, jealousy in love, politeness, and vigilance. The emerald signified for a man joyousness, transitory hope, and the decline of friendship; for a woman, unfounded ambition, childish delight, and change.

Colored gems, because of the magical powers associated with them, achieved extensive use as talismans and amulets, as predictors of the future, as therapeutic aids, and as essential elements to many religious practices: pagan, Hebrew, and Christian.

Zodiac Stones

The following list of the zodiacal gems and their special powers has been passed on from an early Hindu legend.

Aquarius (Jan. 21–Feb. 21)	*Garnet*—believed to guarantee true friendship when worn by an Aquarian
Pisces (Feb. 22–Mar. 21)	*Amethyst*—believed to protect a Pisces wearer from extremes of passion
Aries (Mar. 22–Apr. 20)	*Bloodstone*—believed to endow an Aries wearer with wisdom
Taurus (Apr. 21–May 21)	*Sapphire*—believed to protect from and cure mental disorders if worn by a Taurus
Gemini (May 22–June 21)	*Agate*—long life, health, and wealth were guaranteed to a Gemini if an agate ring was worn
Cancer (June 22–July 22)	*Emerald*—eternal joy was guaranteed to a Cancer-born who took an emerald along his or her way
Leo (July 23–Aug. 22)	*Onyx*—would protect a Leo wearer from loneliness and unhappiness
Virgo (Aug. 23–Sept. 22)	*Carnelian*—believed to guarantee success in anything a Virgo tried if worn on the hand
Libra (Sept. 23–Oct. 23)	*Chrysolite* (peridot)—would free a Libra wearer from any evil spell
Scorpio (Oct. 24–Nov. 21)	*Beryl*—should be worn by every Scorpio to guarantee protection from "tears of sad repentance"
Sagittarius (Nov. 22–Dec. 21)	*Topaz*—protects Sagittarians, but only if they always show the stone
Capricorn (Dec. 22–Jan. 21)	*Ruby*—a Capricorn who has ever worn a ruby will never know trouble

An old Spanish list, probably representing an Arab tradition, ascribes the following stones to the various signs of the zodiac:

Aquarius—Amethyst	*Leo*—Topaz
Pisces—(indistinguishable)	*Virgo*—Magnet (lodestone)
Aries—Crystal (quartz)	*Libra*—Jasper
Taurus—Ruby and diamond	*Scorpio*—Garnet
Gemini—Sapphire	*Sagittarius*—Emerald
Cancer—Agate and beryl	*Capricorn*—Chalcedony

The Evolution of Birthstones

The origin of the belief that a special stone was dedicated to each month, and that the stone of the month possessed a special virtue or "cure" that it could transmit to those born in that month, goes back to at least the first century. There is speculation that the twelve stones in the great breastplate of the Jewish high priest may have had some bearing on this concept. In the eighth and ninth centuries, the interpreters of the Bible's book of Revelation began to ascribe attributes of the twelve apostles to each of those stones. The Hindus, on the other hand, had their own interpretation.

But whatever the reason, one fact is clear. As G. F. Kunz points out in *The Curious Lore of Precious Stones,* "There is no doubt that the owner of a ring or ornament set with a birthstone is impressed with the idea of possessing something more intimately associated with his or her personality than any other stone, however beautiful or costly. The idea that birthstones possess a certain indefinable, but none the less real significance has long been present, and still holds a spell over the minds of all who are gifted with a touch of imagination and romance."

The following is the list of birthstones adopted in 1952 by major jewelry industry associations.

Present-Day Birthstones

Month	Birthstone	Alternative Stone
January	Garnet	
February	Amethyst	
March	Aquamarine	Bloodstone
April	Diamond	
May	Emerald	
June	Pearl	Moonstone or alexandrite
July	Ruby	
August	Sardonyx (carnelian)	Peridot
September	Sapphire	
October	Opal	Tourmaline
November	Topaz	Citrine
December	Turquoise	Lapis lazuli, zircon

Besides the lists of birthstones and zodiacal or talismanic stones, there are lists of stones for days of the week, for hours of the day, for states of the union, for each of the seasons, and even for anniversaries!

Anniversary Stones

1	Gold jewelry	13	Citrine
2	Garnet	14	Opal
3	Pearl	15	Ruby
4	Blue topaz	20	Emerald
5	Sapphire	25	Silver jubilee
6	Amethyst	30	Pearl jubilee
7	Onyx	35	Emerald
8	Tourmaline	40	Ruby
9	Lapis lazuli	45	Sapphire
10	Diamond	50	Golden jubilee
11	Turquoise	55	Alexandrite
12	Jade	60	Diamond jubilee

The Importance of Color and Its Mystical Symbolism in Gems

The wide spectrum of color available in the gemstone realm was not lost on our forebears. Not only did strong associations with specific stones evolve, but also associations of color with personal attributes. Over time, a fairly detailed symbolism came to join color with character. Those attributes, as they have come down to us, include the following:

Yellow	Worn by a man, denotes secrecy (appropriate for a silent lover); worn by a woman, indicates generosity.
White (colorless)	Signifies friendship, integrity, and religious commitment for men; purity, affability, and contemplation for women.
Red	On a man, indicates command, nobility, lordship, and vengeance; on a woman, pride, haughtiness, and obstinacy.
Blue	On a man, indicates wisdom and high, magnanimous thoughts; on a woman, jealousy in love, politeness, vigilance.
Green	For men, signifies joyousness, transitory hope, decline of friendship; for women, unfounded ambition, childish delight, and change.
Black	For men, means gravity, good sense, constancy, and strength; for young women, fickleness and foolishness; but for married women, constant love and perseverance.
Violet	For men, signifies sober judgment, industry, and gravity; for women, high thoughts and spiritual love.

What Colored Stones Are Available Today?

New Stones Add Exciting Choices

Today, gems are worn primarily for their intrinsic beauty and are chosen mainly for aesthetic reasons, not for mythical attributes. While we may own a birthstone that we wear on occasion, our choice of stones is usually dictated by personal color preferences, economics, and fashion. The world of colored gems today offers us an almost endless choice. New gems have been discovered and are being made available through the major jewelry companies. If you like red, there are rubies, garnets, red tourmalines, red spinels, and even red diamonds and red "emeralds" (gemologically, red emerald is known as red beryl—see emeralds in chapter 15). If you prefer blue, there are sapphires, iolite, blue spinel, blue topaz, blue tourmaline, tanzanite, and blue diamonds. For those who prefer green, there are emeralds, tsavorite and demantoid (green garnets), green zircons, green tourmalines, green sapphires, peridots, and even green diamonds. And for those who love unusual shades of blue and green, and dazzling neon shades in sparkling, transparent stones, there are the remarkable, rare, Paraiba (also called Hetorita) tourmalines discovered in Brazil in the 1980s.

The following chapters will look at colored stones in more detail and will suggest a variety of stones available in every hue. With colored gems available for almost everyone, in almost any color, at almost any price, you have a wide range of affordable options.

11

Determining Value in Colored Gems

Color is the most important determinant of value in colored gems. It is also, too often, the principal determinant in erroneous identification because, unfortunately, most people don't realize how many gems look alike in color. Even professionals in the trade can be misled or caught off guard. Too often, recognition and identification are based on color alone because so few jewelers and customers are aware of the large number of similarly colored stones that are available.

Until recently, the gemstone industry has promoted very few colored stones, concentrating instead on the more precious and profitable gems. But the growing popularity of colored stones has expanded the market so that consumers now find they have many choices. If you want an emerald-green stone but can't afford a fine emerald, you might choose a green garnet (tsavorite), a green or "chrome" tourmaline, or perhaps green tanzanite (tanzanite is the blue variety of zoisite; now there is a green variety, which is sometimes called green tanzanite). There are at least four gem materials from which to choose, no matter what color you prefer. New gems are being discovered each year, and known gems are being discovered in new colors. Increasingly, fine jewelers and designers are creating exciting pieces using the full color spectrum. It's a wonderful time to explore the jewelry world and to start discovering the possibilities at local jewelers!

The Four Cs of Colored Gems

We've already discussed the four Cs to consider in choosing a diamond (see chapter 3), but colored gems have four Cs of their own: color, color, color, and color! This statement may sound like an exaggeration, but not so much as you might think. Generally speaking, the finer and rarer the color, the less impact cutting, clarity, and carat weight have on the value of the gem. On the other hand, the more common the color, the more impact these other factors have.

When we discuss color, we are not talking simply about hue. Color science and the evaluation of color constitute a very complex area. But if you understand the various elements that must be factored into the evaluation of color, you can begin to look at colored gems in a totally different light.

Color is affected by many variables that make it difficult to evaluate precisely. Perhaps the most significant factor is light; the type of light and its intensity can affect color dramatically. In addition, color can be very subjective in terms of what is considered pleasing and desirable. Nonetheless, there has been extensive research and development in the field of color science, and experts are working to develop a viable color grading system. For the time being, however, a great degree of subjectivity reigns where colored gems are concerned, and no system has yet replaced the age-old eye-and-brain combination, coupled with years of experience in the colored-stone field.

The Key Elements in Describing Color

The color we see in gems is always some *combination* of the pure spectral colors—which range from pure red to pure violet—coupled with varying degrees of brown, white, black, and gray. It is these latter colors, in combination with the spectral colors, that affect the *tone* of the color seen and that make the classification of color so difficult. For example, if white is present with red, you will have a lighter tone or shade of red; if black is present, a darker tone or shade. Depending on the degree of gray, white, black, or brown, an almost infinite number of color combinations can result.

As a general rule, the closer a stone's color is to the pure spectral hue, the better the color is considered to be; the closer it comes to a pure hue, the rarer and more valuable. For example, if we are considering a green stone, the purer the green, the better the color. In other words, the closer it comes to being a pure spectral green, having no undertone (tint) of any other color such as blue or yellow, the better the color. There is no such thing in nature, however, as a perfectly pure color; color is always modified by an undertone of another hue. But these undertones can create very beautiful, unusual, distinctive colors that are often very desirable.

In describing color we will often refer to these factors:

- *Hue*—the precise spectral color (red, orange, yellow, green, blue, violet, indigo)
- *Intensity* (or saturation)—the brightness or vividness (or dullness or drabness) of the color
- *Tone*—how much black, white, gray, or brown is present (how light or dark the stone is)
- *Distribution*—the even (or uneven) distribution of the color

Both the intensity and the tone of color can be significantly affected by the proportioning of the cut. In other words, a good lapidary (stone cutter) working with a fine stone will be able to bring out its inherent, potential beauty to the fullest, increasing the gem's desirability. A poor cutter may take the same rough material and create a stone that is not really pleasing, because the cut can significantly reduce the vividness and alter the depth of color, usually producing a stone that is much too dark to be attractive, or one in which the color seems washed out or watery.

In general, stones that are either very light (pale) or very dark sell for less per carat. There seems to be a common belief that the darker the stone, the better. This is true only to a point. A rich, deep color is desirable, but not a color so deep that it appears black. The average consumer must shop around and train the eye to distinguish between a nice depth of color and a stone that is too dark.

As a general rule, it is even more important to shop around when considering colored stones than it is when buying diamonds. You must develop an eye for all of the variables of color: hue, intensity, tone, and distribution. Some stones simply exhibit a more intense, vivid color than other stones (all else being equal), but only by extensive visual comparison can you develop your eye to perceive differences and make reliable judgments.

For example, let's discuss the variations among rubies for a moment. The finest red rubies from Burma are perhaps the most coveted because of their color. While they are not truly "pure red" (there may be a slight bluish undertone), the color comes closest to being a pure red. The tone may vary, however, from very light to very dark. As with most stones, the very light stones and the very dark sell for less per carat. Burmese rubies are the most highly prized and the most expensive because of the desirability of their color and their scarcity. They also exhibit a beautiful red in all light, while rubies from most other locations may exhibit a lovely red only in incandescent light (such as you find in candlelight, lamplight, chandeliers, and most evening light) and become pinkish or purplish when seen in fluorescent or daytime light.

Thai rubies can vary tremendously in hue and tone, going from a light to a dark red with varying degrees of a bluish undertone, giving them a purplish cast and making them look like the much cheaper reddish purple gemstone, the garnet. While some Thai rubies can have very fine color rivaling the Burmese (these are very expensive), most Thai stones are much less expensive than the Burmese, primarily because the color can't compare.

African rubies from Tanzania usually have a tint or undertone of brown or orange, which makes them also much cheaper than the Burmese reds, but depending on the precise shade, often more valuable than the Thai ruby, depending on the latter's color. Rubies from newly discovered deposits in Kenya, Cambodia, Vietnam, Kashmir (Pakistan), and parts of China are very close in hue and tone to Burmese rubies, and may also retain their color in all light. These stones can command very high prices if other quality factors are fine.

Ceylon rubies are also encountered with relative frequency. However, these are usually paler in tone. In the United States they are called pink sapphire when the tone is too light, not ruby. The saturation of color is too weak to be technically described as ruby, since ruby should be red, not pink. You should be aware that in the United States, the color must be deep enough to be considered red to be called ruby, while in other parts of the world, the name *ruby* may be applied if the stone falls anywhere in the pink-to-red range. (It should be noted that sapphire and ruby are the same stone, physically and chemically. The red variety is called ruby, and the equally popular blue is called sapphire. Both belong to the corundum family).

Next, let's look at the spectrum of emerald colors. Some of the finest emeralds today come from Colombia and are the color of fresh, young green grass—an almost pure spectral green with a faint tint of either yellow or blue. The color in the finest of these emeralds is unique to Colombia. Emeralds from other countries can also be very fine, with exceptional color, but few can match the color of the finest Colombian. Unfortunately, very fine Colombian emeralds with exceptional color are extremely rare now, and thus very costly.

African emeralds can also exhibit a lovely shade of green, but usually with a bluer undertone and a slightly dark tone, probably caused by traces of iron, which may make the stone less desirable and thus less valuable than a fine emerald from Colombia. However, the African stones usually have fewer inclusions (flaws) than the Colombian, and cut a more vivid stone. Therefore, some of the African stones, depending on depth of color, compare very favorably to the Colombian, aesthetically, while costing less per carat.

Light and Environment Affect the Color You See

The color of a stone can be drastically affected by the kind of light and the environment in which the examination is being conducted; that is, variables as disparate as the color of the wallpaper or the tint of a shirt can alter a stone's appearance. If examined under a fluorescent light, a ruby may not show its fullest red because most fluorescent lights are weak in red rays; this causes the red in the ruby to be diminished and to appear more as a purple red. The same ruby examined in sunlight or incandescent light (an ordinary electric lightbulb), neither of which is weak in red rays, will appear a truer, fuller red. Because the color of a ruby is dependent upon the "color temperature," or type of light used, it will always look best in warm light. A ruby looks even redder if examined against a piece of orange-yellow paper. For this reason, loose rubies are often shown in little envelopes, called parcel papers, that have a yellow-orange inner paper liner to show the red color to the fullest.

Blue sapphire, another intensely colored gem, comes in numerous tones of blue—from light to very dark, some so dark that they look black in incandescent (warm) light. Most sapphires, however, look bluest in fluorescent light, or daylight. Many contain some degree of green. The more green, the lower the price. Some even exhibit a color change—we've seen blue sapphires that were a magnificent blue in daylight turn to an amethyst purple in incandescent light. Some, like the stones from the Umba Valley in Tanzania, turn slightly lavender over time. The lighter blues are generally referred to as Ceylon-colored sapphire; the finest and most expensive blue sapphires generally come from Burma (now called Myanmar) and Kashmir and exhibit a rich, true blue in all kinds of light. Those from Kashmir exhibit a more subdued, soft, velvety look by comparison with Burmese or Ceylon-type sapphires.

An environment that is beneficial to your stone can also be created by the setting in which the stone is mounted. For example, an emerald-cut emerald mounted in a normal four-prong setting will not appear to have as deep a color as it will if mounted in a special box-type setting that completely encloses the stone so that light is prevented from entering its sides. The "shadowing" effect created by this type of enclosure deepens the color of the stone. This technique, and other types of special mounting, can be used to improve the color of any colored gemstone where it is desirable to intensify the color.

Another example is found with a fine, expensive imperial jade. A fine jade cabochon (a smooth, rounded cut that has no facets) is often mounted with a solid rim around the girdle (bezel set), with the back of the ring constructed much deeper than the actual bottom of the stone, and the back side of the ring nearly completely closed except for a small opening at the bottom center. This is done either to hide a stone's defect or to improve its body color.

Opal, too, is often set in ways that enhance color. The environment in this case is a closed, flat backing, which has been blackened to intensify the play of color (fire) seen in the stone.

A Word about Color Distribution, or Zoning

Even though zoning doesn't really describe color, and is sometimes evaluated as part of the clarity grade, we think it should be discussed as part of color evaluation.

In some stones, the color isn't always evenly distributed but exists in

Zones of color
in a stone

zones; in some stones, the pattern created by alternating zones of color and colorlessness resembles stripes. Zoning is frequently observed in amethyst, ruby, and sapphire. These zones are most easily seen if you look through the side of the stone and move it slowly, while tilting and rotating it.

Sometimes a stone in the rough is colorless, or nearly so, but has a spot or layer of color. If the cutter cuts the stone so that the culet is in the color spot, the whole stone will appear that color. If there is a layer and the cutter cuts the stone so that the layer lies in a plane nearly parallel to the table, the whole stone will look completely colored. Evenness of color and complete saturation of color are very important in determining the value of colored gems. Even though you may not notice the zones themselves when looking at the stone from the top, a heavily zoned stone will lack the color vibrancy of another stone without such zoning. Normally, if the zoning isn't noticeable from the top, value is not dramatically reduced, but a stone with even color will appear more vivid from the top—the face-up position, as seen when mounted—and will cost more. And, depending upon the hue and tone, possibly much more.

A Word about Color-Change Stones

Some stones exhibit a very strange phenomenon when viewed in different types of light: they change color completely. These stones are called color-change gems. There are color-change spinels, color-change sapphires, color-change garnets, and so on. In these gem families, however, the color change phenomenon is rare. The gem alexandrite, on the other hand, *always* exhibits a color change, and its value is based largely on the degree of change. There are even color-change synthetics, such as the inexpensive synthetic color-change sapphire that is often misrepresented and sold as genuine alexandrite. Alexandrite is a bluish green gem in daylight or under daylight-type fluorescent light, and a deep red or purple red under incandescent light (see chapter 15).

Clarity

As with diamonds, *clarity* refers to the absence of internal characteristics (inclusions) or external blemishes. Flawlessness in colored stones is perhaps even rarer than in diamonds. However, while clarity is important, and the cleaner the stone the better, flawlessness in colored stones does not usually carry the premium that it does with diamonds. Light, pastel-colored stones will require better clarity because the inclusions are more readily visible in these stones; in darker-toned stones, they may not be as important a variable because they are masked by the depth of color.

The *type* and *placement* of an inclusion is more important than the presence of inclusions in and of themselves when considering a colored gemstone. For example, a large crack *(feather)* that is very close to the surface of a stone—especially on the top—might be dangerous because it weakens the stone's durability. It may also break the light continuity, and may show an iridescent effect as well. Iridescence usually means that a fracture or feather breaks through the surface somewhere on the stone. Such a flaw would detract from the stone's beauty and certainly reduce its value. But if the fracture is small and positioned in an unobtrusive part of the stone, it will have minimal effect on durability, beauty, or value. Some flaws actually help a gemologist or jeweler to identify a stone, since certain types of flaws are characteristic of specific gems and specific localities. In some cases, a particular flaw may provide positive identification of the exact variety or origin and actually cause an increase in the per-carat value. (For more information on the types of inclusions found in colored gems, we recommend our book *Gem Identification Made Easy.*) We should note, however, that a very fine colored gem that really is flawless will probably bring a disproportionately much higher price per carat because it is so rare. Because they are so rare, flawless rubies, sapphires, emeralds, and so on should always be viewed with suspicion; have their genuineness verified by a gem-testing lab. The newer synthetic gems are often flawless and are easy to confuse with genuine, natural gems. Colored gemstones are also classified into three categories—I, II, and III—reflecting the degree to which inclusions are typically eye-visible. You should learn what the clarity classification is for any stone you are seeking so you know what to expect. Then, by comparing numerous stones, you will come to know what is typical, what is too many, and what is rare for the stone you desire.

If inclusions weaken the stone's durability, affect color, are easily noticeable, or are too numerous, they will significantly reduce price. Otherwise, they may not adversely affect price, and in some cases, if they provide positive identification and proof of origin, they may actually increase the cost rather than reduce it, as with Burmese rubies and Colombian emeralds.

Again, it is important to shop around, become familiar with the stone you wish to purchase, and train your eye to discern what is "normal" so you can decide what is acceptable or objectionable.

Gemstones

Rare and Distinctive—
Fancy Natural-Color
Diamonds

Diamonds occur naturally in more colors and more shades of color than any other gemstone—virtually every color in the rainbow.

Red and Pink Gemstones to Warm Any Heart

Red gems occur in a wide range of hues and tones to please every taste and budget.

Rhodolite Garnet

Morganite

Rubellite
(Red Tourmaline)

Kunzite

Tourmaline

Topaz

Topaz

Ruby

Red Beryl
(Red "Emerald")

Sapphire

Spinel

Morganite

Rare red beryl, also referred to as red "emerald"—

Left: The crystal as it occurs in nature.

Right: A brilliantly cut and polished gem waiting to be set.

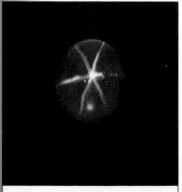

A six-rayed **star ruby.**

Right:
Rhodochrosite,
an oval cabochon and a rare round faceted stone.

Blue Gemstones Offer Heavenly Choices

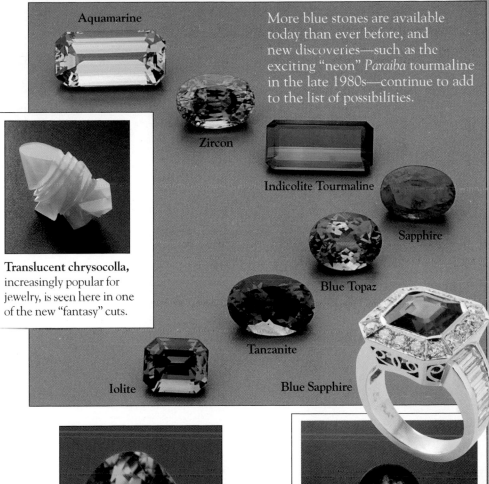

Aquamarine

Zircon

Indicolite Tourmaline

Sapphire

Blue Topaz

Tanzanite

Iolite

Blue Sapphire

More blue stones are available today than ever before, and new discoveries—such as the exciting "neon" *Paraiba* tourmaline in the late 1980s—continue to add to the list of possibilities.

Translucent chrysocolla, increasingly popular for jewelry, is seen here in one of the new "fantasy" cuts.

"Neon" tourmaline
from Paraiba, Brazil.

Exceptionally fine **star sapphire,** showing strong star, can be very costly today.

Moonstones, exhibiting their magical "adularescence"—a bright, billowing, milky sheen moving within the stone.

Yellow and Orange Gems to Brighten the Day

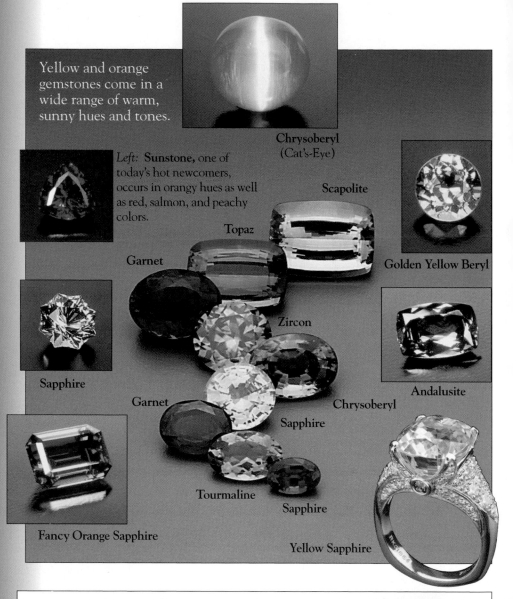

Yellow and orange gemstones come in a wide range of warm, sunny hues and tones.

Chrysoberyl (Cat's-Eye)

Left: **Sunstone,** one of today's hot newcomers, occurs in orangy hues as well as red, salmon, and peachy colors.

Scapolite

Topaz

Garnet

Golden Yellow Beryl

Zircon

Sapphire

Andalusite

Garnet

Chrysoberyl

Sapphire

Tourmaline

Sapphire

Fancy Orange Sapphire

Yellow Sapphire

Precious topaz, also known as "imperial" topaz.

Notice the similarity in color between some citrine and topaz. Citrine is often mistaken and misrepresented as topaz. Citrine is a lovely gem, but it is less brilliant, less rare, and less costly than topaz.

Citrine, a member of the quartz family, comes in shades from pale yellow to rich amber.

Green Gems That Everyone Will Envy

Tsavorite Garnet

If green is your color, choices abound from pastel yellow-green to rich grass green.

Peridot

Tourmaline

Tourmaline

Emerald

Sapphire

Chrome Tourmaline

Tanzanite

Demantoid Garnet

Zircon

Emerald, cut in the shape that bears its name—the "emerald cut."

Paraiba Tourmaline

Fine Art Deco period brooch with very fine green **jadeite** centerpiece.

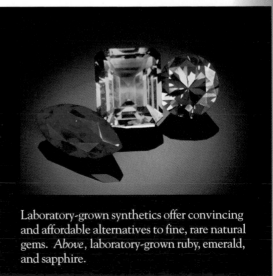

Laboratory-grown synthetics offer convincing and affordable alternatives to fine, rare natural gems. *Above,* laboratory-grown ruby, emerald, and sapphire.

Opals—A Fiery World of Color

In addition to the widely available white opal, very affordable "fire" opals and rare, costly black opals create excitement.

Australian Andamooka crystal opal and **Andamooka matrix opal** beads.

Above: Gaia Pelikan's boulder opal in 18K red gold and *forged stainless steel.*
Left: Magnificent pendant by Kreg Scully, sculpted from white opal with semi-black opal inlay.

Above: **Mexican "fire" opals.**

Below left: **Boulder opal**
Below center: **Fine black opal**
Below right: **Boulder opal**

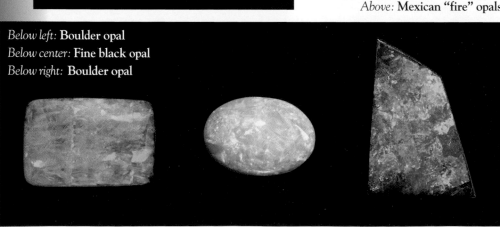

Ornamental Stones and Decorative Art

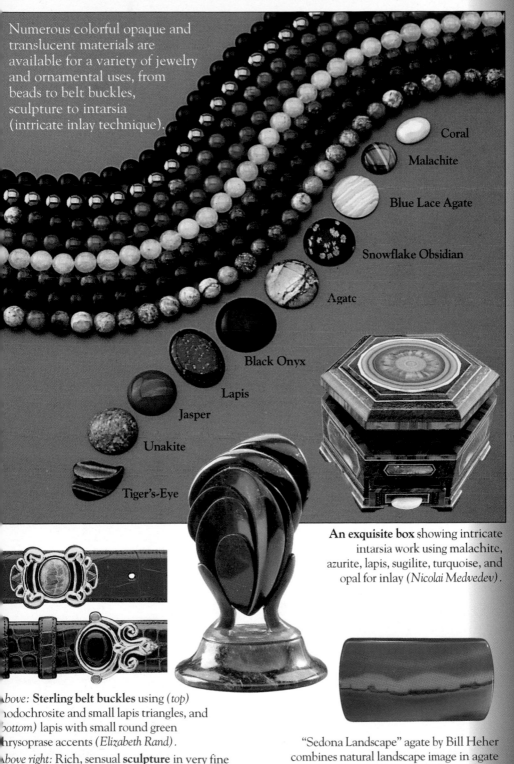

Numerous colorful opaque and translucent materials are available for a variety of jewelry and ornamental uses, from beads to belt buckles, sculpture to intarsia (intricate inlay technique).

Coral

Malachite

Blue Lace Agate

Snowflake Obsidian

Agate

Black Onyx

Lapis

Jasper

Unakite

Tiger's-Eye

An exquisite box showing intricate intarsia work using malachite, azurite, lapis, sugilite, turquoise, and opal for inlay (*Nicolai Medvedev*).

Above: **Sterling belt buckles** using (*top*) rhodochrosite and small lapis triangles, and (*bottom*) lapis with small round green chrysoprase accents (*Elizabeth Rand*).

Above right: Rich, sensual **sculpture** in very fine lapis (*Michael Dyber*).

"Sedona Landscape" agate by Bill Heher combines natural landscape image in agate with dye pigments to create blue sky and reddish-brown earth tones.

Popular Diamond Shapes ... Old & New

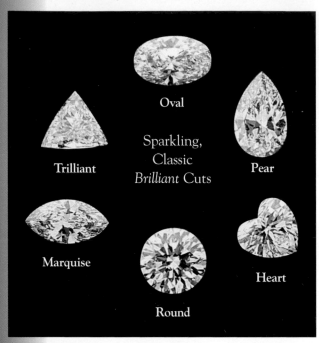

Oval

Sparkling, Classic *Brilliant* Cuts

Trilliant

Pear

Marquise

Heart

Round

Step-cut **trapezoids** are a nice complement to **classic emerald cu**

Step-cut **half-moons** add a distinctive touch to new **Crisscut®**

Elegance is easily achieved with the **Royal Asscher®**, which often stands alone.

A square brilliant **radiant** cut.

Similar to radiant and princess cuts in personality, the **Tiana™** has a softer outline which is similar to the cushion-cut.

Tiffany's new square **Lucida™**.

The whimsical **Lily Cut®**.

Shield   Tapered   Epaulette
         Bullet

Shapes from bygone eras enjoy renewed allure for use as side stone

Above left: **Quadrillion™** princess cut.
Above: Striking engagement ring draws attention to the princess-cut center stone.

Above left: **Spirit Sun®**, a revolutionary sixteen-fac diamond with pointed crown that achieves greater brilliance and reflectivity. *Above center:* The startlingly simple and luminous **Context®** cut. *Above right:* **EightStar®**, a "super ideal" cut exhibiti eight perfectly aligned arrows.

Gemstone Clarity Classifications Used by the Gemological Institute of America (GIA)

Gemstone	Type I	Type II	Type III
Andalusite		X	
Apatite	X		
Beryl			
Aquamarine	X		
Emerald			X
Red			X
Deep blue		X	
All other colors (pink, yellow, green)	X		
Chrysoberyl			
Alexandrite		X	
All other colors	X		
Corundum*		X	
Diopside		X	
Feldspar (Moonstone/sunstone)		X	
Garnet		X	
Iolite		X	
Opal (Fire)		X	
Peridot		X	
Quartz		X	
Spinel		X	
Topaz			
Blue	X		
All other colors		X	
Tourmaline			
Green	X		
Watermelon			X
All other colors		X	
Zircon			
Colorless and blue	X		
All other colors		X	
Zoisite (tanzanite)	X		

* While most ruby is classified as Type II, ruby of exceptional color from Burma (Myanmar) and certain other locations are more typically graded similarly to Type III gemstones.

Terms Used to Describe Optical Effects in Faceted and Nonfaceted Gems

The physical characteristics of colored stones are often described in terms of the way light travels through them, their unique visual effects, and the way they are cut. Here are a few terms you need to know:

- *Transparent.* Light travels through the stone easily, with minimal distortion, enabling one to see through it easily.
- *Translucent.* The stone transmits light but diffuses it, creating an effect like frosted glass. If you tried to read through such a stone, the print will be darkened and obscured.
- *Opaque.* The stone transmits no light; you cannot see through it even at a thin edge.

Special Optical Effects

- *Adularescence.* A billowy, movable, colored cloud effect seen in some stones, such as moonstone; an internal, movable sheen.
- *Asterism.* Used to describe the display of a star effect (four- or six-rayed) seen when a stone is cut in a nonfaceted style (star ruby, garnet, and sapphire.)
- *Chatoyancy.* The effect produced in some stones (when cut in a cabochon style) of a thin, bright line across the stone that usually moves as the stone is moved from side to side; sometimes called a cat's-eye effect.
- *Iridescence.* A rainbow color effect produced by a thin film of air or liquid within the stone. Most iridescence seen in stones is the result of a crack breaking their surface. This detracts from the value, even if it looks pretty.
- *Luster.* Usually refers to the surface of a stone and the degree to which it reflects light. Seen as the shine on the stone. Diamond, for example, has much greater luster than amethyst. Pearls are also evaluated for their luster, but pearls have a softer, silkier-looking reflection than other gems. The luster in pearls is often called orient.
- *Play of color.* Used frequently to describe the multi-color effect seen in opal.

Cut

Colored gems can be either *faceted* or cut in the *cabochon,* or unfaceted, style. Generally speaking, the preference in the United States until recently was for faceted gems, so the finest material was usually faceted. However, this was not always the case in other eras and other countries. In Roman times, for example, it was considered vulgar to wear a faceted stone. Preference also varies with different cultures and religions, and the world's finest gems are cut in both styles. Don't draw any conclusions about quality based solely on style of cut.

Cabochon cut
Note the smooth top of
this *sugarloaf* cabochon.

Cabochon. A facetless style of cutting that produces smooth rather than faceted surfaces. These cuts can be almost any shape. Some are round with high domes; others look like squarish domes (the popular "sugarloaf" cabochon); others are "buff-topped," showing a somewhat flattened top.

Many people around the world prefer the quieter, often more mysterious personality of the cabochon. Some connoisseurs believe that cabochons produce a richer color. Whatever the case, today we are seeing much more interest in and appreciation for cabochons around the world, and more beautiful cabochons than have been seen in the market in many years.

Faceted. A style of cutting that consists of giving to the stone many small faces at varying angles to one another, as in various diamond cuts. The placement, angle, and shape of the faces, or facets, is carefully planned and executed to show the stone's inherent beauty—fire, color, brilliance—to fullest advantage. Today there are many "new" faceted styles, including "fantasy" cuts, which combine rounded surfaces with sculpted backs.

The Importance of Cut

As stated earlier, cutting and proportioning in colored stones are important for two main reasons:

1. they affect the *depth* of color seen in the stone; and
2. they affect the *liveliness* projected by the stone.

Color and cutting are the most important criteria in determining the beauty of a colored stone. After that, carat weight must be factored in; the higher carat weight will usually increase the price per carat, generally in a nonlinear proportion. If a colored stone was of a good-quality material to begin with, a good cut will enhance its natural beauty to the fullest and allow it to exhibit its finest color and liveliness. If the same material is cut poorly, its natural beauty will be lessened, causing it to look dark, too light, or even "dead."

Therefore, when you examine a colored stone that looks lively to your eye and has good color—not too dark and not too pale—you can assume the cut is reasonably good. If the stone's color is poor, or if it lacks liveliness, you must examine it for proper cut. If it has been cut properly, you can assume the basic material was poor. If the cut is poor, however, the material may be very good and can perhaps be recut into a beautiful gem. In this case you may want to confer with a knowledgeable cutter to see if it is worthwhile to recut, considering cutting costs and loss in weight. If you don't know any cutters, a reputable jeweler, gemologist-appraiser, or local lapidary club may be able to recommend one.

There are also many new styles of gemstone cutting being created today by top cutters. New techniques such as concave faceting or optical inlay produce amazing effects, and their innovators are being recognized as true artists in stone (see *Colored Gemstones: The Antoinette Matlins Buying Guide* for more information on this exciting, evolving field).

Evaluating the Cut of a Colored Gem

When you are examining the stone for proper cut, a few considerations should guide you:

Is the shade pleasing, and does the stone have life and brilliance? If the answer is yes to both questions, then the basic material is probably good, and you must make a decision based on your own personal preferences and budget.

Is the color too light or too dark? If so, and if the cut looks good, the basic uncut material was probably too light or too dark to begin with. Consider purchase only if you find the stone pleasing, and only if the price is right, i.e., significantly lower than stones of better color.

Is the stone's brilliance even, or are there dead spots or flat areas? Often the brilliance in a colored gemstone is not uniform. If the color is exceptional, subdued brilliance may not have a dramatic effect on its allure, desirability, or value. However, the less fine the color, the more important brilliance becomes.

Weight

As with diamonds, weight in colored stones is measured in carats. All gems are weighed in carats, except pearls and coral. Coral and pearls are sold by the grain, momme, and millimeter. A grain is ¼ carat; a momme is 18.75 carats.

Normally, the greater the weight, the greater the value per carat, unless the stones reach unusually large sizes, for example, in excess of 50 carats. At that point, size may become prohibitive for use in some types of jewelry (rings or earrings), selling such large stones can be difficult, and price per carat may drop. There are genuine cut topazes, weighing from 2,500 to 12,000 carats, which could be used as paperweights.

As with diamonds, do not confuse *weight* with *size*. Some stones weigh more than others, because the density (specific gravity) of the basic material is heavier. Ruby is heavier than emerald, so a 1-carat ruby will have a different size than an identically shaped and proportioned emerald; the ruby will be smaller in size, since it is heavier. Emerald weighs less than diamond, so a 1-carat emerald cut in the same shape and with the same proportioning as a diamond will look larger than the diamond, because it is lighter, and more mass is required to attain the same weight.

Some stones are readily available in large sizes; tourmaline, for example, often occurs in stones over 10 carats. For other stones, sizes over 5 carats may be very rare and therefore considered large, and will also command a proportionately higher price. Examples include precious topaz, alexandrite, demantoid and tsavorite garnets, ruby, and red beryl. With gems that are rare in large sizes, a 10-carat stone can command any price—a king's ransom. A 30-carat blue diamond was sold in 1982 for $9 million. Today, $9 million would be considered a bargain for that stone!

Scarcity of certain sizes among the different colored stones affects the definition of *large* in the colored-gem market. A fine 5-carat alexandrite or ruby is a very large stone; an 18-carat tourmaline is a "nice size."

As with diamonds, stones under 1 carat sell for less per carat than stones over 1 carat. But here it becomes more complicated. The definition of large or rare sizes differs tremendously, as does price, depending on the type of stone. For example, an 8-carat tourmaline is an average-size stone, fairly common, and will be priced accordingly. A 5-carat tsavorite is extremely rare, and will command a price proportionately much greater than a 1-carat stone. Precious topaz used to be readily available in 20-carat sizes and larger, but today even 10-carat stones of very fine color are practically nonexistent, and their price has jumped tremendously.

The chart of colored gemstones in chapter 14 indicates the availability of stones in large sizes; and it shows where scarcity may exist, and at what size.

Colored Gemstone Certificates

Systems for grading colored gemstones are not yet established worldwide. As a result, certificates or grading reports for colored gemstones vary widely in the information provided. Reports for colored stones have a more limited value in some respects than diamond reports, which are widely relied on to describe and confirm diamond quality using precise, universally accepted standards, but they are *very* important nonetheless. Today's synthetics, newly discovered gemstone materials, and increased use of treatments are creating a need for reports that verify *identity* (the type of gem), *genuineness* (whether it is synthetic or not), indicate the presence of *treatments*, and, if treated, the *degree of treatment*. For any expensive colored gemstone today, especially gems of unusual size or exceptional quality and rarity, we recommend obtaining a report from a recognized laboratory (see appendix). The most widely recognized reports for colored gemstones include those issued in the United States by the American Gemological Laboratories (AGL), Gemological Institute of America (GIA) Gem Trade Laboratory, and the American Gem Trade Association (AGTA) Gemological Testing Center; in Switzerland, leading firms are laboratory Gübelin and Swiss Gemmological Institute (SSEF); in the UK, the Gemmological Association and Gem Testing Laboratory of Great Britain.

At the least, colored gemstone reports should identify the gemstone and verify whether it is natural or synthetic. You can also request a *grading report,* which will provide, in addition to identity, a full description of the stone and a rating of the color, clarity, brilliance, and other important characteristics. These provide essential information pertaining to the stone's quality. This information is always useful for insurance purposes and can also be helpful if you are comparing several stones with an eye toward purchase.

Where sufficient gemological data can be compiled from careful examination and with proper testing, some reports will also disclose whether or not the stone's color and clarity are *natural* or *enhanced* and, if enhanced, by what method and to what degree—that is, faint, moderate, heavy, and so on. Also, depending on the information the gemologist can obtain from the gemstone during examination, some laboratories will indicate country of origin, if requested. The AGL, the AGTA Lab, SSEF, and Laboratory Gübelin will indicate origin where possible; GIA will not indicate country of origin.

Fees for colored gemstone reports vary depending on the type of gem; the type of report requested; and the time, skill, and gemological equipment necessary to perform conclusive tests. An estimate can usually be provided by a telephone call to the laboratory.

When you are considering a colored gemstone that is accompanied by a report, keep in mind the different types of reports available. Also keep in mind that the information provided on the report is only as reliable as the gemologist performing the evaluation, so be sure the report is issued by a respected laboratory; if in doubt, check with one of the labs listed in the appendix to see if they are familiar with the laboratory in question. Next, ask yourself what the report is really telling you—is it confirming identity and genuineness only? If so, remember that *quality* differences determine value—a genuine one-carat ruby, sapphire, or emerald can sell for $10 or $10,000 or more, depending on the quality of the particular stone. *Being genuine doesn't mean a stone is valuable.*

Treatment disclosure is essential. Whether or not a gem has been treated, and, if so, the degree of treatment, affect value and durability as well as appearance. Furthermore, it is important to know whether or not the treatment is permanent and whether it necessitates special care. Take time to look at many stones, ask questions, and make comparisons. In this way you can develop a good eye and an understanding of the differences that affect quality rating, beauty, and value.

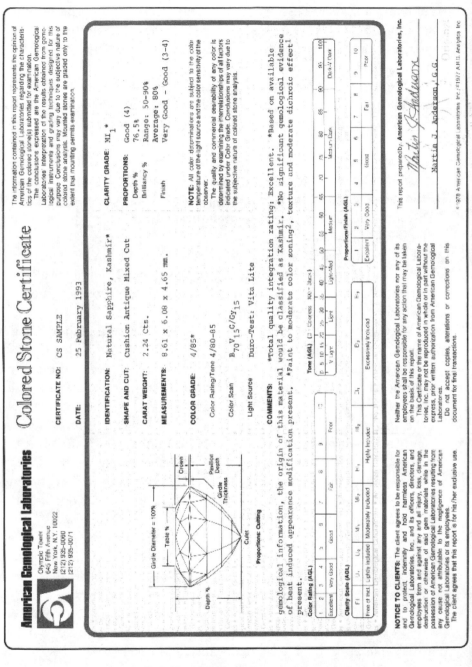

A sample AGL colored gemstone report, providing
treatment data, overall quality evaluation, and country of origin

AGTA GEMOLOGICAL TESTING CENTER

EMERALD IDENTIFICATION REPORT

Date: SAMPLE
Report No. SAMPLE

The item described below has been examined by at least two professional staff gemologists of the AGTA Gemological Testing Center. The results of the examination are presented here subject to the limitations printed on the reverse of this report

Item Description: Loose Stone

Number of gems examined:	1
Color:	Green
Transparency:	Transparent
Weight (ct):	6.90
Dimensions (mm):	13.33 x 12.80 x 8.21
Shape:	Octagonal
Cut:	Emerald-cut
Enhancement:	Moderate clarity enhancement[1]

Result: **NATURAL EMERALD**

Origin: **COLOMBIA**[2]

Comments: [1]The identity of the clarity enhancing substance was determined to be an oil. As indicated on the reverse, emeralds are commonly clarity enhanced. [2]The data obtained during the examination of this stone indicates that the probable geographic origin is as stated (see below for testing techniques).

The reverse of this page is an integral part of the report, it contains important information that may help in the interpretation of the information on this side.

Garry Du Toit

Susan Paralusz
For and on behalf of the
AGTA GEMOLOGICAL TESTING CENTER

Tests Carried Out to Establish the Identity of the Emerald Described Herein						
Refractive index ☒	Specific gravity ☐	Hand spec ☒	Microscope ☒	Polariscope ☐	FTIR ☐	Others ☒
Radiography ☐	Raman ☒	UV/vis/NIR ☒	Image spec ☐	XRD ☐	EDXRF ☒	

American Gem Trade Association Gemological Testing Center, 18 East 48 th Street, Suite 1002, New York, NY 10017, USA
Tel: **212.752.1717** Fax: **212.750.0930**

A sample AGTA Emerald Identification Report,
providing treatment data and country of origin

12

Colored Gemstone
Treatment & Synthesis

In addition to the wide variety of natural gemstone alternatives from which to choose today, treated materials and numerous synthetics are available. They make attractive jewelry, but you must understand what you have, and pay the appropriate price for it.

Gemstone Treatment Is Routine in Today's Jewelry Scene

The use of various treatments to improve the appearance of gemstones is not new. We find evidence of treatment in antique jewels, and ancient writings from Roman times and before attest to a long-standing knowledge of ways to improve the appearance of many gemstones. What is new, however, is the *routine* use of treatments, which began in the 1960s, necessitated by an ever-declining supply of natural, fine-quality gemstones. *Natural* emeralds, rubies, and sapphires—that is, gems not subjected to any type of artificial treatment or enhancement—have never been rarer than they are today. It is fair to say that if it were not for the use of various treatments, the supply of beautiful gemstones would be virtually depleted by now, and only the wealthiest and most powerful would be enjoying them!

While they can still be found, locating a natural gem in a particular size and quality can take months of intensive searching. When one is found, it can command a price prohibitive to all but the most serious collector or connoisseur. We were recently retained to help a couple acquire an exceptionally fine Colombian emerald. After discussing the options with us, and learning about different fillers and degrees of treatment used on emerald, they were willing to accept a stone with "minor traces of oil." They did not want a stone treated with other types of filler, however, or a stone with more than minimal treatment. It took several months to find the 3.64-carat emerald they selected, and the cost—at wholesale—was almost $100,000! Helping another couple search for an exceptionally fine 5-carat natural sapphire of Kashmir origin took almost as long, and the wholesale cost was over $50,000. This is not what people usually want, and most retail jewelers don't keep such gems in their regular inventory.

Most treatments simply continue the process that Mother Nature started; all gems are exposed to heat, and many to radiation, as they are forming in nature. Today, most rubies, sapphires, and many other gemstones are routinely treated with heat or exposed to some type of radiation to change or enhance their color and improve clarity, and pricing is based on the assumption that enhancement has occurred. On the other hand, if the color of a gem is very fine, and if it can be documented that the color is natural and that there is no clarity enhancement, the stone will command a much higher price. Since such gems are very rare today, some of the best sources of fine, natural-color gems are major estate pieces that sometimes reenter the market when well-known auction houses hold their "magnificent" or "important" jewelry sales.

Whether from an auction house or another source, fine, rare gems with natural color and clarity normally will be accompanied by a gemtesting report verifying this. Without a report, or any representations to the contrary, assume that the color of any gemstone sold today has been enhanced in some manner and that the clarity may also have been improved in the process. When you are buying any expensive rare gem represented to be natural, be sure it is accompanied by a report from a respected gem-testing lab that verifies this fact, or make the purchase contingent on getting a report.

Affordable Beauty

Treated gemstones can be a way for consumers to own lovely pieces at affordable prices. The most important consideration, here as in all purchases of gemstones, is to know exactly what you are buying. While some fraudulent practices involving treated stones certainly exist (see chapter

13), the selling of treated gemstones is perfectly legitimate so long as all the facts are disclosed, the type of treatment used for enhancement is acceptable in the trade, and all important representations are stated on the bill of sale. With these safeguards you can be reasonably secure about the purchase you are contemplating and can enjoy the fine color and beauty of a treated stone for many years to come.

Some of the most common types of treatment include the following.

Heating

Subjecting certain gems to sophisticated heating procedures is a practice that is accepted within the jewelry industry as long as the change induced is *permanent*. Most sapphires and rubies are heated. The treatment may lighten, darken, or completely change the color and improve the clarity by melting some of the fine "silk" inclusions often present. A skilled gemologist or gem-testing laboratory can often determine whether or not the color of these gems has been altered by heating by examining the stone's *inclusions* under the microscope. Sapphire and ruby, for example, can withstand high temperatures, but often the heat causes small crystal inclusions present inside the stone to melt or explode. These altered inclusions then provide the evidence of heating.

It may be easy to determine that a stone *has* been heated, but it is often impossible to know for certain that it has *not* been—that is, that its color is natural. Making this determination can require a high degree of skill and sophisticated equipment, often only available at a major laboratory, and even then, it may not be possible to ascertain definitively. Gemologists must carefully examine the internal characteristics of the particular stone. Sometimes they see an unaltered inclusion that would lead to a conclusion that the color is natural; other times they see an altered inclusion that indicates treatment; and sometimes the inclusions, or changes and abnormalities in them, that one seeks to make a positive determination simply are not present. When there is nothing inside the gem to indicate whether it has or has not been heated, we cannot be sure.

Most rubies and sapphires sold since the 1960s have been heated to enhance their color and clarity. Other gemstones that are routinely heated today include amber, amethyst, aquamarine, pink beryl (morganite), carnelian, citrine, kunzite, tanzanite, pink topaz, several varieties of tourmaline, and zircon.

Radiation

Radiation techniques are relatively new. Frequently used on a wide range of gemstones, radiation is sometimes combined with heating. The effect is permanent on some stones, and accepted in the trade; it is not acceptable on other stones because the color fades or changes back to its original over a relatively short time. There are still some questions regarding radiation levels and the long-term effects on health. The Nuclear Regulatory Agency has been working to establish standards, and the GIA Gem Trade Laboratory now has a facility with the capability to test gemstones for "acceptable" and six "unacceptable" radiation levels.

Virtually all blue topaz sold in jewelry stores has been irradiated to obtain the various blue shades that have become so popular. Other gemstones that may have been irradiated to obtain color include deep blue beryl (called *maxixe*; this color will always fade); yellow beryl; diamond; kunzite; yellow or orange sapphire (not stable; will fade quickly); yellow and green topaz; and red, pink, and purple tourmaline.

Diffusion Treatment

Diffusion is a recent addition to the world of gemstone treatments. There are several different processes being used—you will hear terms such as *surface* diffusion, *deep* diffusion, *bulk* diffusion, *lattice* diffusion, or *elemental* diffusion—but the basic process is similar. It involves exposing the surface of the material to chemicals and heating it over a prolonged period, sometimes altering the atmosphere in which it is being heated. By so doing, the color of the treated material can be transformed into much "rarer" and more desirable colors. At present, diffusion is being used extensively to produce various colors of topaz and and much more desirable colors in sapphire—including various shades of blue, yellow, orange, and the rare pinkish-orange "padparadscha" color. Even "ruby" is being created from very common, inexpensive corundum. Diffusion is also used to create very natural looking "star" rubies and sapphires. Diffusion treated gemstones should sell for *much less* than those treated by traditional heating techniques—about one-tenth the price of material treated by routine heating.

Usually the material being treated by diffusion techniques is colorless, pale, or heavily zoned, but extremely dark, almost black, material can also be improved by diffusion techniques. Early techniques produced stones in which color was confined to the surface (if you cut the stone in half you would see a very shallow rim of color around the perimeter of the stone, and a colorless interior) and a competent gemologist could easily identify them as diffusion treated. New processes are being used today that result in much deeper color penetration. These stones are much more difficult to detect and often require more sophisticated gemological testing and, in some cases, the services of a major gem-testing laboratory.

It is important to know whether or not the stone's color results from diffusion treatment so that you know you are paying an appropriate price. Furthermore, stones treated by some diffusion techniques require special care to prevent damage such as chipping, which might require recutting or polishing; if the color is confined to the surface, recutting or polishing could remove the color altogether. Note: should this happen, the stone can be retreated to restore the original color.

Unfortunately, diffused sapphires and rubies have been mixed in with parcels of non-diffused stones and some may have been inadvertently set in jewelry and sold without disclosure. So it is especially important to buy fine sapphires and rubies only from a reputable source, and to take what you purchase to a competent gemologist who can either verify your purchase, or determine that the services of a major gem-testing laboratory are required to know for sure.

Diffusion-treated stones offer beautiful choices at affordable prices. Just take care to know whether or not the stone has been treated by diffusion techniques. If it has, pay the right price and exercise some care in wearing and handling it.

While diffusion treatment is being used routinely today on sapphire, ruby, and topaz, this treatment could have applications to other gemstone materials in the future. It should also be noted that sapphire produced in some parts of the world, such as Montana, are not subjected to diffusion treatments and are accompanied by *guarantees* that no diffusion treatment is being used, only routine heating.

Fracture Filling

Fractures can interrupt light as it travels through a colored gemstone, creating a whitishness in the area of the fracture or, in some cases, reflecting back and making the fracture more noticeable. If a surface-reaching fracture is filled with the proper substance, the light will continue to pass through without blockage or reflection, so the color is not diminished and reflective fractures are much less noticeable because the reflectivity is greatly reduced. Certain gemstones, such as emerald, have more fractures than other gemstones because they form under extremely violent geological conditions. For this reason, emeralds are usually treated with fillers to reduce the visibility of fractures. The jewelry trade has always considered the oiling of emerald an acceptable practice, and it has been used routinely for many years. We don't know when the oiling of emerald began, but the practice was known during the Roman period, and we find many antique emerald pieces that still show traces of oil when examined with a microscope.

Today, gemstone treaters use various substances to fill fractures, including oil, wax, paraffin, glass, and various formulations of epoxy resin. Gemstones that may be treated with one of these substances include emerald, aquamarine, peridot, jade, turquoise, ruby, sapphire, and, in rare cases, alexandrite and garnet. Be especially alert to the possibility of fillers in ruby and sapphire; many rubies and sapphires from several new deposits contain reflective inclusions, so the use of oil and wax to improve the appearance of ruby and sapphire is increasing.

All Synthetics Are Not the Same

Scientific advances and new technology have resulted in a whole world of *synthetic* gemstone materials, but it's important to understand that a synthetic is *not* an imitation. Technically, the term synthetic indicates that the material is artificially made by *using the same chemical ingredients found in natural products*—in other words, using Mother Nature's recipe. This means that a synthetic gemstone will have essentially the same physical, chemical, and optical properties observed in natural gemstones. From a practical standpoint, this also means that they will respond to various gem-identification tests in the same way as do natural stones. This can make them difficult to distinguish from the natural gem.

An *imitation* is also artificially made but not by using "nature's recipe," so it is very different physically and chemically from the gem it is imitating, and it is very easy to distinguish it from the natural gem with standard gem-identification techniques. For example, a glass "gem" is an imitation. Red glass could imitate ruby. But it resembles ruby only in *color;* a quick examination with a simple jeweler's loupe would reveal tell-tale signs that it is glass, and any gemological test would clearly corroborate this conclusion.

Today there are numerous synthetic gems, but they are not all produced the same way. Some are produced inexpensively, and although they are made with nature's recipe, they don't really look like the natural gem. Some are made quickly by a process very different from nature's. These are often confused with imitations because of their unnatural appearance and low cost. This type of synthetic is widely available today and has been made for almost a hundred years.

In recent years, technological advances have enabled scientists to create environments that come much closer to duplicating what is found in nature. As a result, crystals can actually be "grown" in laboratories, creating a product that very closely resembles the natural gem. These are often called flux-grown, created, or laboratory-grown synthetics. These laboratory-grown synthetics are expensive to produce and cost much more than other synthetics; in fact, the cost can be so high that consumers sometimes mistakenly conclude they are natural gemstones. Next to the natural, there is nothing that can compare to a fine lab-grown synthetic, and even though the stone may be expensive, the cost is only a fraction of that of a rare, natural gem with a comparable appearance.

Synthetics can make excellent alternatives for buyers unable to afford natural gems in the quality they desire. Be sure, however, not to confuse terms such as *created* or *grown* with *naturally* created or grown. All synthetic products are made by humankind. Also, remember that inexpensive synthetics are abundant, so if you are paying a premium for the stone, be sure you have a lab-grown synthetic and not an inexpensive type. As you shop around and compare various synthetic products, you will find that there are significant visual differences among them. Develop an eye for the type you want.

13

Fraud & Misrepresentation in Colored Gems

We would like to begin by emphasizing here, as we did in the chapter on diamonds, that the percentage of misrepresentation and fraud among total jewelry transactions is quite low, and that most jewelers are reputable professionals in whom you can place your trust. In the colored gem market, there is a greater occurrence of misrepresentation than in the diamond market, however, primarily because of the scientifically complex nature of colored stones. So it is even more important to be aware of the deceptive practices you might encounter when buying a colored gem, both to protect yourself from the more obvious scams and to better understand the importance of dealing with a reliable jeweler. We also stress the importance, to an even greater degree, of seeking verification from a qualified gemologist—one with extensive experience with colored gems—when buying any expensive colored gem to ensure that your gemstone is what it is represented to be.

Misrepresenting Synthetic as Natural

Today it is very important to verify the genuineness of any fine, valuable gemstone because the new generation of synthetic products is so similar to the natural that the two can be easily confused. As we discussed in chapter 12, many very fine synthetics are available, and they can make attractive jewelry choices when properly represented. Still, you should protect yourself from intentional and sometimes unintentional misrepresentation.

Synthetics have been on the market for many years. Good synthetic sapphires, rubies, and spinels have been manufactured commercially since the early 1900s, and very good synthetic emeralds since the 1940s. While these early synthetics were attractive and popular because of their very low price, they didn't really look like natural stones. Most looked "too good to be true," so that they were readily distinguished from the real thing by a competent jeweler.

Today, this is often not the case. While older techniques for producing synthetics are still used and their products are still easy to recognize, new, sophisticated methods result in products that no longer possess the signature characteristics with which gem dealers and jewelers have long been familiar. To further complicate matters of identification, synthetics now often contain characteristics very similar to their natural counterparts. As a result, some are being sold as natural, intentionally and unintentionally. A gemologist with extensive experience, or a gem-testing laboratory such as the GIA or AGL, can differentiate between them and verify genuineness.

A true experience dramatically illustrates why making the extra effort required to verify genuineness is so important. We know a jeweler with an excellent reputation for honesty, reliability, and professional expertise. He had been in the business for many years and had extensive gemological training. Nonetheless, he bought a new type of synthetic ruby as a natural stone, then sold it to a customer for just under $10,000.

His customer, who had purchased the stone at a reasonable price, proceeded to resell it to a third party for a quick profit. The third party took it to a very competent gemologist with a reputation for having the skill and equipment necessary to identify new synthetic materials. The truth about the stone quickly came to light. The second and third parties in this case lost nothing (one of the benefits of buying from a reputable jeweler). The jeweler, however, suffered both a heavy financial loss and considerable damage to his reputation.

You may ask how he made such a mistake. It was easy. He was knowledgeable, like many other jewelers, and thought he knew how to distinguish a natural from a synthetic stone. But he had not kept current on technological advances and new synthetic products entering the marketplace. So he made an over-the-counter purchase of this lovely stone from a private party who had procured it in the Orient. Many of these new synthetics are produced in the United States and then find their way to the Orient—the source of many natural stones—where they are more easily sold as the "real thing." The jeweler had no recourse because he had no way of locating the seller, who had simply walked in off the street.

As this story shows, it is essential to have a highly qualified gemologist verify authenticity, particularly for fine rubies, emeralds, and sapphires. Thousands of dollars may be at stake, for jewelers may innocently buy one of these stones, believing it to be natural, and pass their error on to the customer. Don't delude yourself into believing that if a piece is purchased from a well-respected firm it is always what it is represented to be; even the best-known firms have made mistakes in this area. It may be inconvenient to obtain an expert analysis, and it may require an additional expense, but we believe it is better to be safe now than sorry later.

With sophisticated modern equipment and a greater knowledge of crystals, humans can now "create" or "grow" almost any gemstone. As a general rule, remember that any gem—amethyst, alexandrite, ruby, emerald, sapphire, opal, or even turquoise—could be synthetic, that many synthetics are themselves expensive, and that most have become more difficult to distinguish from their natural counterparts, resulting in inadvertent misrepresentation. So make sure you take time to verify a stone's true identity.

Simulated Stones

As already discussed (see chapter 12), simulated or imitation stones should not be confused with synthetics, which possess essentially the same physical, chemical, and optical properties of the natural gem. A simulated stone is usually a very inexpensive artificial imitation that resembles the natural stone in color, but little else. Many imitations are glass, but they can also be plastic. Imitations, or simulants as they are also called, are very easily differentiated from the genuine by careful visual examination and simple gemological testing. There are glass simulations of all the colored stones, and glass and plastic simulated pearls, turquoise, and amber are also common.

Imitations are frequently found in estate jewelry, sometimes mixed with natural gems in the same piece.

Look-Alike Substitution

Another form of deception involves misrepresenting a more common, less expensive stone for a rarer, more expensive gem of similar color.

Today, as more and more natural gemstones in a wide variety of colors enter the market, both deliberate and accidental misrepresentation can occur.

Color Alteration

As we discussed in chapter 12, color enhancement of gemstones is ages old, and many of the techniques used today have been used for generations. Many are routine and do not in themselves constitute fraud. Some treatments, however, should not be applied to certain gems, normally because the results are not permanent and the color may revert to the original. Such treatments are not accepted by the trade.

Because color enhancement is so common, it's important for the consumer to understand exactly which procedures are acceptable in the industry and which represent deceptive or fraudulent practices aimed at passing off inferior stones as much more expensive ones.

Here we will discuss various treatments and explain which are routine and which may constitute fraud or misrepresentation.

Heat-Treated Stones

Subjecting stones to sophisticated heating procedures is the most commonly used method of changing or enhancing a gem's color and is used routinely on a variety of gems to lighten, darken, or completely change color. Heat treatment is not a fraudulent practice when used on certain gems, on which the results are permanent. This procedure is an accepted practice routinely applied to the following stones:

- *Amber*—to deepen color and add "sun spangles"
- *Amethyst*—to lighten color; to change color of pale material to "yellow" stones sold as citrine
- *Aquamarine*—to deepen color and remove any greenish undertone to produce a "bluer" blue
- *Carnelian*—to produce color
- *Citrine*—often produced by heating other varieties of quartz
- *Kunzite*—to improve color
- *Morganite*—to change color from orange to pinkish
- *Sapphire*—to lighten or intensify color; to improve uniformity
- *Tanzanite*—to produce a more desirable blue shade

- *Topaz*—in combination with radiation, to produce shades of blue; to produce pink
- *Tourmaline*—to lighten the darker shades, usually of the green and blue varieties
- *Zircon*—to produce red, blue, or colorless stones

The color obtained by these heating procedures is usually permanent.

Radiated Stones

Radiation techniques are now in common use, produced by any of several methods, each of which has a specific application. Sometimes radiation is used in combination with heat treatment. As long as the technique produces stable results, color enhancement by radiation techniques is not considered fraudulent.

Radiation techniques are routinely used for the following stones:

- *Diamond*—to change the color from an off-white color to a fancy color (green, yellow, etc.)
- *Kunzite*—to darken color
- *Pearl*—to produce blue and shades of gray ("black" pearls)
- *Topaz*—to change from colorless or nearly colorless to blue; to intensify yellow and orange shades and create green
- *Tourmaline*—to intensify pink, red, and purple shades
- *Yellow beryl*—to create yellow color

Some very deep blue topazes have been found to be radioactive and may be harmful to the wearer. Most blue topaz sold in the United States since 1992 has been tested for radiation level by the GIA or other centers established for that purpose. Exercise caution when purchasing deep blue topaz outside the United States, in countries where radiation testing is not required.

As far as we know now, the color changes resulting from radiation treatment on the above stones are usually permanent. Some stones subjected to radiation, however, obtain a beautiful color that is temporary. Beryl can be irradiated to produce a deep "sapphire" blue *maxixe* type, but the color fades quickly. Irradiated "blue," "orange," and "yellow" sapphire will fade quickly. Irradiated "*maxixe* beryl" and irradiated sapphire are not accepted in the trade. We have seen nice "yellow" sapphires treated by radiation quickly lose their color when exposed to the flame of a cigarette lighter. If you are considering a "yellow," it may be worthwhile to try this simple flame test if the jeweler will permit. If not, be sure to have it fade tested by a qualified gemologist or gem lab.

When diamonds are irradiated to produce fancy colors, labs can usually determine that they have been treated. However, for most other gems on which radiation is used, testing procedures for determining whether or not color is natural have not been developed as of this date.

Diffusion-Treated Stones

Sapphire and ruby. Diffusion treatment is a method used to transform a colorless, pale, or heavily zoned stone into a much more desirable—and valuable—color by introducing chemicals into its surface and heating it over a prolonged period of time. Initially, the chemicals used were the same chemicals used by nature and created color on the surface only. Today, other chemicals are also used and color penetration is often much deeper and more difficult to detect. Colors produced by diffusion include yellow, orange, blue, red, and the rare orangey-pink known as "padparadscha."

Diffused rubies and sapphires are now being produced in many colors and are being substituted for non-diffused stones by unscrupulous merchants and purchased by dealers and jewelers unknowingly in parcels of stones that are subsequently mounted in jewelry. They are also being set in antique and estate jewelry. When you are buying any fine sapphire today, it is important to purchase from a knowledgeable, reputable jeweler. Be especially wary of bargains. Diffusion-treated "ruby" is less common than treated sapphire, but when buying *any* fine ruby or sapphire, in *any* color, we recommend getting a report from a respected gem-testing lab (see Appendix).

Topaz. Diffusion treatment creates a lovely green color not found in nature, and the iridescent "mystic" topaz that results from coating the surface with chemicals and applying heat. "Pink" topaz can also be created by diffusion treatment.

There is nothing wrong with buying diffused stones as long as you know it and pay the right price (approximately $1/10$th the cost of a comparable stone that has been subjected to routine heating only). You must also be aware that extra care may be required when wearing diffusion-treated stones to reduce the risk of chipping.

Dyed Stones

Gemstones have been dyed since earliest times. Numerous examples of dyed chalcedony (an inexpensive variety of quartz) can be found in antique jewelry, imitating other gems. Gems that are frequently dyed include jade, opal, coral, lapis, and to a lesser degree poor-quality star rubies, star sapphires, and emeralds.

Dyed material may be very stable, but it can also be very temporary. We've seen dyed lapis in which the "blue" came off with a cotton ball moistened in fingernail polish remover. Dyed gems may be genuine stones that have been dyed to enhance their color (as in dyeing pale green jadeite to a deeper green), or they may be a different gem altogether.

Dyed gems should always cost less than gems with natural color. Fine lapis and jadeite should always be checked for dyeing.

Here are some gemstones that are often *faked* using dyeing techniques:

- *Black onyx*—dyed chalcedony (onyx rarely occurs naturally)
- *Banded agate*—dyed chalcedony, with white bands alternating with strong colored bands
- *Carnelian*—chalcedony dyed reddish brown
- *Chrysoprase*—chalcedony dyed green
- *Jade (jadeite)*—chalcedony dyed green to imitate fine jadeite
- *Swiss lapis*—jasper dyed blue and sold as "lapis" or "Swiss lapis"

Here are some gemstones that are often dyed:

- *Jade (jadeite)*—color frequently improved by dyeing to a beautiful emerald or young grass green color, to look like "imperial" jade (while jade occurs naturally in almost every color, it may also be dyed other colors)
- *Coral and lapis*—dyed to deepen the color, or create more uniform color

Blackening Techniques

These are used to alter color, not by dyeing but by introducing a chemical reaction (sugar-acid chemical reaction) that creates black carbon, which blackens the color. The following stones are commonly faked by using this treatment:

- *Black opal*—blackened white opal (black opal is more valuable and precious)

- *Black onyx*—blackened chalcedony (most of the "black onyx" sold today in jewelry is actually chalcedony)

Waxing

This is a process consisting of rubbing the stone with a tinted waxlike substance to hide surface cracks and blemishes and to slightly improve the color. It is used often on cheaper Indian star rubies and sometimes on star sapphires.

Oiling

This technique is commonly used on emeralds. The emerald is soaked in oil (which may or may not be tinted green). Its purpose is to fill fine cracks, which are fairly common in emerald. These cracks look whitish and therefore weaken the green body color of the emerald. The oil fills the cracks, making them "disappear," and thereby improves the color by eliminating the white. It can also reduce the reflectivity of cracks.

This is an accepted procedure and will normally last for many years. However, if the stone is put in a hot ultrasonic cleaner (which is dangerous to any emerald and is *never* recommended), or soaked in an organic solvent such as gasoline, xylene, or substances containing these, such as paint remover, the oil may be slowly dissolved out of the cracks and the whitish blemishes will then reappear, weakening the color. If this should happen, the stone can be re-oiled. Using green-tinted oil, however, is not an accepted trade practice.

Oiling is now used on many other gems, including sapphire and ruby.

Painting

This technique is often used with cabochon (nonfaceted) transparent ("jelly") or semitransparent opals to create a stone that looks like precious black opal. This is done by putting the stone in a closed-back setting that has a high rim (bezel). A black cement or paint is spread on the inside of the setting so that when the opal is placed inside, the light entering it gets trapped and reflected back, giving the opal the appearance of a fine black opal. (See also the section below, describing composite stones and opal doublets.)

Foil-Backed Stones

This technique is not frequently encountered in modern jewelry but is relatively common in antique jewelry, and anyone interested in antique jewelry should be aware of it. It is seen with both nonfaceted and faceted stones, set usually in a closed-back mounting. This technique involves lining the inside of the setting with silver or gold foil to add brilliance and sparkle (as with foil-backed glass imitating diamond), or with colored foil to change or enhance color by projecting color into the stone. Always be apprehensive when considering a piece of jewelry that has a closed back.

We recently examined a heavy, yellow-gold cross set with five fine flawless emeralds, which appeared to have exceptionally fine green body color. The stones were set "in the gold" so that the backs of the stone couldn't be seen. Our suspicions were aroused, since the emeralds were all flawless and the color was so uniformly fine. Upon closer examination it became clear that the green body color was projected into the stones by a fine emerald-green foil back. The stones were probably not even emerald, but near-colorless aquamarines. Since both aquamarine and emerald belong to the same mineral family, beryl (emerald is the name given to the rare green variety of beryl, while we call the more common blue variety aquamarine), an inexperienced jeweler or gemologist using standard, basic procedures to identify the stones could have erroneously identified them as fine emeralds.

Smoking

This is a technique used only on opals. It is used to give off-white to tan-colored opals from Mexico a more desirable, moderately dark coffee brown color that greatly enhances the opal fire. It consists of taking a cut and polished opal, wrapping it tightly in brown paper, and putting it in a covered container over moderate heat until the paper is completely charred. When cooled and removed, the opal now has a much more intense brown body color and fire. But if this smoke-produced color coating were to be badly scratched, the underlying color would show through and the stone would have to be resmoked.

This treatment can be easily detected by wetting the stone (preferably with saliva). While it is wet, some of the fire disappears; then it reappears after the surface has dried.

Fracture Filling with Glass and Epoxy Resins

As with diamonds, fractures that break the surface of a colored gem can be filled with a liquid glass or glasslike substance, or with an epoxy resin-type filler. Fillers make cracks less visible and improve a stone's overall appearance. A coloring agent can also be added to the filler to simultaneously improve a stone's overall color. Selling a filled gem without disclosure is not an accepted trade practice. To do so knowingly constitutes fraud. Nonetheless, the number of glass-filled rubies encountered in the marketplace and being sold without disclosure has increased dramatically, and emeralds filled with epoxy resin are now in wide circulation and often sold without disclosure of the presence of epoxy resin.

Composite Stones

Composite stones are exactly what the term implies: stones composed of more than one part. Composites come in two basic types. Doublets are composite stones consisting of two parts, sometimes held together by a colored bonding agent. Triplets are composite stones consisting of three parts, usually glued together to a colored middle part.

Doublets

Doublets are especially important to know about because, while they were widely used in antique jewelry before the development of synthetics, today they are making a comeback and reappearing throughout the jewelry market.

In antique pieces, the most commonly encountered doublet, often referred to as a *false doublet,* consists of a red garnet top fused to an appropriately colored glass bottom. With the right combination, any colored gem could be simulated by this method. Garnets were used for the top portion of these false doublets because they possessed nice luster and excellent durability and were readily available in great quantity, which made them very inexpensive.

Another form of the doublet is made from two parts of a colorless material, fused together with an appropriately colored bonding agent. An "emerald" (sometimes sold as *soudé* emerald) can be made, for example, using a colorless synthetic spinel top and bottom, held together in the middle (at the girdle) by green glue. Red glue or blue glue could be used to simulate ruby or sapphire.

True doublets are created by using two genuine stone parts and fusing them together with an appropriately colored glue to create a "larger" gem of better color than the original components. For example, we sometimes see emerald doublets composed of two parts of genuine pale green emerald, fused with deep green glue to create a large, deep green "gem" emerald.

A clever version of a true doublet that we sometimes still encounter is a "sapphire" doublet composed of two pieces of genuine sapphire, but pale yellow sapphire fused together with blue glue. This creates an especially convincing "fine blue sapphire." The same techniques are used to make ruby doublets, although they don't look as convincing. And the same basic procedures can produce emerald doublets, using beryl instead of sapphire.

Opal doublets also occur, usually consisting of a thin top layer of genuine opal cemented to a base that can be either a poorer grade of opal or some other substance altogether. The most commonly encountered opal doublets are those made to look like the precious black opal. This doublet is usually composed of a translucent or transparent top, cemented by

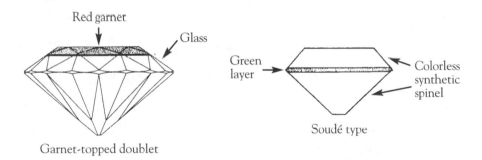

Garnet-topped doublet

Soudé type

When some composite stones are immersed in liquid (such as alcohol or methylene iodide), one can often see two or three distinct parts. With soudé emeralds, the top and bottom may seem to disappear, leaving only a green plane visible across the girdle area. (*Note:* Immersion will not reveal garnet-topped doublets.)

black cement to a bottom portion of cheaper opal or other material that acts as a support. Please note that the tops of these "black opal" doublets are usually not genuine black opal, though they certainly look like it.

Opal doublets are also made by cementing a thin piece of fine opal to a larger piece of less fine opal to create a larger overall appearance. The doublets can be identified by observing the *join* of the two pieces at the girdle; you can see the dark line of the cement between the two pieces.

Because so many doublets are flooding the market, those who love sapphire, ruby, and emerald must be particularly careful and buy only from reputable jewelers. We know a woman who paid $16,000 recently for a pair of "genuine" emerald earrings from a jeweler on New York's 47th Street. They contained four soudé emerald doublets and were worth only a couple of hundred dollars—and that was for the gold and diamonds in the settings. Luckily, this woman had all the right information on the bill of sale, took them for an independent evaluation by a gemologist-appraiser, and discovered the error in time to return the pieces and get her money back from the jeweler.

It is alarming to see the large number of ruby and sapphire doublets consisting of genuine tops—usually nearly colorless or a very inexpensive greenish brown color—and synthetic sapphire and ruby bottoms that are being sold as genuine. Avoid "bargains" from any merchant unless you can check them out. Be especially wary of street peddlers when you are traveling in Asia and South America. We've seen an incredible number of doublets in jewelry and "unmounted" stones brought back by unsuspecting travelers, especially those journeying to exotic spots known for gems.

Many of the doublets now appearing in jewelry sold by reputable firms were originally slipped in with genuine stones shipped to buyers around the world. Since doublets are difficult to spot and will even pass four gemological tests providing positive identification, it is easy for one to be passed on to a customer unknowingly, especially when it is set in sleek, modern bezel settings.

There is nothing wrong with buying a doublet as long as you know what you are buying, and pay a fair price. Just be careful not to buy a doublet unknowingly. Be sure to verify all the facts.

Triplets

Triplets are frequently encountered in the opal market and have substantially replaced the doublet there. The triplet is exactly like the opal doublet except that it has a cabochon-shaped colorless quartz cap (the third part) that covers the entire doublet, giving the delicate doublet greater protection from breakage and providing greater luminescence (brightness) to the stone.

With careful examination, a competent jeweler or gemologist should be able to easily differentiate a doublet or triplet from a natural. We should note, however, that detection of an opal doublet may be very difficult if it is set in a mounting with a rim (bezel set) covering the seam where the two pieces are cemented together. It might be necessary to remove the stone from its setting for positive identification. Because of opal's fragile nature, removal must be performed only by a very competent bench jeweler (a jeweler who actually makes or repairs jewelry), and the jeweler may agree to do so only at your risk, not wanting to assume responsibility for any breakage. In the case of a black opal worth several thousand dollars, it is well worth the additional cost and inconvenience to be sure it is not a doublet worth only a few hundred dollars. Always be apprehensive when buying a "flat-topped opal" that is bezel-set.

Misleading Names

Another form of misrepresentation occurs when colored stones are called by names that lead the buyer to believe they are something they are not. This practice is frequently encountered, especially outside the United States. When any stone is described with a qualifier, as in "Rio topaz" or "Zambian emerald," be sure to ask whether the stone is a genuine, natural stone. Ask why there is a qualifier.

Let's examine two examples: "Japanese amethyst" and "Ceylon sapphire." In the case of Japanese amethyst, the stone is not genuine but synthetic, and the name, therefore, is clearly misleading. However, in the case of the Ceylon sapphire, *Ceylon* refers to the location from which that gem was mined, and most Ceylon sapphires are always a particular tone of blue (a lighter shade, and very lively). Their color makes them much more desirable than certain other varieties, such as Australian or Thai, which are often overly dark and less brilliant. Therefore, in this case, *Ceylon* is very important to the stone's complete description.

Let's look at one more example, Ceylon-*colored* sapphire. In this case, the qualifier is the word *colored*. In most cases, this word implies some type of color alteration or treatment. A Ceylon-colored sapphire is not a Ceylon sapphire but a sapphire that has been treated to obtain the Ceylon color.

There is nothing actually wrong with selling "Japanese amethyst" or "Ceylon-colored sapphire" or other similarly named stones, as long as they are properly represented and priced. Then the decision becomes yours: either you like it or you don't; it meets your emotional need for an amethyst or Ceylon sapphire or it doesn't; and the price is right or it isn't. The following tables provide some examples of names to be aware of: "descriptive" names that are important to the stone's complete description; and misnomers—misleading names that are meant to do exactly that, mislead.

Descriptive Names

Misnomers (and What They Really Are)

Diamond

Canary diamond (fancy natural *intense* or *vivid* yellow diamond)
Chameleon diamond (diamond that changes color when heated or left in dark)
Fancy diamond (natural-colored diamond)

Alaska diamond (hematite)
Arkansas diamond (quartz) (although genuine diamond is found in Arkansas)
Bohemian diamond (quartz)
Ceylon diamond (colorless zircon)
Herkimer diamond (quartz)
Kenya diamond (rutile)
Matura diamond (zircon)
Mogok diamond (colorless topaz)
Pennsylvania diamond (pyrite)
Rainbow diamond (rutile)
Rangoon diamond (zircon)
Rhine diamond (quartz; original "rhinestone")

Emerald

African emerald (emerald mined in Africa)
Brazilian emerald (emerald mined in Brazil)
Colombian emerald (emerald mined in Colombia. The best quality Colombian emerald is considered by connoisseurs to be the finest. It is rare and very expensive.)
Indian emerald (emerald mined in India)
Pakistan emerald (emerald mined in Pakistan)
Zambian emerald (emerald mined in Zambia)

Chatham emerald (synthetic)
Esmeralda emerald (green tourmaline)
Evening emerald (peridot)
Lannyte emerald (doublet)
Mascot emerald (doublet)
Oriental emerald (green sapphire)
Soudé emerald (doublet)

Jade

Ax stone (nephrite jade)
California jade (both jadeite and nephrite jade)
Greenstone (nephrite jade, New Zealand)
Imperial jade (fine, gem-quality jadeite jade)

African jade (green massive garnet)
Australian jade (chrysoprase quartz)
Colorado jade (amazonite feldspar)
Fukien jade (soapstone)
Honan jade (soapstone)
Indian jade (aventurine quartz)
Korea jade (serpentine [bowenite])

Descriptive Names	Misnomers (and What They Really Are)
Jade (both jadeite and nephrite jade)	*Manchurian jade* (soapstone)
Kidney stone (nephrite)	*Mexican jade* (dyed green calcite)
Maori (nephrite jade, New Zealand)	*New jade* (serpentine [bowenite])
Spinach jade (nephrite jade)	*Oregon jade* (dark green jasper [quartz])
	Soochow jade (serpentine or soapstone)
	Swiss jade (dyed green jasper [quartz])
	Virginia jade (amazonite, variety feldspar)

Opal	
Andamooka opal (a type of opal from Andamooka, Australia)	*Gilson opal* (imitation or synthetic)
Black opal (a rare type of genuine opal with a dark body color)	*Japanese opal* (plastic imitation)
Boulder opal (genuine opal in which brown host rock may be seen)	*Slocum opal* (imitation)
Fire opal (opal with strong reddish or orangish color, mostly from Mexico)	
Harlequin opal (very rare genuine opal that exhibits a "harlequin" pattern)	
Jelly opal (a transparent type of opal that has a jellylike appearance)	

Pearls	
Biwa pearl (freshwater cultured pearl grown in Lake Biwa, Japan)	*Atlas pearl* (imitation satinspar-type gypsum beads)
Burmese pearl (natural or cultured pearl from Myanmar [Burma]; very rare today)	*Conch pearl* ("pearls" produced by the conch; not truly pearls, but as rare and costly as many natural pearls)
Chinese pearl (freshwater or seawater cultured pearl, produced in China)	*Girasol pearl* (imitation)
Cultured pearl (pearl with a tissue graft or nucleus implanted by humans to start the production of the pearl coating, called *nacre* [nay'-ker])	*Laguna pearl* (imitation)
	Majorica pearl (imitation)
	Red Sea pearl (coral beads)
	Tecla pearl (pink conch pearl)

Descriptive Names	Misnomers (and What They Really Are)

Pearls (*cont.*)
Mexican pearl (natural or cultured pearl produced in Mexico)
Oriental pearl (genuine, *natural* pearl; rare and very costly in fine quality)
Potato pearl (near-round, cultured freshwater, all-nacre pearl)
South Sea pearl (natural or cultured pearl produced in the waters of Australia and the Pacific Ocean)
Tahitian pearl (natural or cultured pearl that occurs in shades of gray, black, and exotic colors naturally)

Ruby

African ruby (ruby from Africa)	*Almandine ruby* (garnet)
Burma ruby (ruby from Myanmar [Burma]. The finest are considered by connoisseurs to be the most desirable; they are rare and costly.)	*Australian ruby* (garnet)
	Balas ruby (spinel)
	Bohemian ruby (garnet)
	Cape ruby (garnet)
Ceylon ruby (ruby from Sri Lanka [Ceylon])	*Chatham ruby* (synthetic)
	Ramura ruby (synthetic)
Thai ruby (ruby from Thailand)	*Ruby spinel* (spinel)
	Siberian ruby (tourmaline)

Sapphire

Australian sapphire (sapphire from Australia)	*Brazilian sapphire* (blue tourmaline; Brazil also has sapphire, but it is called simply sapphire)
Burmese sapphire (sapphire from Myanmar [Burma]; in fine quality, rare and expensive)	*Chatham sapphire* (synthetic)
	Lux sapphire (iolite)
Ceylon sapphire (sapphire from Sri Lanka [Ceylon]. Lighter blue than Burmese; fine quality also rare and expensive)	*Water sapphire* (iolite)
Kashmir sapphire (sapphire from Kashmir; fine-quality stones are considered by connoisseurs to be the finest; rare and costly)	
Montana, or Yogo, sapphire (sapphire from Montana)	

Descriptive Names	Misnomers (and What They Really Are)
Oriental sapphire (old term to denote "genuine") *Thai sapphire* (sapphire from Thailand)	

Topaz

Precious (imperial) topaz (usually fine apricot orange)	*Madeira topaz* (citrine quartz) *Occidental topaz* (citrine quartz)* *Palmeira topaz* (citrine quartz) *Rio topaz* (citrine quartz) *Saffranite topaz* (citrine quartz) *Scottish topaz* (citrine quartz) *Smokey topaz* (smokey quartz) *Spanish topaz* (citrine quartz)

*Much of the citrine quartz seen on the market today is produced by heating the purple variety (amethyst). This heating alters the color from purple to shades of yellow, yellow-brown, or golden yellow.

Other Names You Might See

Names	What They Really Are
Aquagem	Light blue synthetic spinel
California moonstone	Chalcedony quartz
California turquoise	Variscite
Chortanite	Imitation tanzanite (YAG)
Cortanite	Imitation tanzanite (YAG)
Esmeralda	Green tourmaline
Forsterite	Imitation tanzanite
German lapis	Dyed blue jasper (quartz)
Goldstone	Artificial glass with copper crystals
Imperial yu stone (*yu* is the Chinese word for jade)	Fine green aventurine quartz
Japanese amethyst	Synthetic amethyst
Oriental chrysoberyl	Yellow-green sapphire
Oriental topaz	Yellow sapphire
Rose zircon	Synthetic pink spinel
South Sea cat's-eye	Operculum, "door" of a univalve shellfish
Swiss lapis	Dyed blue jasper (quartz)
Tsavolite	Imitation tsavorite (synthetic corundum)

14

Buying Colored Gems

When you go to buy colored gemstones today, you will find yourself immersed in color—every hue, every shade of the spectrum. There has never been a more exciting time to search for a colored gem because there have never been so many alternatives. Whatever color you prefer, and whatever your budget, there is a sparkling natural gem awaiting your discovery.

You will see "new" gems only recently discovered: emerald green garnets (tsavorite), blue and green tanzanite (gemologically, the green variety is known as green zoisite, the mineral name for this gemstone, since the gem named tanzanite was blue), and "neon" tourmalines from Paraiba, Brazil (also called Hetorita), in blue and green shades never seen before. Sapphires abound in virtually every color, as do tourmalines. Even diamond can now be seen in a wide variety of natural "fancy" colors (some at very "fancy" prices).

The new colors are exciting, but so are the new cuts; there are unusual shapes in both faceted and cabochon (nonfaceted) cuts, "fancy" and "fantasy" cuts, and "sculpted" cuts.

In the following pages we present some of the most popular gemstone alternatives by color; a table that indicates the effect of treatments on gemstone value; a list of gemstones that are not routinely treated; and a guide to how gemstones compare in terms of price, availability, and wearability. The gems will be discussed individually in chapter 15—beginning with "precious" and followed alphabetically by the other popular gem families. It should be noted that the terms *precious* and *semiprecious* are discouraged today, since they can be misleading; rubies, sapphires, and emeralds are only "precious" in rare qualities, and there are many "semiprecious" gemstones today that are rarer and more valuable than so-called precious gems.

Gem Alternatives by Color

Color Family	Popular Name of Stone	Gem Family
Red— *from red* *to shades* *of pink*	Andalusite—pink to reddish brown	Andalusite
	Diamond—all shades of pink and red	Diamond
	Garnet—several red color varieties	
	Almandine—violet to pure red	Garnet
	Malaya—brownish red to orangy red	Garnet
	Pyrope—brownish red to red	Garnet
	Rhodolite—red to violet	Garnet
	Kunzite—violet-pink to pink-violet	Spodumene
	Morganite—pink to orange-pink	Beryl
	Pink sapphire—pinkish red	Corundum
	Red "emerald"—red	Beryl
	Rose quartz—pure pink	Quartz
	Rubellite—red to violet-red and pink	Tourmaline
	Ruby—bluish red to orange-red	Corundum
	Spinel—red to brownish red and pink	Spinel
	Sunstone—rich red to orange-red	Feldspar
	Zircon—brownish red to deep, dark red	Zircon
Orange	Diamond—various shades including yellow-orange to brownish orange	Diamond
	Garnet—a few orange varieties	
	Hessonite—orange-brown to brown-orange	Garnet
	Malaya—red-orange to orangy brown	Garnet
	Spessartite—orange to red-orange to brown-orange	Garnet
	Morganite—pale orange to orangy pink	Beryl
	Padparadscha sapphire—pinkish orange	Corundum
	Spinel—brown to orange	Spinel
	Sunstone—rich orange to orange-red	Feldspar
	Topaz—brownish orange, yellow-orange, pinkish orange	Topaz
	Tourmaline—all shades of orange	Tourmaline
	Zircon—orange to golden brown	Zircon
Yellow	Beryl (heliodor)—golden yellow	Beryl
	Chrysoberyl—yellow, yellow-green, yellow-brown	Chrysoberyl
	Citrine—yellow to yellow-brown	Quartz
	Diamond—all shades of yellow to chartreuse	Diamond
	Garnet—a couple of yellow varieties	
	Andradite—honey yellow to greenish yellow	Garnet
	Grossularite—yellow to greenish yellow to brownish yellow	Garnet
	Sapphire—yellow	Corundum

	Sphene—green-yellow to golden yellow to brown	Sphene
	Sunstone—orangy yellow, yellow, greenish yellow	Feldspar
	Topaz—brownish yellow to yellow	Topaz
	Tourmaline—all shades	Tourmaline
	Zircon—yellow to yellow-brown	Zircon
Green	Alexandrite—daylight: bluish to blue-green; artificial light: violet-red	Chrysoberyl
	Diamond—blue-green to yellow-green to gray-green	Diamond
	Emerald—yellowish green to bluish green	Beryl
	Garnet—a couple of green varieties	
	Demantoid—yellow-green to emerald green	Garnet
	Tsavorite—yellowish green to bluish green	Garnet
	Peridot—yellow-green to green	Peridot
	Sapphire—yellow-green to blue-green to gray-green	Corundum
	Sphene—grass green to yellow-green	Sphene
	Sunstone—yellowish, grayish, brownish green	Feldspar
	Tanzanite—gray-green to blue-green	Zoisite
	Tourmaline—several green color varieties	
	Chrome—rich green to slightly yellow-green	Tourmaline
	Paraiba—light to deep green to blue-green	Tourmaline
	Verdelite—all shades of green	Tourmaline
	Zircon—green to yellow-green to gray-green	Zircon
Blue	Aquamarine—blue to blue-green	Beryl
	Diamond—all shades	Diamond
	Iolite—violet to gray-blue	Iolite
	Sapphire—cornflower blue to greenish blue to inky blue	Corundum
	Spinel—blue, gray-blue, greenish blue	Spinel
	Tanzanite—violet-blue	Zoisite
	Topaz—blue to blue-green	Topaz
	Tourmaline—a couple of blue color varieties	
	Indicolite—inky blue, greenish blue	Tourmaline
	Paraiba—intense blue to violet-blue to green-blue	Tourmaline
	Zircon—pastel blue	Zircon
Violet	Amethyst—lilac to violet to reddish purple to brownish purple	Quartz
	Benitoite—blue to violet-blue to gray-blue	Benitoite
	Diamond—all shades	Diamond
	Kunzite—pinkish violet to red-violet	Spodumene
	Morganite—pinkish violet	Beryl
	Paraiba—violet to blue-violet	Tourmaline
	Rhodolite—red-violet	Garnet
	Sapphire—purple to violet	Corundum
	Spinel—grayish violet to pure purple	Spinel

The Effect of Treatments on the Value of Gemstones

The following table provides an indication of price adjustment for *natural* versus *treated* ruby, sapphire, and emerald. Keep in mind that untreated sapphire and ruby from certain locations, such as Burma or Kashmir, command a premium greater than indicated below. Also, note that there are rare gems of exceptional quality above the extra fine rating below, and such stones will command a much greater premium if untreated.

How Treatments Affect Prices of Colored Gems*

Emerald	GOOD	FINE	EXTRA FINE
Untreated	+10% to +25%	+25% to +50%	+50% and up
Slight treatment	0%	0%	0%
Moderate treatment	–5% to –10%	–10% to –15%	–15% to –25%
Extensive treatment	–15% to –20%	–20% to –25%	–25% to –35%
Ruby			
Unheated	+5% to +20%	+20% to +35%	+35% to +50% and up
Moderate heat	0%	0%	0%
High heat with slight glass residue	–5%	–5% to –10%	–10% to –15%
moderate glass residue	–5% to –10%	–10% to –15%	–15% to –20%
extensive glass residue	–15% to –20%	–20% to –25%	–25% to –35%
Glass-filled cavity	–10% to –50%	–10% to –50%	–10% to –50%
Sapphire			
Unheated	+5% to +10%	+10% to +20%	+20% to +30% and up
Heated	0%	0%	0%
Oiled (no data; often goes undetected)			

*The information presented above is based on information from several sources, including *The Guide* (Gemworld International) and *JCK Magazine*.

The Rarest of Them All—The *Natural* Gems

There has been so much focus on the extensive use of treatments to enhance gems that it is easy to forget that there are also natural gems: those that have not been artificially enhanced in any way. Within every gemstone family there is the occasional beauty that is just as nature made it. Unfortunately, as we discussed earlier, sometimes we cannot distinguish what is natural from what is not. Such is the case with blue topaz, for example. Blue topaz does occur naturally, in lovely pastel shades. It is one of nature's rarest and loveliest gems, but alas, we do not yet have the means to definitively distinguish what is natural from what has been irradiated. Thus, regardless of its rarity and true preciousness (and value), it commands a very small price.

There are also natural rubies, sapphires, and emeralds. Most are not the color and clarity we've come to expect (from the standards applied to the treated gems), but we are starting to see interest in a wider range of qualities, especially for stones in the lighter shades of color. And exceptionally fine-quality rubies, sapphires, and emeralds also exist. Fortunately, where ruby, sapphire, and emerald are concerned, it is usually possible to distinguish the natural from the treated, and as the natural stones become even rarer and rarer, prices are starting to reflect their preciousness, as you've seen in the table above.

There is yet another group of gems about which little has been said until recently: gemstones and gemstone families that are not routinely treated to alter color or clarity at this time. When you buy one of the following gemstones, the color is generally natural, and in most cases these gemstones are not enhanced in any way. Included in the list below

---

Gemstones That Are Not Routinely Enhanced*

Alexandrite	Iolite	Tourmaline (rare
Andalusite	Moonstone	chrome green
Chrysoprase	Fire opal	variety and cat's-
Chrysoberyl	Peridot	eye tourmaline)
(all colors)	Spinel (all colors)	Zircon (brown and
Garnet (all colors)†	Tanzanite (green)	green varieties)
Hematite		

*The color of these gems is normally natural. In rare instances, surface-reaching fractures or cavities may be filled with oil, wax, or resin.
†Demantoid garnets may be treated with a low-heat process used to create green color.

are many beautiful choices in a rainbow of colors. If you are not familiar with them, there is more information in the following chapters. Whatever your color preference and budget, if you seek something truly
"natural," you should be able to find the right gem from this list. If jewelers in your area don't have what you want, they can contact the American Gem Trade Association (AGTA) to arrange to get stones for you to see.

How to Use the Following Guides

The purpose of the following price guides is twofold: to help you
understand how prices for different gems in a given color compare with
one another; and to demonstrate how significant the price range might be
for a given type of stone, so that you will have a clearer understanding
of the importance of quality differences.

The guides can be especially useful—and help you avoid mistakes—
if you follow these steps:

- *Decide what color you want in a gem, and then make a list of
  the gems available in that color.* If you want an emerald green
  gem, for example, you would use the guide to see what emerald green gems are available: emerald, tsavorite garnet, chrome
  tourmaline, green tourmaline, or green sapphire, for example.
- *Compare their prices* to get a sense of the relative cost of each.
  In comparing prices for these green gems, you would immediately see that emerald is the most expensive, tsavorite garnet is
  next (but still much more affordable than emerald), chrome
  tourmaline costs less than the tsavorite, then green tourmaline,
  and finally the most affordable, green sapphire.
- *Note availability* to determine how easy or difficult it might
  be to locate the particular gem you think you want. In this
  example, you would see that of the choices, green sapphire is
  not as readily available as several other choices and might be
  difficult to find.
- *Note the range in price* for the stones that interest you. *The
  larger the price range in a given stone, the more critical any
  differences in quality become.* A wide price variance would indicate that you must be especially careful to spend time comparing and learning about the stone, developing an eye to spot
  subtle differences in quality.

- *Read about each gem individually.* Now turn to chapter 15 and read about each of the gems you're considering individually. You may find that there is something about the stone or its history, mythology, or wearability that makes it an even more interesting choice for you. Here you will also learn if there is anything special you need to know, to look for, or to look out for as you shop.

Now, you're ready to embark on a sparkling search. But always remember: *being genuine doesn't mean a stone is a "gem" or that it is "valuable."* There are genuine rubies, sapphires, and emeralds that can be bought for a couple of dollars per carat, and some you couldn't pay us to take! A gem must be beautiful and rare, attributes that are related to *quality*. The finer the quality, the more beautiful and the more rare. The quality of the individual stone is what determines whether or not it is a "gem," and it is the *quality* that determines its value. The range in price for any colored gemstone is directly related to quality differences—and it can be enormous. Be sure you have read chapter 11 carefully, and understand the factors that determine quality before making any decision.

After reading these chapters, you will know what to ask the jeweler to show you. But don't forget to do a lot of window-shopping, looking, and asking questions until you really have developed a feel for that particular stone and its market.

Price Guides to Popular Gems

The prices quoted in these price guides are for faceted gemstones unless otherwise noted. Cabochon-cut stones often cost less. Prices shown are for good to extra fine quality. Gems used in mass-produced jewelry sold in many jewelry stores are often of commercial quality and may cost significantly less than the prices indicated here. Also, it is rare to find gems sold by jewelry retailers that exceed the prices shown for extra fine quality. Rare gems in exceptionally fine quality and rare stones of unusual size can sell for much more than the prices indicated here. If the price of a gem you are considering is higher than what we indicate, we strongly recommend taking extra steps to confirm its exceptional quality before purchase; in some cases we would recommend having the seller obtain a quality grading report from a laboratory such as the American Gemological Laboratories (AGL) or the American Gem Trade Association (AGTA) Gemological Testing Center.

The prices shown for gems that are routinely treated or enhanced in some way—ruby, sapphire, emerald, topaz, tourmaline, and so on—reflect prices for treated material (showing evidence of "moderate" treatment). For *natural* gemstones, or heavily treated stones, see price adjustment chart on page 148.

Guide to Popular Gems and Their Prices*

Family	Popular Name	Color(s)	Approx. Retail Cost Per Carat	Brilliance	Wearability	Availability
Andalusite	Poor man's alexandrite	Changes color from grayish green to reddish brown, emerald green to bright yellow	1 to under 5 cts: $75–375 5 to under 10 cts: $150–525	Good	Good	Large: poor; smaller: fair
Apatite	Apatite	Various shades of blue and green varieties	1 to under 3 cts: $50–200) 3 to under 5 cts: $75–275	Fair	Fair, soft, scratches easily	Good
Benitoite	Benitoite	Blue, violetish blue, bluish violet	½ to under 1 ct: $875–2,250 1 to under 2 cts: $1,250–5,000 2 to under 3 cts: $2,000–7,500	Very good	Fair to good	1 ct: good; larger: fair to poor
Beryl[1]	Aquamarine	Pastel blue to medium deep blue	1 to under 5 cts: $75–1,500 5 to under 10 cts: $125–1,500	Good	Good	Good
	Golden beryl (heliodor)	Yellow, brownish yellow	1 to under 5 cts: $75–150 5 to under 10 cts: $100–250	Good	Good	Good
	Green beryl	Pastel grayish green to yellowish green or bluish green	1 to under 5 cts: $50–325 5 to under 10 cts: $50–500	Good	Good	Good
	Emerald[2]	Yellow-green to blue-green	1 to under 2 cts: $700–13,000 2 to under 4 cts: $1,000–20,000	Fair to good	Fair to good	Very fine Colombian: rare; others: good
	Morganite	Pink to orange-pink	1 to under 5 cts: $25–1,000 5 to under 10 cts: $75–1,250	Good	Good	Fine: rare; medium: good
	Red beryl[3] (Red Emerald™)	Light to deep orangish red to purplish red	under 1 ct: $300–15,000 1+ to 3+ cts: $2,000–40,000	Fair to good	Fair to good	Very fine: rare; medium: good

Chart continues on next page.

*Prices compiled from *The Guide*, Gemworld International, Inc., and adjusted to retail.

[1]Beryl also comes in green (different from emerald green), lilac, salmon, and orange. Most are still not readily available, but some, such as the lovely orange variety, can be found for under $75 per carat and offer excellent value.

[2]Cabochon-cut rubies, sapphires, and emeralds usually cost much less; finest gems can cost much more.

[3]Prices are based on information provided by www.redemerald.com.

Family	Popular Name	Color(s)	Approx. Retail Cost Per Carat	Brilliance	Wearability	Availability
Chrysoberyl	Alexandrite	Changes from greenish in daylight to reddish in incandescent light	½ to under 2 cts: $1,750–16,000 2 to under 5 cts: $3,750–40,000	Good	Excellent	Large: poor; small: fair
	Chrysoberyl	Yellow to yellow-brown to yellow-green	1 to under 5 cts: $50–250 5 to under 10 cts: $100–625	Good	Excellent	Fair
	Precious cat's-eye	Greenish to brownish yellow with "eye" effect	1 to under 3 cts: $750–4,200 3 to under 5 cts: $1,500–6,400	Negligible	Excellent	Fair to good
Corundum	Ruby[2]	Red to bluish or purplish red to yellow-red	½ to under 1 ct: $300–3,800 1 to under 2 cts: $525–8,000 2 to under 4 cts: $750–13,600	Fair to good	Excellent	Fine, natural color: rare; others: good
	Blue sapphire[2]	Bright blue to inky blue	½ to under 1 ct: $150–2,175 1 to under 2 cts: $325–4,000 2 to under 4 cts: $700–8,000	Good	Excellent	Natural color, Burmese and Kashmir: rare; others: good
	Colorless sapphire	White (colorless)	½ to under 1 ct: $25–150 1 to under 2 cts: $50–275	Good	Very good	Fair
	Green sapphire	Clear green to brownish or bluish green	1 to under 3 cts: $75–700 3 to under 5 cts: $200–1,000	Good	Excellent	Clear green: rare; others: good
	Pink sapphire	Light to very dark pink (almost red)	1 to under 2 cts: $200–2,075 2 to under 3 cts: $300–3,125	Good	Excellent	Good in sizes under 1 ct
	Yellow sapphire	Yellow (most are heat-treated; natural yellow usually less brilliant)	1 to under 5 cts: $100–1,250 5 to under 10 cts: $250–1,500	Good	Excellent	Large: poor; others: fair
Feldspar	Labradorite	Deep gray-blue to brownish blue with strong iridescent play of color	16" strand of 8 mm beads: $200–250 1 to under 5 cts: $25–125	Not applicable	Good	Good

Chart continues on next page.

Feldspar (cont.)	Moonstone	Milky white to blue-white	1 to under 5 cts: $25–175 5 to under 20 cts: $50–250	Not applicable	Good	White: good; blue: fair
	Sunstone⁴	Red, orange, yellow, deep blue, green	under 1 ct: $75–2,500 1 to under 5 cts: $100–2,500	Fair to good	Good	Small sizes: good; others: fair
Garnet	Almandine (common garnet)	Purplish red to pure red	1 to under 5 cts: $15–50 5 to under 10 cts: $25–75	Fair to good	Good	Fair
	Demantoid	Yellow-green to emerald green	1 to under 2 cts: $1,000–6,000 2 to under 3 cts: $1,950–10,000	Very good	Good	Good
	Grossularite	Yellow to yellowish green to yellowish brown	1 to under 5 cts: $50–250 5 to under 10 cts: $125–575	Fair to good	Good	Good
	Malaya	Pink-orange to brownish red	1 to under 5 cts: $75–700 5 to under 10 cts: $200–950	Good	Good	Poor
	Pyrope (common garnet)	Yellowish red to dark red	1 to under 5 cts: $15–50 5 to under 20 cts: $25–125	Fair to good	Good	Good
	Rhodolite	Red-violet	1 to under 5 cts: $25–150 5 to under 20 cts: $75–375	Good	Good	Good
	Spessartite	Brownish orange to reddish brown to brownish red	1 to under 5 cts: $25–125 5 to under 30 cts: $50–200	Good	Good	Good
	Mandarin	Intense orange to fiery reddish orange	1 to under 5 cts: $200–1,250 5 to under 10 cts: $500–1,875	Fair to very good	Good	Large: rare; others: good
	Tsavorite	Yellowish green to bluish green	1 to under 2 cts: $625–1,750 2 to under 3 cts: $1,000–3,375 3 to under 5 cts: $1,700–6,400	Good	Good	Good
Iolite	Iolite	Violet-blue to gray-blue	1 to under 5 cts: $50–200 5 to under 10 cts: $75–250	Good	Fair	Fair

Chart continues on next page.

²Cabochon-cut rubies, sapphires, and emeralds usually cost much less; finest gems can cost much more.
⁴Bicolor, tricolor, and color change sunstones also occur but are rare. Prices for these are much higher than indicated for other colors of sunstone.

Family	Popular Name	Color(s)	Approx. Retail Cost Per Carat	Brilliance	Wearability	Availability
Pearls[5] (cultured)	Round[6]	Silver, silver-white, pink-white, white, cream	*16–18" strands* 6–6.5 mm: $1,050–3,000 7–7.5 mm: $1,350–6,250 8–8.5 mm: $2,125–11,000 9–9.5 mm: $5,500–27,000	Not applicable	Good	Gem-quality over 8 mm: rare; others: good
	South Sea (round)	Silver, silver-white, pink-white, white, cream	*price per pearl[7]* 11–12 mm: $1,000–3,300 12–13 mm: $1,200–3,600 14–15 mm: $2,400–9,000	Not applicable	Good	Gem-quality: very rare; fine-quality over 16 mm: rare; others: fair to good
	Baroque	White to creamy white	*16–18" strands* 7.5–8 mm: $450–1,500 8.5–9 mm: $575–2,000	Not applicable	Good	Good
	Freshwater rice	All colors	4–5 mm: $15–50	Not applicable	Good	Good
	Potato/near round	All colors	4–5 mm: $25–225	Not applicable	Good	Good
	Black/gray (round Tahitian)	Deep gray to black with various overtones of blue, green, and pink—*not* dyed	*price per pearl[7]* 8.5–9 mm: $125–425 10–10.5 mm: $250–650 11.5–12 mm: $425–1,100	Not applicable	Good	Small sizes: fair; larger sizes: rare
Peridot (olivine)	Peridot	Yellow-green to deep green to rich chartreuse	1 to under 5 cts: $50–225 5 to under 10 cts: $75–375	Fair to good	Fair, will scratch easily	Large: poor; smaller: good
Quartz	Amethyst	Purple, reddish purple to brownish purple	1 to under 5 cts: $10–75 5 to under 10 cts: $15–100 10 to under 25 cts: $25–125	Fair to good	Good	Very good
	Ametrine	Shades of yellow and purple in same stone	1 to under 5 cts: $10–40 5 under 20 cts: $15–60	Good	Good	Good

[5]Natural pearls are very rare and much more expensive than cultured. Pricing information is insufficient to provide guidelines. *Chart continues on next page.*

6¾-round pearl, which may appear to be fully round, sell for approximately 50% less than full round pearl.

Category	Variety	Color	Size/Price			
Quartz (cont.)	Citrine	Yellow to yellow-brown	1 to under 5 cts: $10–55 5 to under 25 cts: $15–75	Good	Good	Good
	Rose quartz, Smokey quartz	Pure pink; some murky; some clear, transparent; brown shades	most sizes: $10–30 per stone	Good	Good	Good
Spinel	Blue spinel	Medium gray-blue to deep blue to violet	1 to under 3 cts: $175–1,500 3 to under 5 cts: $225–2,250	Good	Very good	Good
	Pink spinel	Lively or bright pink to brownish pink	1 to under 3 cts: $200–1,500 3 to under 5 cts: $250–1,750	Very good	Very good	Fair
	Red spinel	Red to brownish red	1 to under 3 cts: $250–3,250 3 to under 5 cts: $625–4,200	Very good	Very good	Ruby red: poor; others: good
Spodumene	Kunzite	Lilac, violet, pink	1 to under 5 cts: $15–225 5 to under 20 cts: $75–250	Good	Poor for rings or bracelets	Good
Topaz	Blue topaz	Blue	1 to under 5 cts: $3–25 5 to under 20 cts: $10–30	Good	Fair	Good
	Imperial topaz	Golden with pinkish/reddish overtone	1 to under 3 cts: $100–2,250 3 to under 5 cts: $150–2,750	Good	Fair	Fair to good except in very large sizes
	Pink topaz	Pink (red also available, but very rare and much more expensive)	1 to under 3 cts: $250–1,875 3 to under 5 cts: $250–2,000	Good	Fair	Fair to good
	Yellow/golden topaz	Yellow/golden (no pink/red overtone)	1 to under 5 cts: $100–1,500 5 to under 20 cts: $150–2,000	Good	Good	Good
Tourmaline	Chrome	Deep green	1 to under 3 cts: $200–1,500 3 to under 5 cts: $625–1,575	Good	Fair to good	Poor
	Indicolite	Inky blue to blue-green	1 to under 5 cts: $125–1,125 5 to under 10 cts: $200–1,375	Good	Fair to good	Good
	Paraiba (neon)	Wide range of "neon" blue, green, blue-green, and purplish blue	under 1 ct: $1,000–8,000 1 to under 5 cts: $4,800–40,000	Excellent	Fair to good	Under 1 ct: fair; over 1 ct in fine-quality: poor

Chart continues on next page.

Family	Popular Name	Color(s)	Approx. Retail Cost Per Carat	Brilliance	Wearability	Availability
Tourmaline (cont.)	Pink	Pink or rose	1 to under 5 cts: $50–500 5 to under 10 cts: $125–650	Good	Fair to good	Good
	Rubellite	Red to violet	1 to under 5 cts: $150–575 5 to under 10 cts: $225–750	Good	Fair to good	Good
	Verdelite (green)	Green—all shades except chrome tourmaline	1 to under 3 cts: $50–500 3 to under 5 cts: $75–575 5 to under 20 cts: $100–500	Good	Fair to good	Good
	Golden	Yellow, orange, and brown varieties	1 to under 5 cts: $75–500	Good	Fair to good	Fair
	Bicolor, tricolor	Red/black, red/green, red/green/colorless	1 to under 5 cts: $50–625 5 to under 10 cts: $125–750	Good	Fair to good	Good
Zircon	Zircon	Pastel blue (usually heat-treated)	1 to under 5 cts: $50–500 5 to under 10 cts: $100–500	Good	Fair—Zircon is not recommended for rings or bracelets	Large: poor
		Green to yellow-green	1 to under 5 cts: $25–150 5 to under 10 cts: $75–225	Good		Good
		Colorless (usually heat-treated)	Comparable to green	Good		Good
		Orange to golden brown	Comparable to green	Good		Good
		Red to brownish red	Prices unknown (rare)	Good		True red: poor; other reds: good
		Yellow to yellow-brown	Comparable to green	Good		Good
Zoisite	Tanzanite (blue-violet)	Strong blue to weak violet, blue-violet	1 to under 3 cts: $325–1,325 3 to under 10 cts: $500–1,625 10 to under 20 cts: $575–1,500	Good	Poor for rings or bracelets	Good
	Green tanzanite	Blue-green to gray-green	1 to under 3 cts: $1,600–5,000	Good	Good	Small: fair; large: poor

Opal Price Guide*
Approximate Retail Cost Per Carat

There are numerous varieties of opals and wide ranges in quality. Quality differences are often difficult for the amateur to distinguish, but these may significantly affect price. The following prices provide only a guide. For more detailed information, see Selected Readings.

Popular Opal Varieties

Type	Size	Good	Fine	Extra Fine
White base, jelly opal	1 to under 15 cts	$75–100	$150–250	$450–825
Crystal, white	1 to under 15 cts	$75–100	$175–275	$500–875
Semi-crystal, gray base	1 to under 15 cts	$100–200	$350–750	$1,100–2,400
Fire (faceted)	5 to under 10 cts	$100–300	$275–550	$525–1,200

Black and Crystal Black Opal

Color	Size	Good	Fine	Extra Fine
Red-orange	1 to under 15 cts	$450–1,200	$2,400–6,800	$12,250–25,000
Green-blue	1 to under 15 cts	$250–950	$1,650–3,600	$5,000–10,000
Crystal	1 to under 15 cts	$225–600	$1,350–2,800	$4,700–8,750

Boulder Opal—Price per stone

	Size	Good	Fine	Extra Fine
Small	1 to 5 cts	$100–1,500	$1,500–4,500	$4,500–9,000
Medium	5 to 10 cts	$1,500–2,700	$2,700–6,000	$6,000–18,000
Large	10 to 15 cts	$1,700–3,500	$3,500–7,000	$7,000–30,000
Very large	15 to 30 cts plus	$2,500–5,600	$7,000–24,000	$25,000—100,000

Opal Triplets—Price per piece

Size	Good	Fine	Extra Fine
8x6 mm	$25–50	$75	$100
10x8 mm	$50–100	$125	$150
12x10 mm	$75–125	$175	$250
14x10 mm	$100–175	$225	$325

*Prices compiled from *The Guide*, Gemworld International, Inc., and adjusted to retail.

15

Colorful Choices in Colored Gemstones

The Big Three—Emerald, Ruby, and Sapphire

Emerald

Emerald is a green variety of the mineral beryl. One of the rarest members of the beryl family—only the red variety (sometimes called red emerald) is rarer—it is one of the most highly prized of all the gems. Aside from being the birthstone for May, it was historically believed to bestow on its wearer faithfulness and unchanging love, and was thought to enable the wearer to forecast events.

Contrary to popular belief, emerald is *not soft*. It ranks 7½ to 8 on Mohs' scale—an internationally recognized standard that ranks hardness on a scale from 1 to 10, with 1 being the softest and 10 the hardest. It is more fragile than other varieties of beryl and other gems, however, because it is more brittle and under more stress from fractures resulting from the violent geologic conditions under which it formed. This is why it is important to exercise care when you are wearing and handling emerald.

The highest-quality emerald has the color of fresh young green grass—an almost pure spectral green, possibly with a very faint tint of blue, as in the finest emerald from Colombia, which is considered by connoisseurs to be the world's finest. Other sources include Brazil, Zambia, Pakistan, Afghanistan, Russia, and India. Flawless emeralds are rare, so their flaws have come to serve almost as fingerprints, while flawless emeralds are immediately suspect.

Because of emerald's popularity and value, imitations are abundant. Glass, manufactured complete with "flaws," and doublets or triplets, like "aquamarine emeralds" and "Tecla emeralds" (see chapter 13), are often encountered. New products such as the "Lannyte emerald doublet" are also entering the market; when properly represented, they can make an interesting jewelry choice, but a second or third party may fail to mention that they are doublets.

Also, fine synthetic emeralds are being produced (see chapter 12) with nearly the same color, hardness, and brilliance as genuine emerald. These synthetics are not inexpensive themselves, except by comparison with a genuine emerald of equivalent quality.

Techniques to enhance color and reduce the visibility of flaws are also frequently used. A common practice is to fill surface-reaching cracks with oil (sometimes tinted green)—a practice that goes back to early Greek times. Today emeralds are oiled by use of a vacuum/heat technology. This is a widely accepted trade practice, since it is actually good for the stone in light of its fragile nature. Oiling hides some of the whitish flaws, which are actually cracks, filling the cracks so they become less visible. The oil becomes an integral part of the emerald unless it is subjected to some type of degreasing procedure. The development and use of the ultrasonic cleaner has brought to light the extensiveness of this practice. *Never clean emeralds in an ultrasonic cleaner.* (An ionic cleaner is fine for emeralds as well as for all other jewelry.)

A good friend of ours took her heirloom emerald ring to her jeweler for a "really good cleaning." Luckily for the jeweler, she never left the store and was standing right there when the ring was put into the cleaner and removed. She couldn't believe her eyes. She was shocked by the loss of color and the sudden appearance of more flaws. The ultrasonic cleaner had removed the oil that had penetrated the cracks, and an emerald several shades lighter and more visibly flawed emerged. Had she not been there, she would never have believed the jeweler hadn't pulled a switch.

Oiling is considered an acceptable practice, but be sure the price reflects the actual quality of the stone. If necessary, most emeralds can be re-oiled.

Epoxy resin fillers are a recent newcomer. This treatment is gaining popularity and is now used on many emeralds mined in many parts of the world, including Colombia and Brazil.

As with all highly desired gems, the greater the value and demand, the greater the occurrence of fraudulent practices. Examples of almost every type of technique to simulate emerald can be found: color alter-ation by using green foil on closed backs; use of synthetics; substitution of less valuable green stones, doublets, or other composites, etc. There-fore, be especially cautious of bargains, deal with reputable jewelers when planning to purchase, and *always* have the purchase double-checked by a qualified gemologist-appraiser. Any very fine emerald purchased today should have a laboratory report or be submitted to a lab to obtain one.

Ruby

Prized through the ages as, in the words of the Roman historian Pliny, the "gem of gems . . . surpassing all other precious stones in virtue," ruby is the red variety of the mineral corundum. Historically, it has been symbolic of love and passion, considered to be an aid to firm friendship, and believed to ensure beauty. Today's birthstone for July, ruby has a color that ranges from purplish or bluish red to a yellowish red. The finest color is a vivid, almost pure spectral red with a very faint undertone of blue, as seen in Burmese rubies, which are considered the finest among ardent collectors (see pages 103–104). Other sources of fine ruby are Thailand, Vietnam, Cambodia, Kenya, Tanzania, and Azad Kashmir in Pakistan. The ruby is very brilliant and very hard, ranking 9 on Mohs' scale. Ruby is also very durable and wearable—characteristics that make it an unusually fine choice for any piece of jewelry.

Translucent varieties of ruby are also seen, and one variety exhibits a six-ray star effect when cut as a cabochon. This variety is called *star ruby* and is one of nature's most beautiful and interesting gifts. But, as with so many other beautiful gifts once produced only in nature, these lovely gems are now duplicated in synthetic star rubies, and numerous faked star rubies are also the products of human beings' attempts at mimicry.

Here again, remember that the greater the value and demand, the greater the use of techniques to "improve" or to simulate. Among rubies, as among other gemstones, examples of almost every type of deceptive technique can be found—color and clarity enhancement, synthesis, sub-stitutes, doublets, triplets, misleading names, and so on. Be especially alert to various diffusion treatment and oiling of reflective fractures. The newest laboratory-grown synthetic rubies, like those made by Ramaura and Chatham, are so close to natural ruby in every aspect that many are actually passing for genuine, even among gemologists. When you are getting a very fine, valuable ruby, be sure to verify genuineness with a gemologist who has both many years' experience in colored gems and an astute knowledge of the marketplace today. We would recommend having the jeweler or gemologist also obtain a colored gemstone report from a major gem-testing laboratory.

Here again, be especially cautious of bargains. Deal with reputable jewelers when planning to purchase, and have the purchase double-checked by a qualified gemologist-appraiser.

Sapphire

The "celestial" sapphire—symbol of the heavens, guardian of innocence, bestower of truth and good health, preserver of chastity—is in fact the mineral corundum. While we know it best in its blue variety, which is highly prized, it comes in essentially every color; red corundum is ruby. As with ruby, its sister stone, sapphire is characterized by hardness (9 on Mohs' scale), brilliance, and availability in many beautiful colors, all of which make it probably the most important and most versatile of the gem families.

Blue sapphires can be among the most valuable members of the sapphire family—especially stones from Burma and Kashmir, which are closest to the pure spectral blue. Fine, brilliant, deep blue Burmese sapphires will surely dazzle the eye and the pocketbook, as will the Kashmir, which is a fine velvety-toned deep blue.

The Ceylon (Sri Lanka) sapphires are a very pleasing blue but are a less deep shade than the Burmese or Kashmir, instead tending to fall more on the pastel side.

We are also seeing many Australian sapphires, which are often a dark blue but with a slightly green undertone, as are those from Thailand; both sell for much less per carat. They offer a very affordable alternative to the Burmese, Kashmir, or Ceylon, and can still be very pleasing in their color. Blue sapphires also come from Tanzania, Brazil, Africa, and even the United States. Montana sapphires are very collectible because of their unusual shades of color and because many are *natural* color—that is, not subjected to any treatment. For those who want a gem that is truly "natural," Montana sapphire may be the choice for you.

With sapphire, origin can have a significant effect on price, so if you are purchasing a Kashmir, Burmese, or Ceylon sapphire, that should be noted on the bill of sale.

Like ruby, the blue sapphire may be found in a translucent variety that may show a six-rayed star effect when cut into a cabochon. This variety is known as *star sapphire,* of which there are numerous synthetics (often referred to in the trade as Linde, pronounced Lin´dee).

In addition to blue sapphire, we are now beginning to see the appearance of many other color varieties in the latest jewelry designs—especially yellow and pink (Madagascar has recently emerged as an important source of pink sapphires) and in smaller sizes some beautiful shades of green. These are known as *fancy* sapphires. Compared with the costly blue sapphire and ruby, these stones offer excellent value and real beauty.

A beautiful and rare variety called *padparadscha* (a type of lotus flower) is also in demand. The true padparadscha should exhibit a *pink and orange color simultaneously.* Depending on the richness of color, brilliance, and size, these can be very expensive. A lovely but more common and more affordable variety, available today, is really a rich orange color. It is often sold as padparadscha, but the rarer and more costly gem will always exhibit a strong pink with the orange.

Many sapphires today tend to be too dark, however, because of the presence of too much black and poor cutting (cutting deep for additional weight), but the deep blues can be treated to lighten the color. Inevitably, evidence abounds of every technique known to improve the perceived quality and value of the sapphire—alteration of color, synthesis, composites, and misleading names. Be especially alert to the new types of diffusion treatment, and aware that oil is being used increasingly to conceal fractures and reflective inclusions. Also, watch out for the doublets flooding the market. As always, we urge you to be especially cautious of bargains, deal with reputable jewelers, and have your stone double-checked by a qualified gemologist-appraiser.

Other Popular Colored Gems

Alexandrite

Alexandrite is a fascinating transparent gem that appears grass green in daylight and raspberry red under artificial light. It is a variety of chrysoberyl reputedly discovered in Russia in 1831 on the day Alexander II reached his majority; hence the name. In Russia, where the national colors also happen to be green and red, it is considered a stone of very good omen. It is also considered Friday's stone, or the stone of "Friday's child."

Unlike other stones, which humankind has known about and admired for thousands of years, alexandrite is a relatively recent gem discovery. Nonetheless, it has definitely come into its own and is presently commanding both high appeal and high prices. While fairly common in small sizes, it has become relatively scarce in sizes of two carats or more. A fine three-carat stone can cost $45,000 today. If you see an alexandrite that measures more than half an inch in width, be suspicious of a fake. Alexandrite is a hard, durable stone (8½ on Mohs' scale) and is normally cut in a faceted style, but some cat's-eye–type alexandrites, found in Brazil, would be cut as a cabochon to display the eye effect. These are usually small; the largest we've seen was approximately three carats.

Before 1973, there were really no good synthetic alexandrites. While some varieties of synthetic corundum and synthetic spinel were frequently sold as alexandrite, they really didn't look like the real thing but were hard to differentiate, since so few buyers had ever seen genuine stones. They are, however, easy for a gemologist to spot. In 1973, a very good synthetic alexandrite was produced that is not easy to differentiate from natural stones. While a good gemologist today can identify the synthetics, when they first appeared on the market many were mistaken for the real thing. Be especially careful to verify the authenticity of your alexandrite, since it might have been mistakenly identified years ago and passed along as authentic to you today. It could save you a lot of money!

Amber

Amber is not a stone but rather amorphous, fossilized tree sap. It was one of the earliest substances used for personal adornment. Modestly decorated pieces of rough amber have been found in Stone Age excavations and are assumed to have been used as amulets and talismans—a use definitely recorded throughout history before, during, and since the ancient Greeks. Because of its beautiful color and the ease with which it could be fashioned, amber quickly became a favorite object of trade and barter and personal adornment. Amber varies from transparent to semitranslucent and from yellow to dark brown in color; occasionally it's seen in reddish and greenish brown tones. In addition, amber can be dyed many colors. Occasionally, one can find "foreign" fragments or insects that were trapped in the amber, which usually increases its value because of the added curiosity factor.

Plastics are the most common amber imitations. But real amber, which is the lightest gem material, may be easily distinguished from most plastic when dropped into a saturated salt solution: amber will float, while plastic sinks. One other commonly encountered "amber" type is "reconstructed" amber—amber fragments compressed under heat to form a larger piece. An expert can differentiate this from the real under magnification.

Amber can be easily tested by touching it in an inconspicuous place with a hot needle (held by tweezers). The whitish smoke that should be produced should smell like burning pine wood, not like medicine or disinfectant. If there is no smoke, but a black mark occurs, then it is *not* amber. Another test is to try to cut a little piece of the amber with a sharp pointed knife, at the drill hole of the bead; if it cuts like wood (producing a shaving), it is *not* amber, which would produce a sharp, crumbly deposit.

With the exception of those pieces possessing special antique value, the value of amber fluctuates with its popularity, which in part is dictated by the fashion industry and the prevalence of yellow and browns in one's wardrobe. Nonetheless, amber has proved itself an ageless gem and will always be loved and admired.

Amethyst

Amethyst, a transparent purple variety of quartz, is one of the most popular of the colored stones. Once believed to bring peace of mind to the wearer, it was also thought to prevent the wearer from getting drunk. If the circle of the sun or moon was engraved thereon, amethyst was believed to prevent death from poison.

Available in shades from light to dark purple, this February birthstone is relatively hard (7 on Mohs' scale), fairly brilliant, and overall a good, versatile, wearable stone, available in plentiful supply even in very large sizes (although large sizes with deep color are now becoming scarce). Amethyst is probably one of the most beautiful stones available at a moderate price; buyers should be careful, however, because "fine" amethyst is being produced synthetically today. Most synthetics can be identified by a skilled gemologist.

Amethyst may fade from heat and strong sunshine. Guard your amethyst from these conditions, and it should retain its color indefinitely. We are hearing stories from customers across the country, however, complaining of newly purchased amethyst jewelry fading over just a few months, from *deep purple* to *light lavender.* This should not happen and may result from an unacceptable color treatment. If your stone fades this quickly, return it to your jeweler.

Andalusite (Poor Man's Alexandrite)

Andalusite is now offering interesting new possibilities for jewelry. Brazil is the primary source of these fascinating, fairly hard (7 to 7½ on Mohs' scale), and fairly durable stones. Andalusite is very interesting because it may exhibit several colors: an olive green from one direction, a rich reddish brown from another direction, and grayish green from yet another direction. In an emerald cut, it may look primarily green while exhibiting an orange color at the ends of the emerald shape. In a round cut, you may see the green body color with simultaneous flashes of another color. One benefit andalusite has over alexandrite is that you don't have to change the light in which it is being seen to experience its colors; merely changing the perspective does the trick. A rare and sometimes expensive emerald green variety may exhibit a bright yellow simultaneously, or when viewed from different angles. A pink variety does not exhibit this kind of color phenomenon. While andalusite is not readily available yet, it is finding a market, especially among men.

Aquamarine

To dream of aquamarine signifies the making of new friends; to wear aquamarine earrings brings love and affection. Aquamarine, a universal symbol of youth, hope, and health, blesses those born in March. (Before the fifteenth century it was considered to be the birthstone for those born in October.)

Aquamarine is a member of the important beryl family, which includes emerald, but aquamarine is less brittle and more durable than its green counterpart (7½ to 8 on Mohs' scale). Aquamarine ranges in color from light blue to bluish green to deep blue, the latter being the most valuable and desirable. It is a very wearable gem, clear and brilliant, and unlike emerald is available with excellent clarity even in very large sizes, although these are becoming scarce today. Aquamarines are still widely available in sizes up to 15 carats, but 10-carat sizes with fine color and clarity are becoming scarce and are more expensive. Long considered a beautiful and moderately priced gem, it is now entering the "expensive" classification for stones in larger sizes with a good deep blue color.

Several words of caution for those interested in this lovely gem. First, you may want to think twice before buying a pale or shallow-cut stone, since the color will become paler as dirt accumulates on the back. These stones need constant cleaning to keep them beautiful. Second, be careful not to mistake blue topaz for aquamarine. While topaz is an equally beautiful gem, it is usually much less expensive, since it is usually treated to obtain its desirable color. For those who can't afford an aquamarine, however, blue topaz is an excellent alternative as long as it is properly represented and priced. Finally, note that many aquamarine-colored synthetic spinels are erroneously sold as aquamarine.

Benitoite

This exquisitely beautiful and rare gem is seldom seen in jewelry but is very popular among collectors and connoisseurs. Discovered in San Benito, California—hence the name *benitoite*—it was recently selected as the official state stone of California, and we are beginning to see more of it in fine jewelry houses there.

Benitoite ranges from colorless to dark blue (often with a violet tint) to violet. A rare pink variety has also been identified. Benitoite can display fire, the dispersion of white light into the rainbow colors, comparable to a diamond, and is also very brilliant. Some might easily mistake it at a glance for a blue diamond. It lacks diamond's incredible hardness, however, and is more comparable to amethyst in hardness ($6\frac{1}{2}$ on Mohs' scale). It is difficult to find benitoite in sizes over 1 carat; only about five stones per year are cut that weigh 2 carats or more; only one every five years yields a stone 5 carats or more. Benitoite's rarity keeps it very expensive—a fine 1-carat stone could easily cost $3,000—and 2-carat sizes with fine color are extremely rare and even more costly. The largest fine benitoite known weighs just over $7\frac{3}{4}$ carats and is on display at the Smithsonian Institution in Washington, D.C.

For jewelry, benitoite is a relatively wearable stone, but given its rarity and value, we recommend that it be set in a somewhat protective mounting so that it is not easily subjected to accidental scratching or wear.

Beryl (Golden Beryl, Red Beryl, Morganite)

As early as A.D. 1220, the virtues of beryl were well established in legend. Beryl provided help against foes in battle or litigation, made the wearer unconquerable but at the same time friendly and likable, and also sharpened the wearer's intellect and cured laziness. Today beryl is still considered important, but primarily for aesthetic reasons. The variety of colors in which it is found, its wonderful clarity (except for emerald), its brilliance, and its durability (7½ to 8 on Mohs' scale; again with the exception of emerald) have given the various varieties of beryl tremendous appeal.

Most people are familiar with the blue variety of beryl, aquamarine, and the green variety, emerald. Few as yet know the pink variety, morganite, and the beautiful yellow to yellow-green variety, referred to as golden beryl. These gems have only recently found their place in the jewelry world but are already being shown in fabulous pieces made by the greatest designers. While not inexpensive, they still offer excellent value and beauty.

Beryl has also been found in many other colors—lilac, salmon, orange, sea green—as well as colorless. While most of these varieties are not as yet available to any but the most ardent rock hound, the orange varieties are fairly common and can still be found for under $125 per carat. Some orange varieties are heated to produce the more popular pink color and then sold as morganite.

The rarest color is red, which is even more rare than emerald and is comparable in cost. Until recently, it was known only to serious collectors and was called bixbite after the man who discovered it. The gem variety of red beryl was discovered in Utah, still its only known source. But thanks to the discovery of a new deposit, we are now beginning to see this exciting gemstone in the jewelry market. It faces a major problem, however: what to call it. Some dealers are calling it red emerald because it is the same basic material as emerald and because it is truly comparable to emerald in rarity, beauty, and value. Whatever the name by which it is called—red "emerald," red beryl, or bixbite—it is a beautiful gem that should be loved and cherished by anyone lucky enough to own one.

Bloodstone (Heliotrope)

Believed by the ancient Greeks to have fallen from heaven, this stone has held a prominent place throughout history, and even into modern times, as a great curative. It was (and still is in some parts of the world) believed capable of stopping every type of bleeding, clearing bloodshot eyes, acting as an antidote for snakebite, and relieving urinary troubles. Today there are people who wear bloodstone amulets to prevent sunstroke and headache and to provide protection against the evil eye.

The birthstone for March, bloodstone is a more or less opaque, dark green variety of quartz with specks of red jasper (a variety of quartz) spattering red throughout the dark green field. Particularly popular for men's rings (perhaps they need more protection from illness?) bloodstone is most desirable when the green isn't so dark as to approach black and the red flecks are roundish and pronounced. It is moderately durable (7 on Mohs' scale), and is fairly readily available and inexpensive.

Chrysoberyl and Cat's-Eye

The chrysoberyl family is very interesting because all three of its varieties—alexandrite, cat's-eye, and chrysoberyl—while chemically alike, are quite distinct from one another in their optical characteristics and bear no visible resemblance to one another.

Chrysoberyl in its cat's-eye variety has long been used as a charm to guard against evil spirits. One can understand why, given the pronounced eye effect: the eye, so legend has it, could see all, and it watched out for its wearer. But it was also believed that to dream of cat's-eye signified treachery. On still another level, it symbolized long life for the wearer, perhaps as a result of being protected from the evil eye.

Cat's-eye (8½ on Mohs' scale) is a hard, translucent gem ranging in color from a honey yellow or honey brown to yellowish green to an almost emerald green. It has a velvety or silklike texture and, when properly cut, displays a brilliant whitish line of light right down the center, appearing almost to be lighted from inside. Genuine cat's-eye should not be confused with the common quartz variety, which is often brown and is called tiger's-eye; the latter has a much less striking eye and weaker color altogether. This phenomenon is produced only in cabochons.

To see the effect properly, the stone should be viewed under a single strong light source, coming if possible from directly overhead. If the line is not exactly in the center, the stone's value is reduced. The line does shift from side to side when the stone is moved about—probably another reason ancient people believed it capable of seeing all and guarding its wearer.

The stone called chrysoberyl, on the other hand, is a brilliant, transparent, very clear, and very durable stone (8½ on Mohs' scale) found in yellow, yellow-green, and green varieties. This is another stone that still offers excellent value. It's a real beauty, very moderately priced, and just beginning to be appreciated and used in contemporary jewelry.

Chrysoprase and Carnelian

Chrysoprase has long been the subject of marvelous stories. In the 1800s, it was believed that a thief sentenced to be hanged or beheaded would immediately escape if he placed a chrysoprase in his mouth. Of course, it might be hard to obtain the stone unless he just happened to carry one around! And Alexander the Great was believed to have worn a "prase" in his girdle during battle, to ensure victory.

Chrysoprase is an inexpensive, highly translucent, bright, light green to dark green variety of quartz. While its color is often very uniform and can be very lovely in jewelry, for many years these gems have been dyed to enhance their color, where necessary. Chrysoprase is another stone that is usually cut in cabochon style. It has become very popular for jewelry as a fashion accessory. Do not confuse it with jade, however. It is sometimes called Australian jade and is sometimes misrepresented as real jade.

If you're the timid sort, carnelian is the stone for you. "The wearing of carnelians is recommended to those who have a weak voice or are timid in speech, for the warm-colored stone will give them the courage they lack so that they will speak both boldly and well," reports G. F. Kunz, a turn-of-the-century gemologist and historian.

This stone is especially revered by Moslems, because Muhammad himself wore a silver ring set with a carnelian engraved for use as a seal.

Napoleon I, while on a campaign in Egypt, picked up with his own hands (apparently from the battlefield) an unusual octagonal carnelian upon which was engraved the legend, "The Slave Abraham Relying upon the Merciful [God]." He wore it with him always and bequeathed it to his nephew.

Carnelian, one of the accepted birthstones for August, is a reddish orange to brownish orange variety of quartz. A moderately hard (7 on

Mohs' scale), translucent to opaque stone, its warm uniform color and fair durability have made it a favorite. It is often found in antique jewelry and lends itself to engraving or carving, especially in cameos. It is still a relatively inexpensive stone with great warmth and beauty and offers an excellent choice for jewelry to be worn as an accessory with today's fashion colors.

Coral

Coral, which for twenty centuries or more was classed with precious gems and can be found adorning ancient amulets alongside diamond, ruby, emerald, and pearl, had been "experimentally proved" by the sixteenth century to cure madness, give wisdom, stop the flow of blood from a wound, calm storms, and of course enable the traveler to safely cross broad rivers. It was also known to prevent sterility. This was certainly a powerful gem!

Red coral symbolizes attachment, devotion, and protection against plague and pestilence. And one unique quality: it loses its color when a friend of the wearer is about to die! There is a catch to coral's potency, however. To effectively exercise its power, it should not be altered by the human hand but should be worn in its natural, uncut state. This perhaps is why one often sees this stone in necklaces or pins in its natural state.

Coral lost its popularity for a while but has been steadily gaining in popularity in recent years. It is a semitranslucent to opaque material, formed from a colony of marine invertebrates, that is primarily a skeletal calcium carbonate gem. The formations as seen in the water look like tree branches. Coral occurs in a variety of colors—white, pink, orange, red, and black. One of the most expensive varieties, very popular in recent years and used extensively in fine jewelry, is angel-skin coral. This is a whitish variety highlighted with a faint blush of pink or peach. Today the rarest variety, and the most expensive, is blood coral, also called noble or oxblood coral. This is a very deep red variety and shouldn't be confused with the more common orangy red varieties. The best red comes from the seas around Italy, the whites from Japanese waters, the blacks (which we personally don't find very attractive, and which are also different chemically) from Hawaii and Mexico.

Coral is usually cabochon cut, often carved, but is also fairly frequently found in jewelry fashioned "in the rough" (uncut) in certain countries where the belief persists that coral's magical powers are lost with cutting. It is a fairly soft stone (3½ on Mohs' scale), so some caution should be exercised when wearing. Also, because of its calcium composition, you must be careful to avoid contact with acid, such as vinegar in a salad that you might toss with your hands.

Also, be a cautious buyer for this gem as for others; glass and plastic imitations are commonplace.

Garnet

If you are loyal, devoted, and energetic, perhaps the garnet is your stone. Or if not, perhaps you should obtain some! Red garnets were "known" to promote sincerity, stop hemorrhaging or other loss of blood, cure inflammatory diseases, and cure anger and discord. And if you engrave a well-formed lion image upon a garnet, it will protect and preserve health, cure the wearer of all disease, bring him honors, and guard him from all perils in traveling. All in all, quite a worthwhile stone.

The garnet family is one of the most exciting families in the gem world. One of the few untreated gems, it is moderately hard (ranging from 6½ to7½ on Mohs' scale), durable, and brilliant. It is available in many colors (greens, reds, yellows, oranges) and offers far greater versatility and opportunity for the jewelry trade than has yet been capitalized upon. Depending on the variety, quality, and size, lovely garnets are available for under $40 per carat or more than $5,000 per carat. Garnet can also be mistaken for other, usually more expensive, gems. Green garnet (tsavorite) is one of the most beautiful, and all but a few would assume it was an emerald of the finest quality. In fact, it is clearer, more brilliant, and more durable than emerald itself. There is also a rarer green garnet, called demantoid, which costs slightly more than tsavorite but which, although slightly softer, has more fire. These gems offer fine alternatives to the person desiring a lovely green gem who can't afford emerald. While still rare, expensive gems themselves, these garnet varieties are far less expensive than an emerald of comparable quality. Garnet also occurs in certain shades of red that have been taken for some varieties of ruby. And in yellow it has been confused with precious topaz.

Garnet is found in almost every color and shade, including a rare color-change variety that appears red in incandescent light and blue (the only color not normally seen in garnet) in daylight or fluorescent light. It is best known in a deep red variety but is commonly found in orangish brown shades and brilliant wine red shades as well. Other colors include orange—the new Mandarin garnet being an intense fiery red-orange—red-purple, violet, and pink. A nontransparent variety, grossularite, resembles jade and may be mistaken for jade in cabochons and carvings.

A star garnet found in the United States is a reddish to purple variety that displays a faint four-rayed or six-rayed star, similar to the six-rayed star ruby but not as pronounced.

Hematite and Marcasite

Hematite is a must for the lawyer, for it ensures for its wearer "alertness, vivacity, and success in litigation," claimed an unknown source from ages past. It is also believed to ensure sexual impulse, so if you know of someone with a problem, this may make a "thoughtful" gift.

Hematite is an iron oxide (like iron rust), a metallic, opaque stone found in iron-mining areas. It takes a very brilliant, metallic polish that can look almost like silver, or almost pure black, or gunmetal blue. It was and is popular for use in carving hollow cameo portraits known as intaglio.

Marcasite, the tiny, glittering stone with a brassy-colored luster often seen in old belt buckles and costume jewelry, is a relative of hematite. Most "marcasite" seen in jewelry is not marcasite, but pyrite (fool's gold)—another brassy-colored metallic mineral.

Iolite

This is a transparent, usually very clean, blue gem, ranging from deep blue to light gray-blue to yellowish grey. It is sometimes called dichroite, and in its sapphire blue color is sometimes referred to as *water sapphire* or *lynx sapphire*. It is a lovely, brilliant stone but not as durable as sapphire (7 to 7½ on Mohs' scale). We are just beginning to see this stone in jewelry, and it is still a good value. It is abundant, still very low priced, and one of the most attractive jewelry options for the near future.

Jade

Jade has long been revered by the Chinese. White jade (yes, white) was believed by the early Chinese to quiet intestinal disturbances, while black jade gave strength and power. A very early written Chinese symbol for "king" was a string of jade beads, and jade beads are still used in China as a symbol of high rank and authority. Jade is also an important part of the Chinese wedding ceremony (the "jade ceremony" holds a prominent place here), for jade is considered the concentrated essence of love.

Jade is a very tough, although not too hard, translucent to opaque gem, often seen in jewelry and carvings. There are really two types of jade—jadeite and nephrite—which are really two separate and distinct minerals differing from each other in weight, hardness, and color range. Both are called jade.

Jadeite, the more expensive and more desirable variety, was the most sought after by the Chinese after 1740. It is not found in China, however, but in Burma. Some fine jadeite also comes from Guatemala. It is found in a much wider range of colors than nephrite: green, mottled green and white, whitish gray, pink, brown, mauve, yellow, orange, and lilac. In fact, it occurs in almost every color. But with the exception of green, which comes in shades that vary from light to a beautiful emerald green, colored jade is usually pale and unevenly tinted. The most desirable color is a rich emerald green, sometimes referred to as imperial jade. Smooth, evenly colored pieces of this jadeite are highly prized and, in fact, can be classed as precious stones today. The mottled pieces of irregular green, often seen carved, are less valuable but are still more rare and valuable than nephrite jade.

Nephrite jade, the old and true Chinese jade, resembles jadeite but is slightly softer (jadeite is 7 on Mohs' scale; nephrite, 6½, yet slightly tougher and thus less easily broken) and has a much more limited range of color. Usually fashioned in cabochon cut, or round beads, or in carvings, it is regularly seen in dark green shades sometimes so dark as to look black—hence, black jade. Nephrite green is a more sober green than the apple green or emerald green color of good jadeite. It is closer in color to a dark, sage green or spinach green. Nephrite may also be a creamier color, as in mutton-fat jade. Any fine Chinese carving that is more than 230 years old is carved from nephrite (jadeite was unknown to the Chinese before 1740).

Nephrite has been found in many countries, including the United States, where in the late nineteenth century Chinese miners panning for gold in California discovered large boulders of nephrite jade that they sent back to China to be cut or carved. It is also common in Wyoming, Alaska, and British Columbia.

Nephrite jade is much more common than jadeite and is therefore much less expensive. But it is a lovely, popular stone, used extensively in jewelry and carvings.

One must be careful, however, in purchasing jade. You will often see "imperial" jade that is nothing more than a cheap jade that has been dyed, or dyed quartz. Much jade is treated with polymers or dyed to enhance its value. The dyeing, however, may be very temporary. Black jade is either dyed or very dark green nephrite that looks black. There are also numerous minerals that look like jade and are sold as jade under misleading names, such as "Korean jade," which is serpentine, a soft, green stone similar in appearance to some varieties of jade (see the table of misleading names on page 141). In fact, much of the intricately and beautifully carved jade is actually serpentine, which can be scratched easily with a knife.

Soapstone may also look like jade to the amateur, especially when beautifully carved. This stone is so soft that it can easily be scratched with a pin, hairpin, or point of a pen. It is much less expensive than comparable varieties of jade, as well as softer and less durable.

Jade is a wonderful stone, and imperial jade is breathtaking; no wonder it was the emperor's stone! But jade has long been "copied"—misrepresented and altered. Just be sure you know you are buying what you think you are buying.

Labradorite, Sunstone, and Spectrolite (Feldspar)

Labradorite is a fascinating stone that is starting to appear in some of the more distinctive jewelry salons, especially in beads and carved pieces, and is a member of the feldspar family (6 to 6½ on Mohs' scale). The most frequently seen variety is a grayish, almost opaque stone, within which startlingly brilliant flashes of peacock blue, greens, and/or yellows are visible at certain angles.

A beautiful, shimmering red to orange variety (and occasionally green or bicolor) known as *sunstone* is also beginning to enter the jewelry scene. Mined in Oregon, major United States retailers such as Tiffany are featuring this wonderful, truly American gem. Finland also produces a very lovely variety of labradorite, often called spectrolite, that occurs in colors resembling peacock hues or the colors seen on the wings of butterflies. It can also exhibit a cat's-eye effect.

Labradorite is usually cut in cabochon style, but sunstone also occurs in a transparent material that makes a beautiful faceted gem. There are some glass imitations, but they don't come close to the real thing. This is a stone that is still relatively inexpensive and one to consider seriously if you want something striking and unusual.

Lapis Lazuli

Lapis, a birthstone for December, has been highly prized since ancient Babylonian and Egyptian times. An amulet of "great power" was formed when lapis was worked into the form of an eye and ornamented with gold—in fact, so powerful that sometimes these eyes were put to rest on the limbs of a mummy. In addition, it was recognized as a symbol for capacity, ability, success, and divine favor.

Genuine lapis is a natural blue opaque stone of intense, brilliant, deep blue color. It sometimes possesses small, sparkling gold-colored or silver-colored flecks (pyrite inclusions), although the finest quality is a deep, even blue with a purplish tint or undertone and no trace of those flecks. Occasionally it may be blue mottled with white.

Don't confuse genuine lapis with the cheaper "Swiss lapis" or "Italian lapis," which aren't lapis at all. These are natural stones (usually quartz) artificially colored to look like lapis lazuli. Genuine lapis is often represented as "Russian lapis," although it doesn't always come from Russia. The finest lapis comes from Afghanistan.

Lapis has become very fashionable, and the finest-quality lapis is becoming more rare and more expensive. This has resulted in an abundance of lapis that has been "color improved." It is often fashioned today with other gems—pearls, crystal, coral—that make particularly striking fashion accessories.

Sodalite is sometimes confused with the more expensive, and rarer, lapis and is used as a substitute for it. However, sodalite rarely contains the silvery or golden flecks typical of most lapis. It may have some white veining, but more commonly it just exhibits the fine lapis blue without any markings. The lapis substitutes transmit some light through the edges of the stone; lapis does not, since it is opaque.

Dyed chalcedony (quartz), glass, and plastic imitations are common. One quick and easy test to identify genuine lapis is to put a drop of hydrochloric acid on the stones; this will immediately produce the odor of a rotten egg. This test should be administered only by a professional, however, since hydrochloric acid can be dangerous.

Malachite and Azurite

Malachite must have been the answer to a mother's prayer. According to legend, attaching malachite to the neck of a child would ease its pain when cutting teeth. Also, tied over a woman in labor, it would ensure an easier, faster birth. It could also cure diseases of the eye. More important, however, it was believed capable of protecting from the evil eye and bringing good luck.

Malachite is also popular today, but perhaps more because of the exquisite color and a softness (3½ on Mohs' scale) that makes it very popular for carving. Malachite is a copper ore that comes in a brilliant kelly green, marked with bands or concentric striping in contrasting shades of the same basic green. It is opaque and takes a good polish, but it is soft and should not be worn in rings. This softness, however, makes it a favorite substance for use in carved bases, boxes, beads, statues, spheres, and so on. It is also used in pins, pendants, and necklaces (usually of malachite beads).

Azurite is also a copper ore, but it occurs in a very vivid deep blue, similarly marked. Occasionally one will come across both the green and the blue intermingled in brilliant combinations of color and striking patterns. Both malachite and azurite make beautiful jewelry and lovely carvings.

A particular note of caution: Never clean malachite or azurite with any product containing ammonia. In seconds the ammonia will remove all the polish, which will significantly reduce the stone's beauty.

Moonstone (Orthoclase Feldspar)

Moonstone is definitely a good-luck stone, especially for lovers. As a gift the moonstone holds a high rank, for it is believed to arouse one's tender passion and to give lovers the ability to foretell their future—good or ill. To get this information, however, legend has it that the stone must be placed in the mouth while the moon is full. Perhaps a more important use, however, was in amulets made of moonstone, which would protect wearers from epilepsy and guarantee a greater fruit-crop yield when hung on fruit trees. The stone, in fact, assisted all vegetation.

The name *moonstone* is probably derived from the myth that one can observe the lunar month through the stone—that a small white spot appears in the stone as the new moon begins and gradually moves toward the stone's center, getting always larger, until the spot finally takes the shape of a full moon in the center of the stone.

Moonstone is a member of the feldspar family (6 to 6½ on Mohs' scale). It is a transparent, milky white variety in which can be seen a floating opalescent white or blue light within the stone's body. It is a popular stone for rings because as the hand moves the effect of the brilliant light color is more pronounced. The bluer color is the finer and more desirable, but it is becoming rare in today's market, particularly in large sizes.

There are some glass imitations of moonstone, but compared with the real thing they are not very good.

Obsidian

Obsidian was widely used by the Mexicans, probably because of its brilliant polished surface, for making images of their god Tezcatlipoca and for polishing into mirrors used to divine the future. It has also been found in Egypt, fashioned into masks.

Obsidian is a semitranslucent to opaque glass that is smokey brown to black and sometimes a mixture of both. It is natural glass, not artificial. It is formed by volcanic activity and is also called volcanic glass. One variety, snowflake obsidian, exhibits white spots resembling snowflakes against or mingled with the black; some obsidian exhibits a strong iridescence; and some obsidian exhibits a sheen from within, as seen in moonstone.

Jewelry made from obsidian, which is available in great quantity and is very inexpensive, is a popular fashion accessory. It is particularly popular in Mexican and Indian jewelry and is seen fairly extensively in the West and in Mexico. One must exercise some caution, however, because obsidian is glass (5 on Mohs' scale) and can be scratched or cracked easily.

Onyx

Onyx is not a good-omen stone, and it is certainly not one for young lovers, since it is believed to bear an evil omen, to provoke discord, and separate them. Worn around the neck, it was said to cool the ardors of love. The close union and yet strong contrast between the layers of black and white in some varieties may have suggested onyx's connection with

romance. It was also believed to cause discord in general, create dishar-
mony among friends, bring bad dreams and broken sleep to its wearer,
and cause pregnant women to give birth prematurely.

But there isn't complete agreement as to its unlucky nature. Indians
and Persians believe that wearing onyx will protect them from the evil
eye, and that onyx placed on the stomach of a woman in labor will reduce
the labor pain and bring on earlier delivery. So you choose—good or bad?

Onyx is a lovely, banded, semitranslucent to opaque quartz. It comes
naturally in a variety of colors—reds, oranges, reddish orange, apricot,
and shades of brown from cream to dark, often alternating with striking
bands of white. The banding in onyx is straight, while curved bands occur
in the variety of quartz known as agate. Onyx is used extensively for
cameo and other carving work. It is also frequently dyed.

The "black onyx" that is commonly used in jewelry isn't onyx at all
and isn't naturally black. It is chalcedony (another variety of quartz) dyed
black. It is *always* dyed and may be banded or solid black.

Do not confuse the quartz variety of onyx with cave onyx, which is
found in the stalactites and stalagmites of underground caves. Cave onyx
is a different material altogether. It is much softer, lacks the color variety,
and is much less expensive than quartz onyx.

Opal

The opal has suffered from an unfortunate reputation as being an evil
stone and bearing an ill omen. Ominous superstitions surround this wonderful gem, including the belief that misfortune will fall on those who wear
it. But its evil reputation has never been merited and probably resulted
from a careless reading of Sir Walter Scott's poem *Anne of Geierstein,* in
which the ill-fated heroine received an opal before her untimely death.

Among the ancients, opal was a symbol of fidelity and assurance, and
in later history it became strongly associated with religious emotion and
prayer. It was believed to have a strong therapeutic value for diseases of
the eye, and worn as an amulet it would make the wearer immune from
them as well as increase the powers of the eyes and the mind. Further,
many believed that to the extent the colors of red and green (ruby and
emerald) were seen, the wearer would also enjoy the therapeutic powers
of those stones: the power to stop bleeding from the ruby or the power
to cure kidney diseases from the emerald. The black opal was particularly

highly prized as the luck stone of anyone lucky enough to own one!

This stone, whose brilliance and vibrant colors resemble the colors of fall, is certainly appropriate as a birthstone for October. When we try to describe the opal, we realize how insufficient the English language is. It is unique among the gems, displaying an array of very brilliant miniature rainbow effects, all mixed together.

Its most outstanding characteristic is this unusual, intense display of many colors flashing out like mini-rainbows. This effect is created by opal's formation process, which is very different from that of other gems. Opal is composed of hydrated silica spheres. The mini-rainbows seen in most opals result from light interference created by these spheres. The arrangement of the spheres, which vary in size and pattern, is responsible for the different colors.

Opal is usually cut flat or in cabochon, since there is no additional brilliance to be captured by faceting. In opals, color is everything. The more brilliant the color, the more valuable the gem. It is probably truer of opal than any other stone that the more beautiful the stone and its color, the more it will cost. But it is fairly soft (5 to 6½ on Mohs' scale), so opals should be treated with care.

The finest of all is the black opal. Black opals are usually a deep gray or grayish black with flashes of incredibly brilliant color dancing around within and about the stones as they are turned. One must be careful when purchasing a black opal, however, to ensure that it is not a doublet or triplet: a stone composed of two or three parts of some material fused or glued together. There are many such doublets on the market because of the black opal's rarity, beauty, and extremely high cost; a black opal the size of a lima bean could cost $25,000 today. The black opal doublet provides an affordable option to one who loves the stone but can't afford a natural. But it also provides another opportunity for misrepresentation that can be very costly to the consumer.

Generally speaking, purity of color, absence of dead spots (called trueness), flawlessness, and intensity or brilliance of color are the primary variables affecting value. Opals with an abundance of red are usually the most expensive; those strong in blue and green are equally beautiful but not as rare, so their price is somewhat less. Some opals are very transparent and are classified as jelly, semi-jelly, or water opals. One of the rarest is the harlequin opal, which displays color patterns resembling a checkerboard.

While there are imitations and synthetics, for the most part their quality is such that they are not yet worth considering. The synthetic opal, nonetheless, is being used extensively. Also, since the color of black opals can be improved by treatment, treated opals are encountered frequently. So the usual precautions are in order: make sure you know what you are getting, and before buying, shop around. This holds truer for opal, perhaps, than any other stone.

One word of caution must also be offered: opals require special care because some tend to dry and crack. Avoid exposure to anything that is potentially drying, and immerse your opal in water for several hours periodically to help preserve it. *Never immerse opals in oil;* soaking some opals in oil for only a few hours can cause them to lose some or nearly all of their fire. *Note:* it was once thought that wiping the surface of an opal regularly with oil would protect it. *This is not true and will damage most opals.*

Peridot (Olivine)

Today's birthstone for August, peridot was also a favorite of the ancients. This lovely transparent yellowish green to deep chartreuse stone was quite a powerful gem. It was considered an aid to friendship and was also believed to free the mind of envious thoughts (which is probably why it was an aid to friendship). Because of its yellowish green color, it was also believed to cure or prevent diseases of the liver and dropsy. If that's not enough, worn on the left arm it would protect the wearer from the evil eye.

Peridot is also popular today, but probably more for its lovely shade of green than its professed powers. While peridot is not particularly brilliant, the richness of its color can be exceptional. It comes in shades of yellowish green to darker, purer green colors. Unfortunately, because of its rarity most people never see peridot in the deeper, purer green color that is so prized.

Peridot is still widely available in small sizes, but larger stones are becoming scarce, so prices are now fairly high for good-quality material in higher-carat weights.

Some caution should be exercised in wearing peridot. It is moderately hard (6½ to 7 on Mohs' scale) but can chip and scratch easily. Also, some stones—like green sapphire or green tourmaline—can look like peridot and be mistaken or misrepresented.

Quartz

The most versatile of any of the gem families, quartz includes among its members more variety and a larger number of gems than any other three mineral families together. In the gem trade, the old saying "If in doubt, say quartz" still holds true.

The quartz minerals, for the most part, are relatively inexpensive gems that offer a wide range of pleasing color alternatives in both transparent and nontransparent varieties, from translucent to opaque. They are reasonably hard stones (7 on Mohs' scale) and, while not very brilliant in the transparent varieties, still create lovely, affordable jewelry.

Some of these gems have been discussed in separate sections, but we will provide a list here with brief descriptions of most of the quartz family members.

Transparent varieties. *Amethyst* (see page 167) is lilac to purple in color.

Citrine is often called quartz topaz, citrine topaz, or topaz, all of which are misleading. The correct name for this stone is citrine. It is yellow, amber to amber brown. This is the most commonly seen "topaz" in today's marketplace and is, unfortunately, too often confused with precious topaz because of the careless use of the name. While a pleasing stone in terms of color and fairly durable, citrine is slightly softer and has less brilliance than precious topaz. It also lacks the subtle color shading, the pinker yellow or pinkish amber shades, which lends to precious topaz a distinctive color difference. Much citrine is made by heating pale amethyst.

Citrine is much less expensive than precious topaz. It should never be represented as topaz, which technically is "precious" or "imperial" topaz. Unfortunately, it often is. For example, "topaz" birthstone jewelry is almost always citrine (or a worthless synthetic). So the question to ask the seller is, "Is this citrine or precious topaz?" Get the answer in writing if you are told, "Precious topaz."

Citrine is plentiful in all sizes and can be made into striking jewelry, especially in very large sizes, for a relatively small investment, while precious topaz of fine quality is scarce in sizes over seven carats and is *very* expensive.

Ametrine is a lovely, unusual bicolor quartz in which amethyst and citrine are both present in the same stone. The name is derived by taking the first three letters of amethyst and the last five letters in citrine. Bolivia is the source of natural ametrine, although "ametrine" can also be created in the laboratory.

Praseolite is a pale green transparent variety produced by heating amethyst.

Rock crystal is water clear. It was used in old jewelry for rondelles, a type of small bead resembling a doughnut. Faceted crystal beads were also common in older jewelry. Today, however, *crystal* usually refers to glass.

Rose quartz is light to deep pink. This stone has been very popular for many years for use in carved pieces—beads, statues, ashtrays, fine lamp bases, and pins and brooches. Rarely clear, this stone is usually seen in cabochon cuts, rounded beads, or carvings rather than in faceted styles. Once very inexpensive, it is becoming more costly, particularly in the finer deep pink shades. But the color of rose quartz is especially pleasing and offers an excellent choice for use in fashion accessory jewelry.

You must be somewhat cautious with rose quartz, however, because it tends to crack more easily than most other varieties of quartz if struck or exposed to a blow. The inclusions or internal fractures that are also responsible for the absence of clarity in this stone cause it to be slightly brittle.

Smokey quartz is a pale to rich smokey brown variety, sometimes mistaken for or misrepresented as smokey topaz or topaz. It is also very plentiful and is becoming popular for use in very large sizes for beautiful brooches, large dinner rings, and so forth.

Translucent to opaque varieties. *Agate* and *chalcedony* are found in all colors, and all varieties of markings are seen in this wonderful ornamental gem. Among them you'll find, to mention a few, banded agate; moss agate, a fascinating white or milky agate that looks as though it actually has black, brown, or green moss growing within; eye agate, which has an eyeball effect; or plume agate, which looks as if it's filled with beautiful feather plumes. The colors and "scenes" in agate are infinite. While agate is usually an inexpensive stone, some varieties or special stones with very unusual scenes or markings can be quite expensive.

Carnelian, sard, and *sardonyx* are reddish, orange, apricot, and brown varieties of chalcedony and are often seen in cameo or other carving work. Black onyx is a dyed chalcedony; chrysoprase is green chalcedony, often dyed green.

The unusual colors and markings of agate made it very highly regarded by the ancients and revered throughout history, even to the present day. According to Pliny, it was believed to make wearers "agreeable and persuasive and give them God's favor." Other virtues claimed for agate wearers include giving the wearer victory and strength and also protection from tempests and lightning, guarding its wearer from all dangers, enabling him to overcome all terrestrial obstacles, and imparting to him a bold heart.

Wearing agate ornaments was also seen as a cure for insomnia and could ensure good dreams. In the middle of the 1800s, and continuing to the present in some parts of the world, amulets made from eye agate (brown or black agate with a white ring in the center) were so popular that agate cutters in Germany had time for cutting little else. The "eye" was believed to take on the watchfulness of one's guardian spirit and to protect the wearer from the evil eye by neutralizing its power. At one time these amulets commanded an incredible price.

Whatever their real power, these are fascinating stones, some quite mesmerizing in their unusual beauty. They are often seen in antique jewelry as well as in contemporary pieces. One must be careful, however, to exercise some caution in wear to protect from knocks, as some varieties are more fragile than others. Also, agate is frequently dyed, so it is important to ask whether the color is natural and to be sure that it is not another less valuable stone, dyed to look like a special variety of agate.

Aventurine is a lovely pale to medium green semitranslucent stone with tiny sparkling flecks of mica within. This stone makes very lovely cabochon or bead jewelry at a very affordable price. It is occasionally misrepresented as jade; although the mica flecks are sometimes so small that they cannot be seen easily, they provide an immediate and reliable indicator that the material is aventurine quartz. Be aware, however, that there are some fairly good glass imitations in the marketplace.

Bloodstone (see page 171) is dark green with red spots.

Cat's-eye is a pale yellowish green stone that when cut in cabochon style produces a streak of light down the center that creates an eye effect. This phenomenon is a result of the presence of fiberlike inclusions. This stone has a weaker center line, a paler color, and much lower cost than true cat's-eye from the chrysoberyl family. But it is nonetheless an attractive stone that makes attractive, affordable jewelry.

Chrysocolla—the true chrysocolla— is a very soft copper mineral, too soft for jewelry use. However, quartz that has been naturally impregnated or stained with chrysocolla has good hardness and the same brilliant blue-green, highly translucent color. Chrysocolla is becoming a very popular stone for jewelry, and its price is starting to reflect increased demand.

Chrysoprase (see page 172) is a bright light to dark green, highly translucent stone, often of very even color. It is sometimes misrepresented as or confused with jade.

Jasper is opaque red, yellow, green, and brown (or sometimes gray). It is usually strongly marked in terms of the contrast between the green and other colors in an almost blotchlike or veinlike pattern. The red and green combination is the most popular, although there are more than fifty types of jasper of various colors and patterns.

Jasper was believed in ancient cultures to bring rain and also to protect its wearer from the bites of poisonous creatures. It was believed to have as diverse a power as the colors and veins in which it came, so many uses and magical powers were associated with it.

Jasper offers interesting color contrast and variety and is being used increasingly in today's fashion accessory jewelry.

Petrified wood is sections of trees or limbs that have been replaced by quartz-type silica and transformed into a mineral after centuries of immersion in silica-rich water under extreme pressure. It is usually red, reddish brown, or brown and is not often seen in jewelry.

Tiger's-eye is a golden, yellowish, reddish, and sometimes bluish variety of quartz that produces a bright shimmering line (or lines) of light, which when cut in a cabochon will produce an eye. The eye will move when the stone is turned from side to side. It is inexpensive but very popular for fashion accessory jewelry and men's cufflinks and rings.

Rhodochrosite

Rhodochrosite is a newcomer to the jewelry business. While sought by rock hounds for many years and a favorite of beginning lapidaries, rhodochrosite appeared only occasionally outside of rock and mineral shows frequented by hobbyists. A member of the carbonate mineral group, rhodochrosite is a relatively soft stone occurring in both a rare transparent and a more common nontransparent variety. For practical purposes, we will discuss the latter, more readily available form.

A lovely red to almost white color, often with agatelike curved lines creating a design in contrasting shades of red or pink, rhodochrosite may occasionally occur in an orangy tone, but this is poorer-quality material. The finest color is a medium to deep rose, preferably with curved banding. It has long been popular for certain ornamental objects (spheres, boxes, eggs) but only recently for jewelry. Today, necklaces using rhodochrosite beads alternating with other stones or gold beads are becoming particularly popular. We will see more rhodochrosite on the market in coming years. It is, however, soft (4 on Mohs' scale), and some caution should be used in wearing to avoid unnecessary abuse.

Scapolite

This is an interesting gem that is beginning to appear in more jewelry as it becomes more available. Rediscovered in Brazil after a forty-year hiatus and also recently discovered in Kenya, scapolite is a nice, transparent, fairly durable stone (6½ on Mohs' scale), occurring in a range of colors from colorless to yellow, light red, orange to greenish to bluish gray, violet, and violet blue. The orange, light red, and whitish specimens may also occur as semitransparent stones, which may show a cat's-eye effect (chatoyancy) when cut into cabochons.

The most likely to appear in jewelry are the violets and yellows, and possibly orange cat's-eyes. They might easily be mistaken for yellow beryl or certain quartz minerals like amethyst or citrine.

The bottom line here is that we will have to wait and see what trends evolve around this stone, as its availability will determine its future use and cost.

Serpentine

Serpentine derives its name from its similarity to the green speckled skin of the serpent. Amulets of serpentine were worn for protection from serpent bites, stings of poisonous reptiles, and poison in general. A king was reputed to have insisted that his chalice be made of serpentine, as it was believed that if a poisoned drink were put into a serpentine vessel, the vessel would sweat on the outside. The effectiveness of medicine was increased when it was drunk from a serpentine vessel.

Serpentine is often used as a jade substitute. It is a translucent to semi-translucent stone occurring in light to dark yellowish green to greenish yellow. One variety is used for decorative wall facings and table and counter surfaces, but some of the more attractive green varieties so closely resemble jadeite or nephrite jade that they are used in carvings and jewelry and are often misrepresented as jade. Common serpentine is also sometimes dyed a jadelike color. One lovely green variety, williamsite, which is a very pleasing deep green, often with small black flecks within, is often sold as "Pennsylvania jade." It is pretty, but it is not jade. Another variety of serpentine, bowenite, is also sold today as "Korean jade" or "new jade." Again, it is pretty but it is not jade. Serpentine is softer than jade, less durable, and much more common, which its price should reflect.

It is a lovely stone in its own right and makes a nice alternative to jade. While it has been around for a long time (too often, however, represented as jade), we are just beginning to see this stone used frequently in necklaces and other fine jewelry under its own name.

Sodalite

This stone has already been discussed under *Lapis*. It is a dark blue semitransparent to semitranslucent stone, used frequently as a substitute for the rarer, more expensive lapis. While it may have some white veining, it does not have the golden or silver flecks that are characteristic of lapis. If you do not see these shiny flecks, suspect that the stone is probably sodalite.

Spinel

Spinel is one of the loveliest of the gems, but it has only recently begun to enjoy the respect and admiration it deserves. It is usually compared to sapphire or ruby rather than being recognized for its own intrinsic beauty and value. There is also a common belief that spinel (and similarly zircon) is synthetic rather than natural, when in fact it is one of nature's most beautiful—and truly natural—creations. This misconception probably arose because synthetic spinel is seen frequently on the market, whereas genuine spinel is not often seen.

Spinel is one of the few gems *never* treated or enhanced. It occurs in red orange (flame spinel), light to dark orangy red, light to dark slightly grayish blue, greenish blue, grayish green, and dark to light purple to violet. It also occurs in yellow and in an opaque variety—black. When compared with the blue of sapphire or the red of ruby, the color is usually considered less intense (although some red spinel can look very much like some ruby on the market now), yet its brilliance can be greater. If you appreciate these spinel colors for themselves, they are quite pleasing. The most popular are red (usually a more orange-red than ruby red) and blue (sometimes resembling a strong Bromo-Seltzer–bottle blue).

Spinel may be confused with or misrepresented as one of many stones—ruby, sapphire, zircon, amethyst, garnet, synthetic ruby/sapphire, or synthetic spinel—as well as glass. The synthetic is often used to make composite stones such as doublets. Spinel is a hard (8 on Mohs' scale), fairly durable stone, possessing a nice brilliance, and is still a good value.

This stone is becoming more and more popular today and may, therefore, become more expensive if current trends continue.

Spodumene (Kunzite and Hiddenite)

Spodumene is another gem relatively new to widespread jewelry use. The most popular varieties are kunzite and hiddenite.

Kunzite is a very lovely brilliant stone occurring in delicate lilac, pinkish, or violet shades. Its color can fade in strong light, so it has become known as an "evening" stone. Also, while basically hard (6 to 7 on Mohs' scale), it is nonetheless brittle and can break easily if it receives a sharp blow from certain directions. It is not recommended for rings for this reason unless set in a protective mounting. But it is a lovely gem, whose low cost makes it attractive in large sizes, and is an excellent choice for lovely, dramatic jewelry design.

Hiddenite is rarer. Light green or yellow-green varieties are available, but the emerald green varieties are scarce. As with kunzite, it is hard but brittle, so care must be exercised in wear.

Spodumene also occurs in many other shades of color, all pale but very clear and brilliant. Only blue is currently missing—but who knows what may yet be discovered in some part of the world? Spodumene is still fairly inexpensive and is an excellent choice for contemporary jewelry design. Be careful, however, as it can be confused with and sold as more expensive topaz, tourmaline, spinel, or beryl. Also, synthetic corundum or spinel can be mistaken for this gem.

Sugilite

Named for the Japanese petrologist who discovered it, Ken-ichi Sugi, sugilite first appeared on the jewelry scene in the late 1970s, sold as Royal Azel and Royal Lavulite. Best known today as sugilite, its lovely, deep rich purple to purple red color is unique. An opaque gem, it is usually cut in cabochons or beads, although it is also popular for inlay work (intarsia) by top artisans. Sugilite belongs to the manganese family, and most comes from Africa. The finest color is already becoming scarce, so it is difficult to predict the future for this interesting newcomer.

Tanzanite (see Zoisite)

Titanite (Sphene)

This is another "new" gem that is beginning to appear and offers some interesting possibilities for the jewelry market. While it has been highly regarded for many years, its relative scarcity prevented its widescale use in jewelry. Today, however, new sources have been discovered, and we are beginning to see greater availability.

This is a beautiful, brilliant stone, with a diamondlike (adamantine) luster and fire that is even greater than in diamond. Unfortunately, it is soft. Its colors range from grass green to golden yellow to brown.

There is need for some caution because of this stone's softness (5 to 5½ on Mohs' scale). We suggest that it is especially suitable for pendants, earrings, brooches, and protective ring settings.

Topaz

True topaz, symbol of love and affection, aid to sweetness of disposition, and birthstone for November, is one of nature's most wonderful and least-known families. The true topaz is rarely seen in jewelry stores. Unfortunately, most people know only the quartz (citrine) topaz, or glass, and in the past almost any yellow stone was called topaz. A very beautiful and versatile stone, topaz is a hard, brilliant stone with a fine color range, and it is much rarer and much more expensive than the stones commonly sold as topaz. It is also heavier than its imitators.

Topaz occurs not only in the transparent yellow, yellow-brown, orangy brown, and pinky brown colors most popularly associated with it, but also in a very light to medium red now found naturally in fair supply, although many are produced through heat treatment. It also is found in a very light to medium deep blue, also often as the result of treatment, although blue does occur naturally on a fairly wide scale. Other topaz shades include very light green, light greenish yellow, violet, and colorless. Diffusion-treated topaz is also available in medium to deep green and blue-green.

Blue topaz has become very popular in recent years, most of it treated; unfortunately, there is no way yet to determine which have been treated and which are natural. The blue form closely resembles the finest aquamarine, which is very expensive today, and offers a very attractive and much more affordable alternative to it. Some of the fine, deeper blue treated topazes have been found to be radioactive and, according to the Nuclear Regulatory Commission, may be injurious to the wearer. In the United States, all blue topaz must be tested for radiation levels; the Gemological Institute of America (GIA) now provides this service to the jewelry trade. However, be very careful when buying blue topaz outside the United States. If you do, you may be wise to have it tested when you get home.

There are many misleading names to suggest that a stone is topaz when it is not, for example, "Rio topaz," "Madeira topaz," "Spanish topaz," and "Palmeira topaz." They are types of citrine (quartz) and should be represented as such.

The true topaz family offers a variety of color options in lovely, clear, brilliant, and durable stones (8 on Mohs' scale). This family should become more important in the years ahead.

Tourmaline

Tourmaline is a gem of modern times, but nonetheless it has found its way to the list of birthstones, becoming an "alternative birthstone" for October. Perhaps this honor results from tourmaline's versatility and broad color range, or perhaps from the fact that red and green tourmaline, in which red and green occur side by side in the same stone, is reminiscent of the turning of October leaves.

Whatever the case, tourmaline is one of the most versatile of the gem families. It is available in every color, in every tone, from deep to pastel and even with two or more colors appearing in the same stone, side by side. There are bicolored tourmalines (one-half red and the other half green, for example) and tricolored (one-third blue, one-third green, and one-third yet another color). The fascinating "watermelon" tourmaline looks just like the inside of a watermelon: red in the center surrounded by a green "rind."

One of the most exciting gemological discoveries of this century was the discovery of a unique variety of tourmaline in Paraiba, Brazil. These particular beauties, referred to as Paraiba or Hetorita after the man who discovered them, have colors so intense and come in such a wide range of green, blue, and lilac shades that they are referred to as the *neon* tourmalines. Unfortunately, demand has been unprecedented for these particular tourmalines, and supply has dwindled. The result is that many of the finest Paraibas are very expensive, and some rival the finest sapphires in price. Many imitations are now on the market, and we have found apatite, a common, inexpensive stone that occurs in similar colors but is too soft for most jewelry use, being sold as "Paraiba" tourmaline.

It is indeed surprising that most people know of tourmaline simply as a common "green" stone. Nothing could be more misleading. Today, we are finally beginning to see other lovely varieties of this fascinating gem in the jewelry market. In addition to the exciting new Paraiba, other popular varieties include the following:

- Chrome—a particularly rare green hue
- Indicolite—deep indigo blue, usually with a green undertone
- Rubellite—deep pink to red, as in ruby

While many tourmalines are very inexpensive, the chrome, indicolite, and rubellite varieties are priced (depending on size and quality) anywhere from $300 to $1,000 per carat or more. And the incomparable Paraiba varieties can sell for $2,000 to $4,000 per carat for a top-quality one-carat stone—up to $15,000 *per carat* for a five-carat stone, if you can find one. So much for the "common and inexpensive" myth!

Tourmaline is a fairly hard (7 to 7½ on Mohs' scale), durable, brilliant, and very wearable stone with a wide choice of colors. It is also still available in large sizes. It is a stone that without question will play a more and more important role in jewelry in the years ahead.

Turquoise

A birthstone for December, and ranking highest among all the opaque stones, turquoise—the "Turkish stone"—is highly prized throughout Asia and Africa, not only for its particular hue of blue (a beautiful robin's-egg or sky blue) but especially for its supposed prophylactic and therapeutic qualities. The Arabs consider it a lucky stone and have great confidence in its benevolent action. Used in rings, earrings, necklaces, head ornaments, and amulets, it protects the wearer from poison, reptile bites, eye diseases, and the evil eye. It was also believed capable of warning of impending death by changing color. Also, the drinking of water in which turquoise has been dipped or washed was believed to cure bladder ailments. Buddhists revere the turquoise because it is associated with a legend in which a turquoise enabled Buddha to destroy a monster. Even today it is considered a symbol of courage, success, and love. It has also long been associated with American Indian jewelry and art.

Turquoise is an opaque, light to dark blue or blue-green stone. The finest color is an intense blue, with poorer qualities tending toward yellowish green. The famous Persian turquoise, which can be a very intense and pleasing blue, is considered a very rare and valuable gem. The United States (Arizona and New Mexico) is also an important source of fine turquoise and is now the major source of turquoise used in jewelry worldwide.

All turquoises are susceptible to "aging," turning greenish or possibly darker with age. Also, care must be taken to avoid contact with soap, grease, or other materials that might discolor it and to protect it from abuse, since turquoise scratches fairly easily (6 on Mohs' scale).

But exercise caution when buying turquoise. This is a frequently simulated gem. Very fine glass imitations are produced that are difficult to distinguish from the genuine. Enhanced, coated, and "stabilized" stones, and reconstructed stones (from turquoise powder bonded in plastic), saturate the marketplace, as does synthetic turquoise. There are techniques to quickly distinguish these imitations or treated stones, so, if in doubt, check it out (and get a complete description on the bill of sale: "genuine, natural turquoise").

Zircon

Known to the ancients as hyacinth, this gem had many powers, especially for men. While it was known to assist women in childbirth, for men it kept evil spirits and bad dreams away, gave protection against "fascination" and lightning, strengthened their bodies, fortified their hearts, restored appetite, suppressed fat, produced sleep, and banished grief and sadness from the mind.

Zircons are very brilliant transparent stones available in several lovely colors. Unfortunately, many consumers suffer from a strange misconception that zircon is a synthetic or artificial stone rather than a lovely natural creation. Perhaps this belief is based on the fact that they are frequently color treated, as in the blue zircons so often seen. Zircons also occur naturally in yellow, brown, orange, and red.

Many might mistake the colorless zircon for diamond because of its strong brilliance, which, coupled with its very low cost, makes colorless zircon an interesting alternative to diamonds as a stone to offset or dress up colored stones. But care needs to be exercised because zircon is only moderately hard (6½ to 7½ on Mohs' scale), and it is brittle, so it will chip or abrade easily. For this reason, zircon is recommended for earrings, pendants, brooches, or rings with a protective setting.

Zoisite (Tanzanite)

Zoisite was not considered a gem material until 1967, when a beautiful rich, blue to purple-blue, transparent variety was found in Tanzania (hence tanzanite). Tanzanite can possess a rich, sapphire blue color, possibly with some violet-red or greenish yellow flashes. A gem green variety has recently been discovered, which is being called green tanzanite or chrome tanzanite. The green can be a very lovely shade, ranging from a slightly yellowish green to gray-green to a bluish green. Supply is still limited, so time will tell whether or not this green variety will be readily available to the public.

Tanzanite has become one of the most popular gems in the marketplace. As a result, many imitations are being produced. Double-check on the identity of any fine tanzanite with a gemologist-appraiser.

This lovely gem can cost over $2,000 per carat today in larger sizes. But one must be cautious because it is not very hard (6½ on Mohs' scale) and scratches easily. It is also brittle and can chip easily, so we do not recommend tanzanite for rings (unless set in a very protected setting) or bracelets, or for everyday wear in which it would be exposed to knocks and other abuse.

16

Pearls

*The richest merchandise of all, and the most sovereign commodity
throughout the whole world, are these pearls.*

—C. Plinius Secundus (Pliny the Elder), Roman historian and writer,
from Natural History, 77 A.D.

Next to the diamond, no gem has fascinated humankind more than the pearl. The oldest known natural pearl necklace is more than four thousand years old. Today's birthstone for June, the pearl was long believed to possess a special mystical quality, symbolized by the glow that seems to radiate from its very center. This glow signified to the ancient world a powerful inner life. In fact, Roman women are believed to have taken pearls to bed with them to sweeten their dreams! Over time, the pearl has acquired strong associations with love, success, happiness, and the virtues of modesty, chastity, and purity, which make it a popular choice for brides on their wedding day.

Pearls offer more versatility than perhaps any other gem. They go well with any style, in any place; they can be worn from morning to evening; they look smart and attractive with sportswear, add an "executive" touch to the business suit, and add elegance to even the most glamorous evening gown. They are also available in a wide variety of types, sizes, shapes, colors, and price ranges. They offer limitless possibilities for creative stringing, which adds up to greater versatility as well as greater affordability.

Pearls have become an essential for any well-dressed woman today, yet most buyers feel overwhelmed and intimidated by all the choices and the widely differing prices. But with just a little knowledge, you'll be surprised by how quickly you can learn to see and understand variations in characteristics and quality. Here, we will provide some of the most essential information to help you understand more about the types of pearls most common in the marketplace today. For more in-depth information about all varieties of natural and cultured pearls—including rare natural Melo Melo, Conch, and Quahog pearls—see *The Pearl Book: The Definitive Buying Guide.*

What Is a Pearl?

A pearl is the gem produced by saltwater oysters (the nonedible variety) or by freshwater mollusks. In either case, a small foreign object (such as a tiny sea parasite from the ocean floor) finds its way into the shell and then into the tissue of the mollusk. If the intruder becomes trapped, and the oyster can't rid itself of it, the foreign body becomes an irritant. To ease the discomfort this irritant creates, the mollusk takes defensive action and produces a blackish substance called conchiolin, over which another substance, a whitish substance called "nacre," is secreted. This is the lustrous pearly coating for which the pearl is prized. The nacre is composed of microscopic crystals, each crystal aligned perfectly with the others so that light passing along the axis of one is reflected and refracted by the others to produce a rainbowlike glow of light and color. The pearl is the result of the buildup of layer after layer of this nacre. The thicker the nacre, the more beautiful the pearl.

The Pearl Market Is a "Cultured" Pearl Market Today

Most pearls sold today are *cultured* pearls. Natural—or Oriental pearls, as they are sometimes called—have become one of the rarest of all gems, with prices to match. Cultured pearls are much more affordable.

One way to understand the difference between a natural pearl and a cultured pearl is to think of the natural pearl as a product of the oyster working alone, and the cultured pearl as a product of humans "helping" nature. In the natural pearl, the irritant around which the oyster secretes the nacre and produces the pearl is a foreign object that accidentally finds its way into the oyster tissue. In the cultured pearl, humans implant the irritant—a mother-of-pearl bead called the "nucleus." After the initial implantation, however, the process by which the cultured pearl is produced is very similar to that in the natural pearl: the oyster produces nacre to coat the irritant, layer after layer building up and producing the pearl. The oyster produces the nacre; the oyster produces the finished pearl. The pearl producers wash the oyster periodically, control available food, try to maintain constant water temperature, and control pollutants, but the oyster itself still has control of the pearl product it produces.

The primary physical difference between the resulting products—natural and cultured pearls—is in the thickness of the nacre. Even though it takes several years to raise the oyster and produce a fine cultured pearl, the pearls are nonetheless harvested much sooner than comparable natural pearls, often when the nacre thickness reaches only ½ millimeter. The nacre on the natural pearl is much thicker because it has taken many more years to produce.

Natural pearls are often less perfectly round than fine cultured pearls, and in strands or jewelry containing numerous pearls, naturals usually appear much less uniform in color and shape than do cultured pearls. The reason for greater uniformity in cultured pearls is that they are available in larger quantity, so it is easier to find and carefully match pearls.

Fine natural pearls are rare and valuable and, for the most part, always have been. Never take anyone's word that their pearls are natural—even "inherited" pearls. Most of the time these inherited heirlooms turn out *not* to be natural, or even cultured, but fake. Imitation pearls have been around for centuries. Even Mrs. Harry Winston and the Duchess of Windsor owned and wore fake pearls. Of course, they also had real pearls in the safe!

If you are buying a strand of pearls represented to be natural, make sure they are accompanied by an identification report from a reliable lab. Natural pearls must be x-rayed to confirm authenticity. Always be sure to have proper documentation, no matter who the owner, or how wealthy, or how old the piece.

Cultured versus Imitation Pearls

Both cultured and natural pearls are produced by the oyster or mollusk. Imitation pearls have never seen the inside of an oyster. They are entirely artificial, made from round glass or plastic beads dipped in a bath of ground fish scales and lacquer, or one of the new plastic substances. The difference between real and simulated pearls can usually be seen when the two are compared side by side. One of the most obvious differences is in the luster. Give it the *luster test;* the real pearl will have a depth of luster that the fake cannot duplicate. The fake usually has a surface "shine" but no inner "glow." Look in the shaded area—in the real pearl you see a clearly defined reflection; in the fake pearl you will not.

Use the Tooth Test to Detect the Fake

There are some fine imitations today that can be very convincing. Some have actually been mistaken for fine cultured pearls. An easy, reliable test in most cases is the tooth test. Run the pearl gently along the edge of your teeth (the upper teeth are more sensitive—and also be aware that the test won't work with false teeth). The genuine pearl will have a mildly abrasive or gritty feel (think of sand at the seaside; real pearls come from the sea), while the imitation will be slippery smooth (like the con artist, slippery smooth signifies a fake!). Try this test on pearls you know are genuine, and then on known imitations to get a feel for the difference. You'll never forget it!

The tooth test may be unreliable when applied to the Majorica pearl, however. This is an imitation pearl, which might easily be mistaken for genuine. An experienced jeweler or gemologist can quickly and easily identify the Majorica for you.

The Six Factors That Affect Pearl Quality and Value

Regardless of the type of pearl, or whether it is natural or cultured, the following factors must be evaluated to determine whether or not it is a fine pearl that will give you lasting beauty.

1. *Nacre thickness and quality.* This is the most important factor in terms of beauty and, with cultured pearls, in knowing how long they will last! For this reason, we consider it the most important factor. Nacre *thickness* determines the pearl's longevity. The thicker the nacre, the longer the life of the pearl; the thinner the nacre, the shorter its life. Nacre *quality* determines how the light travels through the layers. Sometimes pearls with thick nacre fail to exhibit the intensity of luster or orient that is expected because the

nacre layers didn't crystallize properly. The crystals may lack transparency, the layers may not be uniform, or the layers may not be properly aligned. The result is a pearl with lower luster. To have a lustrous, iridescent pearl, the nacre must be thick, and it must also have good crystallization. There are pearls with thick nacre that aren't lustrous because of how the layers crystallized, but any pearl that exhibits a rich lustrousness is one that has thick nacre. So always look for a pearl with high luster because this provides a visual indication of thick nacre, your guarantee of lasting beauty. *Alert: There has been an influx of very low quality pearls that have such thin nacre that it chips and peels off, quickly deteriorating into nothing more than worthless shell beads. Should your pearls do this, return them to the jeweler, or write to Antoinette Matlins c/o GemStone Press.*

2. **Luster and orient.** This is the sharpness and intensity of the images reflected from the pearl's surface *(luster)* and the underlying iridescent play of colors *(orient)* that distinguish the pearl from all other gems. The degree of luster and orient is one of the most important factors in determining the quality and value of the pearl. High luster is perhaps the first thing one notices in looking at a fine strand of pearls. The higher the luster and orient, the finer the pearl. Luster is usually judged from sharp (high) to dull (low). When judging luster and orient, look at the shadow area of the pearl, not the shiny, reflective area (don't confuse "shine" with the deep iridescent glow created by the combination of luster and orient).

3. **Color.** Color is usually considered the most important factor affecting value and cost. Two elements are involved in evaluating color: *body color* and *overtone*. The body color is the basic color, i.e., white, yellow, black. The overtone is a secondary color (its tint), such as the pinkish overtone in fine white pearls. *Color* refers to the combination of the body color and overtone. Very white pearls with a rose-colored overtone (tint) are the rarest and the most expensive. The creamier the color becomes, the less costly they are. However, today the rose tint is often imparted to the pearl through artificial means. If you use a loupe to examine the drill hole, you may be able to detect the color enhancement if you can see the line of demarcation between the mother-of-pearl nucleus and the nacre; if the pearl has been tinted, the line will show a pinkish coloration.

Cultured pearls are available in many colors—gray, black, pink, blue, gold—but often these colors have been produced by surface dyes or irradiation techniques. White pearls that have been drilled for jewelry use (as in a necklace) and then tinted or dyed can usually be detected easily by a qualified gemologist. With rare black pearls it may be necessary to send them to a gem-testing laboratory with sophisticated equipment in order to be sure.

4. *Cleanliness (surface texture or perfection).* This refers to the pearl's freedom from such surface blemishes as small blisters, pimples, spots, or cracks. Imperfections may also appear as dark spots, small indentations, welts or blisters, or surface bumps. While occasional small blemishes are not uncommon, if large or numerous they are unsightly. A pearl with sizable or numerous blemishes may also be less durable. The cleaner the skin, the better. Also, the closer the blemish to the drill hole, the less it detracts from both appearance and value. But keep in mind that a pearl with very thin nacre will often have a clean surface.

5. *Shape.* Shape in pearls is divided into three categories: spherical, symmetrical, and baroque. The rarest and most valuable are the spherical or round pearls; these are judged on their degree of sphericity, or roundness. While perfectly round pearls are extremely rare, the closer to perfectly round, the finer and more expensive the pearl. Button pearls and pear-shaped pearls are symmetrical pearls and are judged on evenness and good symmetry—that is, whether they have a nice, well-proportioned shape. Symmetrical pearls are less expensive than round pearls but much more expensive than baroque pearls, which are irregularly shaped. Any strand of pearls should be well matched for shape and, when worn, give the appearance of uniformity. As with cleanliness, however, thin-nacre pearls are often *very* round because the nucleus is round.

6. *Size.* Natural pearls are sold by weight. They are weighed in grains, four grains being equal to one carat. Cultured pearls are sold by millimeter size (1 millimeter equals approximately $\frac{1}{25}$ inch): their measurement indicates the number of millimeters in the diameter of the pearl. Two millimeter dimensions—length and width—may be given if the pearl is not round. The larger the pearl, the greater the cost. A 2-millimeter cultured pearl is considered very small, whereas those over 9 millimeters are consid-

ered very large. Large cultured pearls are rarer, and more expensive. There is a dramatic jump in the cost of cultured pearls after 7.5 millimeters. The price jumps upward rapidly with each 0.5 millimeter from 8 millimeters up.

Another factor affecting the value of any pearl item that has been strung, as in a necklace, is the precision that went into the matching of the pearls; this is called the make. Consider how well matched the strand is in size, shape, color, luster, and surface texture. Graduated pearls also require careful sizing. Failure to match carefully will detract from both the appearance of the item and its value.

Types of Pearls

Saltwater Pearls

The best-known pearl is the round pearl produced by saltwater oysters. The most famous of these is Japan's Akoya pearl. The finest Akoyas are more perfectly round than other pearls and have the highest luster, which makes them very desirable. Unfortunately, for those who prefer very large pearls, they rarely exceed 10 millimeters in diameter, and when they do, they command a stellar price. For larger pearls, one must turn to white South Sea cultured pearls, and natural-color black pearls, which are very much in vogue but also more costly.

Biwa and Other Freshwater Pearls

Some of the world's most prized—and most beautiful—pearls are *natural* freshwater pearls. These are very expensive and can compare to the price of natural saltwater pearls. Frequently whiter than the natural saltwater pearl, and often with a more intense luster, these are the pearls that were so cherished by the Romans. The only reason the Roman legions ever ventured into England, or so it is rumored, was to search for the rare *pink* freshwater pearls found in Scotland!

Freshwater cultured pearls are grown in freshwater rather than saltwater, in mussels that live in lakes and rivers. One of the best known freshwater cultured pearls is the *Biwa* pearl (named after Lake Biwa in Japan), which is one of the finest and most beautiful of the freshwater pearls. It often occurs in oval, barrel, and coin shapes. Although the term "Biwa" should be used only for pearls from Lake Biwa, it is often used indiscriminately to refer to *any* freshwater pearl; since Lake Biwa once produced almost all of the fine freshwater pearls, it has become a generic label for almost all freshwater pearls. Unfortunately, Lake Biwa production now has virtually ceased, and Chinese freshwater cultured pearls are being sent to Japan and sold as "Biwa."

Freshwater cultured pearls are now grown in many countries. The leading producers include the United States, Japan, and China. Common mussel-type molluscs are used. The process used to produce most freshwater pearls doesn't require a shell nucleus; tissue grafting techniques are used instead, which facilitates mass production. The mollusc is also larger than that used to produce Akoya pearls. As a result, an individual mollusc can produce as many as fifty pearls at a time. The pearls produced in this manner are normally small, elongated, and very inexpensive. Using only mantle tissue, however, they are essentially all nacre, and top quality freshwater pearls are very lovely and offer very good value for the money. They occur in a wide range of colors and shapes. They can have high luster or low, depending upon quality. Japan and China are the leading producers of this type.

The look of freshwater cultured pearls is changing, however. Very lovely *round* freshwater all-nacre cultured pearls are now being produced, and are readily available in 7–9 millimeter sizes and up. Pearls up to 15 millimeters are also becoming available on a limited basis, the finest rivaling the rarer, costlier South Sea cultured pearl in appearance.

Round cultured freshwater pearls require more sophisticated production techniques, including an implant procedure. Several techniques are now being used, but the exact techniques used are closely guarded and undisclosed. Some contain a round implant fashioned from mantle tissue or the abundant supply of inexpensive, all-nacre "rice-krispie" type freshwater pearls. The result is an all-nacre, *round* cultured pearl in appearance. Others contain shell beads, produced in a manner similar to seawater varieties. Unfortunately, when you buy them, you cannot be sure what is at the core. For the costlier, large, round, freshwater pearls, we recommend submitting them to a lab for a nacre-thickness report, just in case there is a bead nucleus.

China is the primary source of these lovely pearls, but Japan has begun producing unusually lustrous, large round *pink* cultured freshwater pearls in Lake Kasumiga, hence their name, "Kasumiga" cultured pearls. We also expect to see quantities of round *American* freshwater cultured pearls in the near future. Round freshwater pearls are more expensive than other types of freshwater cultured pearls, but normally much less expensive than the rarer round, saltwater pearls.

Cultured freshwater pearls also occur in interesting shapes, as do the natural; in fact, natural "angel-wing" pearls from the Mississippi River and other nearby rivers and lakes are very collectible. Cultured pearl producers are also culturing freshwater pearls in special shapes such as crosses, bars, and coins. These are referred to as *"fancy"* shapes.

Freshwater pearls occur in a wide range of colors—a much wider variety than round, saltwater pearls—which gives them a special allure. Colors include light, medium, and dark orange, lavender, purple, violet, blue, rose, and gray. Large natural freshwater pearls in unusual colors can be *very* expensive. Freshwater pearls, natural or cultured, may also be dyed. When buying freshwater pearls, be sure to ask if the color is natural.

Another interesting feature of freshwater pearls is that they can be worn singly or grouped in alternating colors, either hanging straight or twisted for a distinctive effect. In addition to the versatility offered by the many color options, the lower cost of most freshwater pearls makes it possible to buy many strands and create an almost endless variety of looks.

Baroque Pearls

A baroque pearl, technically, is any pearl that is not "round" and has an interesting irregular shape (don't confuse it with a round pearl that is simply "out-of-round"—it must have a distinctive enough shape to be interesting and attractive). Baroque pearls are produced by both saltwater and freshwater mollusks and can be natural or cultured. They have a distinctive appeal because of their very beautiful tints of color and iridescent flashes. Their irregular shape renders them far less valuable than round pearls. Nonetheless, they make beautiful, versatile fashion accessories.

Today's Pearl Market Is Filled with Variety

In addition to the Japanese Akoya and Chinese freshwater cultured pearls, here are some of the most popular varieties from which to choose.

Mabé pearl (Mobe).   A dome-shaped pearl, available in a variety of colors and shapes, the most common being round or pear-shaped. This is an *assembled* "blister" pearl (a hollow blister that forms on the side of the interior of the oyster, which is removed and then filled). It has a very thin nacre coating, an epoxy center, and a mother-of-pearl backing. These pearls are produced very inexpensively and require extra care, but they provide a very large, attractive look at affordable prices, compared with other pearls of similar size. They are especially popular for earrings and rings.

Solid blister pearl.   A dome-shaped pearl similar to the mabé but not assembled, this type of pearl is produced in freshwater lakes in Tennessee. It's available in several shapes and has a distinctive appearance created by a mother-of-pearl background, retained from the shell lining when the pearl is removed. These pearls also have an unusually high luster and a lovely iridescent play of color across the surface. They are more expensive than mabé pearls, but also more durable.

South Sea pearl.   Most are produced in the waters off Australia, Indonesia, and the Philippines in saltwater oysters—a much larger variety than the Japanese oyster, which exceed a foot in diameter. South Sea pearls usually start at about 10 millimeters in size and go up from there. Pearls from 11 to 14 millimeters are the average. Pearls over 16 millimeters are considered very large. The South Sea specimens are often less perfectly round and have a less intense luster than their smaller Japanese counterparts, but they are very beautiful and very expensive. The rarest, most expensive color is a warm pinkish white, but the silvery white is perhaps more in demand and therefore also expensive. Yellow whites also exist, but they are the least popular and sell for much less. "Fancy" intense yellows (truly rich yellow, not in any way to be confused with off-white or yellow white) and a wide variety of hues, including many golden tones, are now in great demand. These are less expensive than the finest whites, but they can still be expensive. South Sea pearls are rare in fine qualities and are more expensive than most other pearls.

"Tahitian" black pearl.   This large pearl is produced by a black-lipped saltwater oyster unique to the waters of French Polynesia and the Cook Islands. The pearls range from gray to black in color, and the color is natural; both *natural pearls* with natural black color and *cultured pearls* with natural black color have been found. These varieties are distinctive because of their unusual shades of color, including tones of gray,

blue gray, gunmetal gray, brown black, or greenish black. The color in the Tahitian black pearl, however, is often not uniform throughout. The pearl can be black on one end and much lighter on the other end. The rarest and most expensive color in Tahitian black pearls is black with an iridescent peacock green overtone. Tahitian black pearls are seldom smaller than 8 millimeters. They are rarely perfectly round. Teardrop-shaped baroque pearls are more common. As with other South Sea pearls, these are rare and expensive. Remember, however, not to confuse natural black color with a natural pearl; most are cultured. In addition, beware of irradiated or dyed black pearls, which are common and inexpensive.

Choosing Your Pearls

When buying pearls, it's important to take the time to compare the various types, sizes, and qualities to develop an eye for differences. Here are some suggestions you might find helpful:

- *Compare the quality factors* as you shop. Pay attention to differences in luster and orient, color/tint, cleanliness, roundness, and size. Pay special attention to the luster and orient. This is the most important quality factor you should learn to judge.

  You should also weigh the innumerable variables in quality against each other: if luster is good, roundness may be poor; if roundness is good, luster may be poor; if luster and color are good, the pearls may not have clean surfaces; shape may be good, but matching in the strand may be poor. You can learn a great deal about pearl quality simply by looking.
- *Examine pearls against your own neck and face* to be sure the color of the pearls suits your skin and hair coloring.
- *Ask whether or not the color is natural,* especially when you are considering colored pearls (gray, blue, black, etc.). Pearls of natural color often sell for much more than white pearls, whereas dyed pearls should sell for much less. If the color is natural, be sure it is so stated on the bill of sale.
- *Compare size.* As you shop, ask what size the pearls are, and compare differences in cost for the same quality in different sizes. A double strand of smaller pearls may create an equally lovely appearance and cost less than a single strand of larger pearls.

Pearl beds being tended in freshwater lakes in Tennessee. American Pearl
Company founder John Latendresse was the leading pioneer
in American cultured pearl production.

- *Be sure to ask whether or not the pearls are genuine or simulated,* and be sure that "genuine cultured" or "genuine natural"
  is in writing on the bill of sale. Don't be afraid to use the tooth
  test; it won't harm the pearls (but remove lipstick first).

Shopping around can be of tremendous help before you buy pearls.
It will help you become familiar with the wide range of pearls available
within your price range; it will also develop your eye to distinguish quality differences, and help you decide what color, size, and shape is best
for you. If you take the time to follow our advice, your pearls will give
you unending pleasure and pride.

There have been many new developments in the field of pearl culturing, and more nations than ever before are now culturing pearls. It is not
possible to adequately cover pearls in the space allocated here. For those
with a special interest in pearls, we recommend *The Pearl Book: The
Definitive Buying Guide—How to Select, Buy, Care For & Enjoy Pearls*
by Antoinette Matlins, which provides comprehensive information about
all types of pearls, from every country, including the latest in treatments
and enhancements.

PART FOUR

Design & Style:
Getting the Look You Want

17

Rare and Precious:
Gold & Platinum

Gold—The Timeless Choice

Gold jewelry is very popular today and is available in more styles, colors, and finishes than ever before. It is also a very popular choice for setting gemstones. But it is very important to understand gold and the differences that affect price, in order to avoid confusion about the wide range of prices that seems to pervade the market for what may *appear* to be the "same thing." As with gems, wherever there are significant price differences there are usually quality differences. The key to getting good value in gold is understanding what accounts for differences in quality and price.

What Is Gold?

Gold is one of the world's most precious metals. It is so soft and workable that one ounce can be stretched into a wire five miles long, or hammered into a sheet so thin that it could cover a hundred square feet. It is one of our rarest metals, and since pure gold doesn't rust or corrode, it can last forever. Interestingly, gold is present almost everywhere around us—in the earth's crust, in seas and rivers, and in plants—but it is very difficult and expensive to extract. Approximately two-and-a-half to three tons of ore are needed to extract one ounce of gold.

Most Gold Used in Jewelry Is an Alloy

Gold is the most popular metal used for jewelry today. The simple gold wedding band probably accounts for more of the world's gold than any other single type of jewelry. But pure gold is very soft, so it is usually

211

mixed with other metals to make it stronger and prevent it from bending too easily. When two or more metals are mixed together, we call the resulting product an *alloy*. Most gold used in jewelry is an alloy—and the metals added to the gold are also called alloys.

What Is a Karat? Or Is It Carat?

In jewelry, the term *carat* (or karat) has a double meaning: *carat* is used as a measurement of weight for gemstones, with one carat weighing ⅕ gram; *carat* is also used in countries around the world to indicate the amount of pure gold in a piece of gold jewelry. In the United States, however, when the word is used to indicate gold content rather than gemstone weight, it is spelled with a K—hence karat—to avoid confusion. Jewelry should always be marked to indicate how much pure gold it contains.

In the United States, a karat mark, abbreviated to K or KT, indicates the amount of pure gold present in the metal. The word *karat* (carat) is derived from the word for the fruit of the carob tree: in Italian, *carato*; in Arabic, *qirat*; in Greek, *keration*. The seeds of the fruit were used in ancient times for weighing gems. Also, the pure gold Byzantine coin called the solidus weighed 24 karats. Therefore, a 24-karat mark (24K or 24KT) became the mark used to indicate that something was pure gold.

To understand the concept as applied to gold, imagine that "pure gold" is a pie divided into 24 equal "slices," or parts. Each karat equals one part of the pie. So, 24K would mean that 24 parts (out of a total of 24) are gold. In other words, 24K would be 100 percent gold, or pure gold. In 18K gold jewelry, 18 parts are pure gold and 6 are another metal (or, 18/24 = ¾ = 75 percent pure gold); in 12K, 12 parts are pure gold, 12 parts another metal (12/24 = ½ = 50 percent pure gold). And so on.

In some cultures, 24K gold jewelry is required for certain jewelry pieces, but it's generally agreed that 24K (pure) gold is too soft for jewelry use. In some parts of the world, 18K or 20K is preferred because of its brighter yellow color and because it is considered "purer" and more precious. In the United States, 14K or 18K gold is preferred because it is more durable than higher-karat gold. We usually caution clients about the risk of high-karat gold (20K, 22K, or 24K) for a gem-studded setting because the prongs can be too easily bent open accidentally, resulting in loss of stones.

In some countries, such as Italy, the percentage of pure gold is indicated by a number representing how many parts—out of a total of 1,000 parts—are pure gold. One thousand parts would be the equivalent of 24K. Seven hundred fifty means that 750 parts out of 1,000 are pure gold: 750/1,000 = 75/100 = ¾ = 75 percent pure gold. This corresponds to 18K.

The following table shows how different international gold markings correspond to one another.

Gold Marks

American Marking (Karatage)	Pure Gold Content (Fineness in Percent)	European Marking
24K	100	1,000
22K	91.6	916
20K	83	833
19K (used in Portugal)	79.2	792
18K	75.0	750
15K (seen in antiques)	62.5	625
14K	58.3	585
12K	50.0	500
10K	41.7	417
9K	37.5	375

New Titanium Alloy Increases Strength and Versatility

A new alloy—gold 990—combines gold with a very small amount of titanium. The result is almost pure gold (990/1,000 gold), with greatly increased durability. The titanium produces a color that is much less yellow than what one expects from such a high-karat gold, closely resembling straw and similar to the color of 14K gold. This has reduced its universal appeal. Nonetheless, it offers the preciousness of high-karat gold with added durability.

A Word about Russian Marks

Old timepieces made in Russia were marked to indicate the content based on its equivalent to a zolotnik. A piece marked 96 contained as much gold as 96 zolotniks, which equals pure gold; 72 equals 18K (750); 56 equals 14K (585).

To Be Called Gold, What Is the Minimum Gold Content?

Many countries have established minimum standards that must be met for items to be legally called gold. The laws governing the actual content of gold required in a piece of jewelry, however, vary. In the United States, to be called gold, the item must be at least 10K; in England and Canada, 9K; in Italy and France, 18K.

The Many Colors of Gold

Pure gold is always yellow. But because pure gold is too soft for most jewelry use and must be mixed with other metals (alloys) to increase its hardness, the color can also be modified by adding varying amounts of these other metals. Those usually added to gold for jewelry use include copper, zinc, silver, nickel, platinum, and palladium (a metal in the platinum family). Depending on which alloys are used, a variety of colors can be produced. Another practice is to plate 14K gold jewelry with 18K for an 18K look—that is, a stronger yellow color. White gold is also frequently plated with rhodium, a rare and more expensive metal from the platinum family, to create a whiter, brighter finish.

Using some combination of one or more metal alloys will result in various colors. Several avant-garde designers are now producing jewelry in exciting new colors—including *black* gold, *brown* gold, and *blue* gold—to create dramatic new looks (see color insert).

What causes skin discoloration with some gold jewelry? Pure gold

---

How Alloys Affect Color

Color	Composition
Yellow gold	Gold, copper, silver
White gold	Gold, nickel,* zinc, silver, platinum, palladium
Green gold	Gold, silver (much more than in yellow gold), copper, zinc
Pink (red) gold	Gold, copper (sometimes a small amount of silver is used)

*Note: some people are allergic to nickel and should not wear white gold containing nickel. For this reason, a white gold alloyed with palladium is being used by some manufacturers. White gold that contains palladium will be more expensive than yellow gold or white gold containing another alloy, but it is still less expensive than all platinum.

doesn't tarnish and won't discolor the skin, but *alloys* in the gold can corrode and produce discoloration to the skin in contact with the gold, especially under moist or damp conditions. The fats and fatty acids present in perspiration can set up a corrosive reaction, and the problem can be worse in warm, humid areas, especially where chloride (salt) is in the air.

Smog can also be a problem. Smog fumes can introduce chemicals that cause the alloys in gold to tarnish. The tarnish then rubs off, discoloring skin or clothing.

Cosmetics may be the culprit. Another common cause of discoloration is metallic abrasion caused by some makeup. Some makeup contains compounds that are actually harder than the jewelry with which it comes into contact. As the harder compounds rub against the jewelry they cause tiny particles of metal to flake off, forming a darkish-looking dust. When this dust makes contact with a soft, absorbent surface such as skin or clothing, it forms a black smudge.

There are several possible solutions to the problem of skin discoloration. First, get into the habit of removing jewelry often and cleansing the skin that has touched it with soap and water. Keep your jewelry clean as well, and wipe it periodically with a soft cloth to remove tarnish. Next, try using an absorbent body powder, one free of abrasives, on all areas of your skin that are in contact with jewelry.

Pay attention to the design of jewelry you select if skin discoloration seems to be a problem. Wide shanks can cause perspiration, and rings with an inner concave surface can cause moisture and contaminants to collect, causing both discoloration and dermatitis.

Finally, try switching to a higher gold content or to a different manufacturer. The higher the gold content, the less likely it is that discoloration will occur, because in the higher-karat gold there is less of the alloy—such as copper, silver, or nickel—that might corrode. People who have a problem wearing 14K gold jewelry may find that the problem disappears with 18K gold.

Sometimes simply changing to a similar product made by a different manufacturer may solve the problem. For example, a 14K yellow gold bracelet made by one manufacturer may cause discoloration, while a similar bracelet made by another manufacturer may not. This does not mean that one product is inferior to the other. Manufacturers often use different combinations of alloys, or different percentages or ratios of alloys.

They may look the same, but you might find you can wear one manu-facturer's line better than that of another.

Since different metals and different ratios are used to produce differ-ent colors, discoloration may result when you are wearing one particu-lar color of gold but not with other colors. If there seems to be a problem with wearing white gold, try a white gold alloyed with platinum rather than nickel, since platinum won't corrode.

Determining Value Requires More Than a Scale!

- *Weight* is one factor that goes into determining the value of a piece of gold jewelry. Gold is usually sold by weight, in grams or pennyweights. There are 20 pennyweights to one ounce; if you multiply grams by 0.643, you will have the number of penny-weights. Weight is important because it is an indication of the actual amount of pure gold in the piece. However, it is only one factor to consider. When you are buying gold from a gold man-ufacturer, for example, factored into the price per gram is the cost of gold *plus* the cost for labor and workmanship. The price always takes into consideration (1) the type of *construction,* (2) the means of *production,* and (3) how the piece is *finished.*

- **Design and construction** are important not only because of the piece's finished look but also because specific details in the over-all design and construction affect comfort, wearability, and ease in putting the piece on or taking it off. Good design requires excellent designers as well as extra care and attention to small mechanical details. This adds to the cost of any piece of jewelry.

  In addition, jewelry design is also becoming recognized as an art, and jewelry designers as artists. Some award-winning designers command top dollar, as do top painters, sculptors, and other artists. A piece of gold jewelry made by a fine design-er, especially if it is a one-of-a-kind or limited-edition piece, will sometimes sell for much more than another piece of mass-produced gold jewelry of the same weight and gold content.

  In looking at a piece of gold jewelry, you must also consider the type of construction necessary to create a particular design or look. Is the construction simple or complex? Did the piece require extensive labor or minimal labor? Did it require special skill, talent, or equipment?

To ignore the design and construction factors and assign a value to a piece of gold jewelry based on gold content (i.e., 14K, 18K) and weight alone would be equivalent to placing a value on a painting based on the cost of paint and canvas alone.

- *Production* can affect price significantly. Is the piece produced by machine or by hand? The type of construction required to create a particular design may require that it be made entirely, or in part, by hand, while others can be completely made by machine. Some designs may be produced either way, but those done by hand will have a different look, feel, and cost.

- *Finish* is where we take into account the care and labor costs associated with the actual finishing of the piece. For example, are any special skills or techniques required to put on the final touches that make the piece distinctive, such as engraving, milgraining, hammering, or granulation? Here we also need to note whether or not the piece has been carefully polished to remove any scratches that might diminish its beauty, or rough edges that might be abrasive or catch or snag on fabric. Consider whether the item was hand polished or machine polished; some pieces are machine made but finished by hand. We must also take into consideration any special finishes to the metal itself, such as a florentine, matte, or sand-blasted finish. Each step in the process, and each special step or skill required, adds—sometimes dramatically—to the cost.

Adding It All Up

Many pieces of gold jewelry look alike at first glance. When they are examined carefully, however, it often becomes clear where the differences lie, both in quality and in cost. Ask your jeweler to help you understand these differences by comparing different qualities for you. Only after carefully evaluating all of these factors can you appreciate gold jewelry and recognize cost differences and real value.

Is That "Bargain" Really a Bargain?

Beware of *underkarating,* which is a serious problem around the world. If a piece of gold jewelry is underkarated, it means that the jewelry is marked to indicate a certain gold content but actually contains less than is indicated. Needless to say, retailers who knowingly sell under-karated gold jewelry create the impression that they are giving you a bargain because their prices are so low, but if there is actually less gold (and more alloy, so the piece would have a comparable weight to that of others you might be considering), you aren't getting any bargain. Unfortunately, most people never learn that they have bought underkarated gold. We know of people who bought gold jewelry marked 14K or 18K and found out later that it was only 8K or 10K—or less! Thus, it is very important to buy gold jewelry from a reputable source, one that makes the effort to check its gold shipments carefully.

Look for a manufacturer's registered trademark. Being sure gold is properly represented in terms of its value is what really matters; you should get what you pay for. Buying from a reliable source is the first step. In addition, be sure to look for a manufacturer's registered trademark: a mark stamped near the karat mark. To avoid being held liable themselves, more and more jewelers are buying only from manufacturers willing to stamp what they make with their own mark: a mark registered with the U.S. Patent and Trademark Office. Buying gold with a manufacturer's trademark is one way to help assure you get what you pay for, since the product can be traced to a specific manufacturer whose name and reputation are on the line.

Fine, expensive gold jewelry should always be tested. While testing for *exact gold content* requires assaying, it is usually relatively easy to detect any underkarating that is serious enough to affect the value of a specific piece of jewelry and the price paid. Any jeweler or gemologist-appraiser can make such a determination, in most cases, quickly and easily, with only a gold tester or by using the streak test. You should be aware that with an electronic gold tester, some very heavily plated pieces might give a false reading indicating gold when the piece is only base metal. For this reason the streak test is better, but the person doing the test must be sure to take a file or carbide scriber and make a very deep scratch in order to penetrate the plating for an accurate test.

There are strict laws pertaining to gold content and marks used to indicate it. Take the time to understand what you are buying, buy only from a reputable source, and be sure to have it tested. If you do, your gold jewelry will give you a lifetime of pleasure.

Platinum: Cool, Classic and Contemporary

Platinum is even more rare and valuable than gold. The platinum family is composed of six elements—platinum, palladium, iridium, osmium, rhodium, and ruthenium. These six silvery-white metals are generally found together in nature, with platinum and palladium the most abundant, and iridium and ruthenium the rarest (and most expensive). Platinum is rarer and heavier than other precious metals and is the purest metal—often referred to as the "noblest." Because platinum is so pure, it does not cause allergic reactions. This is very important to people who are sensitive to the base metals used in many other metal alloys, which can cause a wide range of reactions from skin irritation or discoloration to hay fever and asthma. In addition, platinum is much stronger than other precious metals, and more malleable, which makes it easier for a jeweler to maneuver around a fragile stone with less risk of damaging it. Because of these qualities, fine jewelers often prefer working in platinum, especially for intricate pieces.

Platinum Marks

Unlike gold, platinum is not identified by karat marks. The amount of pure platinum is indicated in *parts per thousand* (ppt) of pure platinum. In the United States, jewelry that contains at least 950 parts-per-thousand pure platinum can be referred to as "platinum," with no qualifiers. Such pieces will be marked with the word platinum, the abbreviation PLAT, or using the numeric indicator, pt950 or 950Plat. Platinum pieces that contain less than 950 ppt must be described accordingly and the pure platinum content indicated in the mark. For example, platinum jewelry that contains 900 parts per thousand pure platinum would be marked "900Plat" or "900Pt." Jewelry containing 850 ppt would be marked "850Plat" or "850Pt" (this usually applies only to platinum chain, which has been alloyed with a higher percentage of other metals for added strength and flexibility). In the United States, a two-letter or four-letter abbreviation for the word platinum is permitted. *Platinum consisting of 500 parts per thousand pure platinum or less cannot be called platinum or marked with the word platinum or any abbreviation for platinum.*

Platinum articles that combine pure platinum with other platinum group members will also be marked accordingly. For example,

900Pt/100Ir would indicate 900 parts per thousand pure platinum and 100 parts per thousand of iridium. This was once the most commonly used platinum alloy in the U.S. Older pieces may be stamped "900Pt" or "900 Plat" without any indication that there is also iridium because it was understood that "900 platinum" would always be alloyed with 100 parts of iridium. Some older pieces will still have the stamp IRIDPLAT or the stamp "90% platinum 10% iridium" inside.

Platinum Alloys Old and New

Typically, platinum is alloyed for added strength, usually combining pure platinum with another rare platinum group metal to maintain its purity. Today there are a growing number of new platinum alloys on the market that have been created for different functions that make platinum easier to manufacture for different types of jewelry. For example, there are *hard cast* alloys that are desirable for "tension" mountings, and *heat treatable* alloys can be hardened for extra durability, after the piece has been made. Platinum/iridium is used for fabrication of jewelry, platinum/ruthenium is used for machine-made wedding rings, and platinum/cobalt is designed to provide the finest detailing in castings. The specific alloy combinations are proprietary, but platinum is most often alloyed with other platinum family members (although copper, tungsten, cobalt and gold can also be used in platinum alloys). Unlike gold alloys, there are very minor color differences regardless of the alloy used. More importantly, the pure platinum content in the various combinations found in today's platinum alloys has remained very high—at least 90 percent (except in platinum chain)—and primarily alloyed only with platinum group metals to protect its reputation as the purest and most "noble" metal.

Low "Karat" Platinum? In recent years, several platinum alloys have entered the marketplace not for the purpose of adding strength or to make it easier to manufacture specific types of jewelry in platinum, but in an effort to provide more affordable white-metal alternatives to 950-platinum.

In our discussion of white gold we have already mentioned the platinum/gold alloy that provides a nickel-free "white" gold alternative. This product eliminates the risk of possible allergic reaction to the nickel used to create "white" gold, and it is also attractive because, while more expensive than nickel-alloyed white gold, it is still more affordable than platinum. This product, however, is not described as a "platinum" product but as a "white gold alternative."

Today, new "platinum" products such as "karat platinum" have been created and are expected to be available soon. These new alloys contain much less platinum (most have only 585 parts per thousand of pure platinum, or less), making them much more affordable than other platinum alloys and more affordable than the platinum-alloyed white gold. The proposed mark for the new "karat platinum" alloy is "585Plat.0PGM." This indicates that there are 585 parts per thousand of pure platinum, and *no platinum group metals;* "karat platinum" is alloyed with a combination of copper and cobalt. This affordable new alloy is already finding retailers eager to offer it to customers. It could become a very attractive alternative to people looking for a nickel free, white-metal alternative that is even more affordable than the platinum/gold alloy currently available.

There is some concern that such platinum alloys will confuse consumers about what they are really buying. More importantly, because they don't meet the purity standards that have long set platinum apart from other precious metals, many jewelry industry groups are recommending that jewelry must contain at least 850 parts per thousand of platinum in order to be marked or sold as "platinum." The FTC is currently examining the issues surrounding "karat platinum" and similar alloys and reviewing its current platinum guide in regard to how such alloys should be described and marked in order to avoid confusion or misrepresentation. This may delay entry into the marketplace but we expect to see exciting new jewelry creations fashioned from these new alloys in the not-too-distant future.

Rhodium Plating Adds Whiteness and Brightness

The brightest and most reflective of all the platinum family members is *rhodium.* Because of these qualities it is frequently used to coat silver, gold, and palladium jewelry, and as an electroplate finish. Rhodium is harder and whiter even than platinum, and highly resistant to corrosion. Because rhodium is so hard, it does not wear off as quickly as yellow gold plating.

Rhodium plating can eliminate allergic reactions to base metals. White gold that has been alloyed with nickel or other base metals *should* be rhodium-plated, especially 10-karat or 14-karat white gold. The rhodium plating eliminates skin contact with the base metal in the alloy and thus eliminates any possible allergic reaction that the wearer might have to one of the alloys used to transform the color of yellow gold to white.

Rhodium alchemy. Another use for rhodium plating is to change the color of yellow gold jewelry to "platinum" white. People who have inherited jewelry, for example, that is yellow gold rather than white, or whose own metal color preference has changed over time, can simply take it to a jeweler to have it rhodium-plated. This will change the color to platinum-white, and because of rhodium's hardness, the color transformation can last for a very long time. When the yellow begins to show through, you can simply have it replated with rhodium at a nominal charge.

Yellow Gold, White Gold, or Platinum— Which One?

The first choice you must make is one of color. This selection usually depends on personal preference, skin tone, and the color of other jewelry you may own. Remember when considering yellow gold that it is available in several different hues, which include a greenish-yellow and a pinkish-yellow.

If your choice is yellow, the only decision you must make is whether you prefer 14-karat, 18-karat, or a higher karat gold. On a limited budget, 14-karat is more affordable. It is also harder than 18-karat. One noticeable difference is that 18-karat yellow gold is a brighter gold (and 20-karat to 24-karat has an even brighter, more vivid yellow color). If you prefer the brighter yellow but can't afford higher karat gold, ask for 14-karat gold with an 18-karat finish. After several years the finish may wear off, but you can have a jeweler restore it at a reasonable price.

If you prefer a white metal, your choice may be more difficult. While white gold and platinum may look quite similar, they are distinctly different metals. As we have mentioned, platinum is much more expensive, so if you have a limited budget, white gold may be the better choice. In addition to being more affordable, 18-karat white gold is harder and more resistant to scratches than most platinum alloys (see below). On the other hand, white gold often exhibits a brownish or yellowish cast which must be covered with rhodium-plating; the plating will wear off over an extended period of time, but as with gold-plating, a jeweler can have it replated at a modest cost.

One significant disadvantage of white gold is that it is more brittle than both platinum and yellow gold. Because of this, be sure to have your jeweler check the prongs of a white gold setting at least once a year. White gold is also subject to stress corrosion, which does not occur in platinum. And there is the allergy consideration; nickel-alloyed white gold can result in a range of allergic reactions, some serious, which has led the European community to ban its use in jewelry. For this reason, platinum-alloyed white gold—or perhaps the new "585Plat" alloy—make a better choice for those who cannot afford platinum.

Platinum is somewhat softer but it is more malleable than white gold, making it an ideal choice for very intricate settings that require intensive labor. It is much easier to use platinum for pavé work—that is, designs in which the stones are set as closely together as possible, as though the surface were "paved" with stones. With platinum, the jeweler can also make a safer setting because a larger prong can be used, since platinum conforms so easily to the shape of the stone, reducing the risk of damage. The most important benefit of platinum is that, while it is softer than white gold and can scratch, it is more durable and does not wear down or abrade like gold. Therefore, over time, platinum settings hold up and last longer than gold ones.

Today there are more styles in platinum, and platinum and gold combinations, than ever before, and the introduction of the new platinum alloys we discussed earlier is also having a positive effect on the increasing availability of platinum designs.

In the final analysis, it is up to you to weigh the advantages and disadvantages of each in terms of your own needs. Whichever precious metal you choose, you can find many beautiful styles and designs. With proper care, whatever choice you make should last a lifetime.

Non-Traditional Metals Find Jewelry Niche: Titanium, Stainless Steel, and Tungsten

Some of today's newest jewelry designers seeking bold, comfortable, and often more-affordable alternatives to gold, silver, and platinum, have focused the spotlight on non-traditional metals: titanium, stainless steel, and tungsten. These metals have a lot to offer. All three are very comfortable, wearable, and low-maintenance. Designers are producing pieces made entirely of one of these metals, which have particular appeal to men as well as women, and also in combination with 14- or 18-karat yellow gold, platinum, and silver. Some incorporate diamonds and gemstones into their creations, while others are having fun with other non-traditional jewelry materials such as rubber, leather, and wood. These new metals are also becoming popular choices for wedding rings.

Titanium

Ed Mirell's winning *titanium* and *blue anodized-titanium* and diamond men's accessory collection.

Best known for its uses in space exploration and bicycle frames, titanium is an affordable newcomer to the jewelry scene that has become very popular. It offers an attractive white-metal look when used alone, or a straw-yellow look when alloyed with gold (see page 213). It can also be alloyed with other metals to create other colors (see color insert), such as black, or to display incredible rainbow iridescence. It is lightweight, resistant to saltwater and sun damage, and hypoallergenic. In addition, it won't dent or tarnish.

William Richey's stainless steel cufflinks include all stainless steel, stainless steel and 18K yellow gold, with or without diamonds.

Stainless Steel

Stainless steel is becoming one of the hottest metals on the jewelry scene. Many designers like to combine it with gold because its gray color blends so well with pink gold and yellow gold to create interesting design contrast (see color insert), but stainless steel is being used increasingly on its own. Forged stainless steel is maintenance-free—it will not rust or oxidize—and this durable metal makes a strong, clean statement at a very affordable price.

Tungsten

Tungsten is an unusually hard, dense metal. Its weight is comparable to 18-karat gold, which makes it especially attractive to men seeking a ring with heft. When processed with carbon and other elements to form tungsten carbide, it becomes a very durable, scratch resistant metal. It is the world's hardest metallic substance—*approximately ten times harder than 18-karat gold, and four times harder than titanium*—and produces an intense polish that will last longer than other metals. For this reason, it requires special equipment and the use of diamond abrasives to work the metal. This adds significantly to its cost, and also limits the type of jewelry currently available. At this time, only rings are being produced from tungsten, and their price is significantly higher than titanium

Rings from Trent West's TrewTungsten® line: tungsten with yellow gold inlay and tungsten with platinum inlay and diamond.

or stainless steel; the cost of tungsten is roughly comparable to the cost of 18-karat or platinum rings (see color insert).

The tungsten customer is not drawn to tungsten for its cost, but rather for its character and durability. Its dark gray color is distinctive on its own, and it also provides a striking contrast when used with gold or platinum inlay. Used alone, or in combination with other precious metals and diamonds, tungsten rings make a singular statement, one that seems destined to shine brightly into future generations.

18

Choosing the Setting

The setting you choose will be determined primarily by your personal taste. Nevertheless, it is a good idea to be familiar with a few of the most common settings so that you have a working vocabulary and some idea of what is available.

Bezel setting. With a bezel setting, a rim holds the stone and completely surrounds the gem. Bezels can have straight edges, scalloped edges, or any molded shape that accommodates the stone. The backs can be open or closed. One advantage of the bezel setting is that it can make a stone look larger. The bezel setting can also conceal nicks or chips on the girdle and protect the girdle of the stone from chips and nicks.

Bezel-set center stones with "grosgrain textured" platinum and 18K gold

Keep in mind that if you use yellow gold in a bezel setting, the yellow of the bezel surrounding the stone will be reflected into the stone, causing a white stone to appear less white. On the other hand, a yellow gold bezel can make a red stone such as ruby look even redder or an emerald look greener.

Partial bezel-set solitaire

A variation on the bezel setting is the collet setting, which has a similar appearance to the bezel setting but involves the use of gold tubing.

Prong setting. Prong settings are perhaps the most common type of setting. They come in an almost infinite variety. There are four-prong, six-prong, and special styles such as Belcher, Fishtail, and six-prong Tiffany. In addition, prongs can be pointed, rounded, flat,

Graceful intertwined prongs
hold these diamonds
in five-stone bands.

V-shaped prongs
protect point of heart.

In this grouping, lower ring
shows gypsy setting; upper
ring shows collet setting.

Channel-set baguettes
in a wedding band

or V-shaped. Extra prongs provide added security for the stone and can make a stone look slightly larger. However, too many prongs holding too small a stone can over-power the stone, making the stone look smaller and the mounting look heavy. When setting a marquise, heart shape, or pear shape, we recommend that the point or points be held by a V-shaped prong, which will best protect the point(s). For emerald-cut stones that have "canted" corners (a corner with a small diagonal edge rather than forming a 90° angle), flat prongs are the preferred choice.

Gypsy setting. In this type of setting, the metal at the top of the ring (around the stone) is much heavier than the shank. The stone is set flush into a hole at the top.

Illusion setting. The illusion setting is used to make the mounted stone appear larger. There are numerous styles from which to choose.

Flat-top and bead settings. In a flat-top setting, a faceted stone is placed into a hole in the flat top of the metal and then held in place by small chips of metal attached by solder at the stone's girdle. Sometimes these metal chips are worked into small beads, so this setting is some-times called a bead setting.

Channel setting. This setting is used exten-sively today, especially for wedding bands. The stones are set into a channel with no metal sep-arating them. In some cases, the channel can continue completely around the ring, so that the piece has a continuous row of stones.

Bar setting. This setting, which resembles a channel setting, combines the contemporary and classic looks. It is used in a circular band, and instead of prongs, each stone is held in the ring by a long thin bar, shared between two stones.

Bar-set bands

Pavé setting. This setting is used for numerous small stones set together in a cluster with no metal showing through. The impression is that the piece is entirely paved with stones. The setting can be flat or dome-shaped, and can be worked so that the piece almost appears to be one large single stone. Fine pavé work can be very expensive.

Cluster setting. A cluster setting usually consists of one large stone and several smaller stones as accents. A cluster setting is designed to create a lovely larger piece from several small stones.

Fine pavé work in diamond and pearl engagement rings and in a wedding band

Micro-pavé. This describes intricate pavé work using extremely small diamonds set into delicate frames, the baskets holding the stones, the front and side sections, and even into the prongs themselves.

Distinctive Contemporary Settings

Today there are many interesting and distinctive designs offering something for everyone. Fine casting houses produce top-quality settings that

Very tiny diamonds cover all visible metal—even the prongs—in this *micro-pavé* ring.

simply await the stones to finish them off. Some firms produce semi-mounts: settings complete with side stones, awaiting only your center stone. These can provide affordable and easy solutions to creating a new ring, or remounting stones from another piece.

An increasing number of custom jewelry designers also cater to today's market (see color section). International jewelry design competitions such as the Spectrum Awards designer competition sponsored by the American Gem Trade Association (AGTA), or the Diamonds-International Awards sponsored by the Diamond Information Center, provide a showcase for their work. The result is an almost limitless choice, ranging from bold sculpted gold and platinum combinations to intricate antique reproductions.

Settings to Suit Your Lifestyle

It is important to consider your lifestyle when selecting any piece of jewelry. Be realistic about the wear and tear a ring or bracelet might take, and remember that no piece of jewelry is indestructible. Remember that even diamond, the hardest natural substance known, can chip or break if exposed to a sharp, accidental blow.

Active outdoor types, for example, might be better off avoiding jewelry like a ring containing a marquise or pear-shaped stone, since both these shapes have points. Points are more vulnerable to chipping or breaking, which could result from the kind of sudden or sharp blow an active person might subject a stone to.

In addition, the shank as well as the prongs of a ring will show the effects of wear; any detailing on a ring will blur over time, as the result of gardening, playing on the beach, mountain climbing, handling ski equipment or bicycles, or any other kind of repeated contact or use.

Classic four- or six-prong settings served a less active generation well but may not be as suitable for today's woman. If your daily schedule features a great deal of activity, you would be wise to consider a sturdier jewelry style, keeping in mind that *sturdy* and *graceful* are not mutually exclusive. For example, a bezel setting might be better suited to your activity level. This choice won't detract from a gemstone's brilliance, yet it will afford you and your fine gems greater security.

Since everyday activities can loosen a setting as easily as more strenuous ones can, it is important to have a reputable jeweler check mountings and settings once every six months. Chlorine attacks soldering links and stress points, so if you swim regularly in a chlorinated pool, take your jewelry off first.

In terms of ring design, while rings are usually round, fingers aren't. Top-heavy rings will turn on the finger unless the diameter, or outline, is square or stirrup-shaped to conform to the shape of the finger. Also, remember that rings worn together side by side quickly begin to wear on each other.

Tips for Selecting the Right Style

1. Set a realistic budget range to eliminate confusion and temptation that can result in disappointment.
2. Shop around and familiarize yourself with current styles to educate your eye and learn what really appeals to you.
3. Try on different styles. Jewelry looks different when you see it *on*. This holds true of rings especially. We've seen many men and women insist they don't like a particular ring in a showcase, and then love it when they try it on.
4. If you're trying to achieve an impressive look with smaller stones, consider interesting jackets for earrings, or inserts or wraps for rings. These enable you to slip your ring or studs into another piece (usually gold, platinum, or silver, sometimes with stones) and instantly create a larger look.
5. If selecting an engagement ring, remember that you will also be wearing a wedding band. Be sure to select a style that will complement the type of wedding band you are considering.

International Ring Size Equivalents

American	English	French/Japanese	Metric
½	A	–	37.8252
¾	A½	–	38.4237
1	B	–	39.0222
1¼	B½	–	39.6207
1½	C	–	40.2192
1¾	C½	–	40.8177
2	D	1	41.4162
2¼	D½	2	42.0147
2½	E	–	42.6132
2¾	E½	3	43.2117
3	F	4	43.8102
3¼	F½	–	44.4087
3¼	G	5	45.0072
3½	G½	–	45.6057
3¾	H	6	46.2042
4	H½	–	46.8027
4¼	I	7	47.4012
4½	I½	8	47.9997
4¾	J	–	48.5982
5	J½	9	49.1967
5¼	K	10	49.7952
5½	K½	–	50.3937
5¾	L	11	50.9922
6	L½	–	51.5907
6¼	M	12	52.1892
6½	M½	13	52.7877
6¾	N	–	53.4660
7	N½	14	54.1044
7	O	15	54.7428
7¼	O½	–	55.3812
7½	P	16	56.0196
7¾	P½	–	56.6580
8	Q	17	57.2964
8¼	Q½	18	57.9348
8½	R	–	58.5732
8¾	R½	19	59.2116
9	S	20	59.8500
9¼	S½	–	60.4884
9½	T	21	61.1268
9¾	T½	22	61.7652
10	U	–	62.4026
10¼	U½	23	63.0420
10½	V	24	63.6804
10¾	V½	–	64.3188
11	W	25	64.8774
11¼	W½	–	65.4759
11½	X	26	66.0744
11¾	X½	–	66.6729
12	Y	–	67.2714
12¼	Y½	–	67.8699
12½	Z	–	68.4684

19

Antique and Period Jewelry: Back by Popular Demand

Interest in beautiful antique and period jewelry has soared in recent years. Lovely pieces from ages past often exhibit unusual design, intricate workmanship, and exceptional gemstones rarely found in new jewelry creations. No one can deny their allure, but as we have discussed in previous chapters, it is important to know what to *look for* and what to *look out for.* Indeed, when it comes to "estate jewelry" (that is, jewelry that is not new), it is even more important, and the older the piece, the more important it becomes to exercise caution. One of the greatest myths of all time is that antique jewelry is more likely to contain "the real thing" than today's jewelry, and that fraud and misrepresentation was less common among jewelers in days gone by than it is today. In reality, just the reverse is true.

Before discussing jewelry from earlier periods, let's begin by clarifying several terms. *Antique jewelry* describes jewelry that is at least 100 years old. Jewelry, for example, from the Georgian or Victorian periods (see below) can be described as "antique" because they are over one hundred years old. *Period jewelry* describes jewelry that has been produced during a particular period in time, one that reflects certain design elements. Period jewelry may be antique or it may be from a much more recent period. Certain periods have become very collectible and command higher prices than jewelry from other periods. *Estate jewelry* is a catch-all term that simply refers to jewelry that is not new, jewelry that has been owned or worn previously. The estate department of a jewelry store can include wonderful antique or period pieces, or affordable used jewelry of no particular antique or period value, but which might, nonetheless, be attractive and offer an unusually good value when compared to new jewelry.

233

For those interested in estate jewelry it is especially important to become knowledgeable about the different periods and how they compare in terms of design and value; some are more collectible than others, and command higher prices. One must also be aware that there are many counterfeit pieces that have been made today to imitate yesterday. There are also many "marriage" pieces, jewelry created from parts of two or more pieces, often done to salvage damaged jewelry or to add value by soldering or adding a collectible "name" to a piece not actually made by that artist or firm.

The best way to learn about fine jewelry from specific periods is to start going to exhibitions where you can see great pieces. Exhibitions are held at select galleries that specialize in antique or period jewelry, museums, and the premier auction houses in your area. Taking time to go view fine jewelry coming up for auction is an excellent way to learn about various periods. At such exhibitions you will not only have an opportunity to see beautiful examples of each period, but also a chance to speak to the auction house experts and examine pieces first hand. Christie's auction house in New York City, for example, sold one of the world's finest collections of Art Nouveau period jewelry by a famous master of the period, Lalique. It provided an excellent opportunity to see exemplary work from this period by a master artist. By examining it carefully, noting its feel, paying attention to particular details, seeing where and how each piece was signed, and so on, you could learn a tremendous amount. In such a way, you can begin to see and appreciate why some pieces are more costly than others, as well as how to separate the fakes and marriage pieces from the real thing. For more information on buying (or selling) at auction, see *Jewelry & Gems at Auction: The Definitive Guide to Buying & Selling at the Auction House & on Internet Auction Sites* by Antoinette Matlins, Gemstone Press.

By taking time to view fine pieces from various periods, and to note overall design characteristics, the use of particular materials, small details such as the type of clasp, closures, enameling techniques, style of the prongs, and so on, you can quickly hone your skills at identifying a particular period. Examining pieces carefully, comparing pieces side by side, and asking the jeweler or expert to explain what makes certain pieces more valuable than others is the best way to learn about estate jewelry. There are also excellent books on jewelry from specific periods that can provide valuable supplemental information.

Collectible Jewelry Periods

Below are brief introductions to some of the most popular jewelry periods, and to some of the most famous jewelers whose names can add significantly to a piece's value. Keep in mind that many periods overlap and that dates are approximate; as you do research, you will also find many inconsistencies with regard to the dates given for the span of any particular period, but nonetheless, they offer a useful guide.

Georgian Period (Approximately 1714–1830)

The Georgian period covers most of the eighteenth century into the early nineteenth century: a period when Great Britain was ruled by the four "Georges." Jewelry of this period was all handmade and designs consisted primarily of themes from nature—birds, flowers, leaves, insects—and also "ribbon and bow" motifs. Along with a very delicate design, you will find jewelry *en tremblant:* with moving parts that would "tremble" as the wearer moved. A new and important discovery of diamonds in Brazil in the eighteenth century resulted in the creation of jewelry that combined many diamonds with colored gemstones such as pink topaz and aquamarine—and foil-backing was used a great deal in this period.

Georgian (George IV) brooch and ear pendants

During the mid-eighteenth century, paste (glass), rhinestones, cut steel, and marcasites became extremely popular. A gold look-alike, known as *pinchback,* was produced from copper and zinc, and it replaced gold in less expensive jewelry.

In the second half of the eighteenth century, intaglios and carved gemstones became popular, and the style became more sentimental, as evidenced by the increased use of hearts, doves, and bows.

French influence can be seen in the beginning of the nineteenth century as Greek mythological subjects, foliate patterns, and scrolls entered the design of the day. Cameos and mosaics, along with amethysts and pearls, were also popular, and pieces "paved" with diamonds (pavé) reached a peak.

Pieces from this period are very rare and very expensive.

Victorian Period (Approximately 1837–1901)

This period began with the reign of Queen Victoria in 1837, but jewelry from several years preceding the start of her reign will include similar design elements. Victoria reigned for almost ¾ of a century, so the jewelry we see covers a range of styles. Jewelry from the early Victorian period (the Romantic period) was light in feel and used small, inexpensive colored stones and seed pearls. Designs consisted of scrollwork, floral spray patterns, and multicolored gold. The 1850s ushered in the Gothic Revival movement, which brought with it a rebirth of the art of enameling, and exquisite pieces returned to the jewelry scene after a long dormant period. In the mid-1850s we also find much greater use of gemstones in all sizes, shapes, and colors, but larger was definitely better. We find massive suites of jewelry with colored gemstones in heavy gold. Diamonds were worn in abundance. Gold necklaces and brooches with festoons and fringe also became popular, with and without gemstones.

After the death of Prince Albert in 1861, "mourning" jewelry was worn. Usually made from jet or black onyx, sometimes with seed pearls, the design was somber. Heavy silver jewelry also came into fashion for daytime wear.

While most Victorian jewelry is associated with England, the finest Victorian period jewelry was made in France. These pieces were of much greater quality overall; they were lighter, more delicate, more finely engraved, and enameled.

Among the great names of the Victorian period you will find Castellani, Carlo Giuliano, Fontenay, Hancock, Falize, Fabergé, and, at the end of the period, Boucheron and Tiffany.

Arts and Crafts Movement (Approximately 1885–1923)

A movement known as Arts and Crafts occurred in reaction to the increase in mass produced jewelry among those who feared the loss of the fine workmanship of high-quality craftspeople. Jewelers who belonged to this movement made each piece by hand, from beginning to end.

Jewelry

Platinum—Rarest and Purest of Precious Metals

Above: Platinum, a natural for this modern *tension* ring by designer Steven Kretchmer.

Platinum's whiteness, strength, and malleability have made it a favorite of fine jewelers since its turn-of-the-century debut. With platinum, jewelers of that era discovered they could create lighter, more delicate settings than ever imagined— the lacey, intricate designs for which Edwardian jewelry remains unparalleled. Today platinum is equally popular for sophisticated, contemporary design.

Above left: Designer Claude Thibaudeau finds platinum a natural for micro-pavé work. *Above right:* Platinum's malleability makes it the ideal choice to create this tanzanite beauty by designer Mark Schneider.

Above: Platinum keepsakes from bygone days.

Modern designers: Scott Keating (*left*) and Etienne Perret (*above*) forge dramatic and playful new looks in platinum.

Gold—A Favorite from Ancient Times...

Prized and coveted for personal adornment since earliest history, gold remains a popular choice for jewelry, for both men and women.

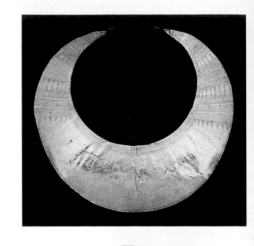

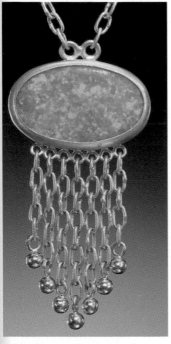

Goldsmith Barbara Berk's *woven* double spiral brooch combines ancient techniques to weave together high-karat gold with bright contemporary designs.

Above: As in ancient times, working exclusively in 24K gold, designer Gurhan loves its look and feel with rare gems such as this black opal. *Below left:* Sensual creations in 18K *brown* gold and 18K *black* gold have moved Yvel into the spotlight.

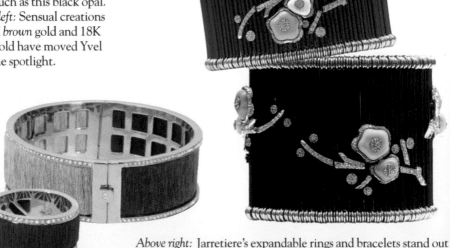

Above right: Jarretiere's expandable rings and bracelets stand out in yellow and white, but are knockouts in *black* and *blue* gold.

No wardrobe is complete without a gold necklace and other accessories.

bove: Limited
ition 18K gold and
atinum necklace by
ilhelm Buchart.

r right: Some popular
ain and necklace styles
p to bottom):
und curb link, open herringbone,
ple herringbone, fancy wheat,
aro, diamond-cut rope,
amond-cut queen, and box.

Right: "Seven Seeds" rings by Maria Kiernik softly cradle a variety of gemstones in complementary shades of gold while her "Ripple" rings are equally striking ... and all can be stacked together.

ght: Ancient
akume Gane
panese
ordmaking
chnique used
designer
eorge Sawyer
eates a unique
w look in jewelry.

Below: A sundial pendant by John David Cooney, as timeless as the ruby set within.

bove: Lemoz uses centuries-old enameling techniques to *eate* exquisite rings with an heirloom feel.

Pearls—Lustrous Beauty for Every Mood

Whatever your personality, whatever the event, pearls fit the occasion.

Gem-quality round pearl earrings.

Striking gold and American cultured abalone pearl ring.

A rainbow assortment of freshwater pearls.

Award-winning platinum ring with *faceted* Tahitian pearl.

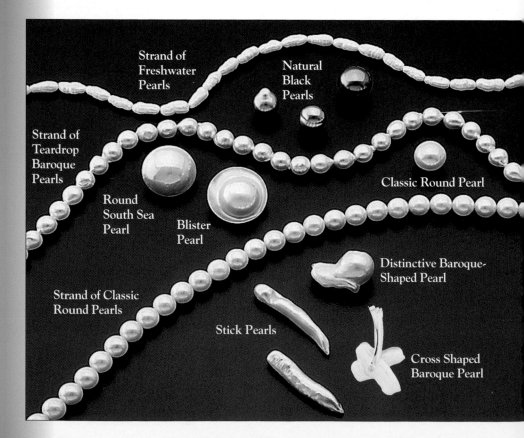

Strand of Freshwater Pearls

Natural Black Pearls

Strand of Teardrop Baroque Pearls

Round South Sea Pearl

Blister Pearl

Classic Round Pearl

Strand of Classic Round Pearls

Distinctive Baroque-Shaped Pearl

Stick Pearls

Cross Shaped Baroque Pearl

Pearls

Left: American (Tennessee) freshwater, cultured solid blister Domé™ pearls, stick pearls, and iridescent natural abalone pearl.

Freshwater cultured "coin" pearls from Tennessee.

Baroque natural pearls.

Natural round pearls.

Above: The beauty of nature is intricately captured in these South Sea cultured pearl rings by Alishan.

Left: Rare natural-color black cultured pearl necklace of exceptional quality and size.

Inset: Natural-color black cultured pearl pendant/enhancer.

Fine Jewelry Design—Art You Can Wear

Fine jewelry designers are gaining recognition as true artists. Major competitions—such as American Gem Trade Association's *Spectrum* awards, De Beers' *Diamonds of Distinction* awards, and Jewelers of America's *Buyers' Choice* awards—are recognizing their accomplishments. Here are examples of work created by some of the most exciting contemporary designers. Note the use of different textures and finishes in the metalwork, and the variety of gemstone materials used.

Right: Striking combination of cabochon and faceted gemstones in this ring by William Richey.

Above: A one-of-a-kind neckpiece holding fantasy cut colored gemstone by Michael Good.

Above: Innovative piece by Virginia Anderson that converts from ring to pendant. *Right:* Contemporary gemstone stacking rings, by Whitney Boin.

Above: Award-winning enamel, diamond and gemstone brooch by Falcher Fusager is magical. *Below:* Brooches have become an essential fashion accessory, like this one by Richard Kimball.

Opal, diamond, gold, and platinum necklace by Jeffrey Dunnington.

Elizabeth Rand's playful nature comes through in her smiling moon-face, carved in moonstone.

Below: A two-tone 18K gold necklace with blue sapphire and diamonds, by Karen Feldman.

Left: Stuller's selection of finished jewelry offers a bold designer look at more affordable prices. *Right:* Intricate engraving creates antique feel in this platinum ring by Russ Copping.

Above: Tanzanite Soleil® suite by Paul Klecka in 18K gold and platinum.

Left: Intricate workmanship, use of color in an exotic theme, and the geometric lines of this one-of-a-kind sapphire, ruby, emerald, and diamond brooch by James Breski are reminiscent of the Art Deco period.

New Metals—New Looks

Left: Tungsten, the hardest of metals, is Trent West's choice, alone or combined with gold, platinum, and diamonds for his unique Trewtungsten® ring line. *Right:* Bold cufflinks by William Richey come in stainless steel with 18K gold, with or without diamonds.

Below: Limitless combinations in *titanium*, yellow gold and diamond bands by Ed Mirell. *Below right:* 18K *red* gold and *forged stainless steel* set Gaia Pelikan's rings apart.

Popular Ring Styles

Three-Stone Rings

Three-stone ring using color for contrast.

Classic round three-stone ring.

Three-stone ring with radiant-cut diamonds.

Ring with three cushion-cut diamonds.

Three variations of the classic "solitaire"

Classic, yet bold.

Solitaire with a "twist."

Floater® ring in platinum and diamond.

Classic Tiffany-style six-prong ring.

Left: Micro-pavé ring from JB International.

Right: A striking 18K white and yellow gold and diamond collection by Alishan.

Old Is New Again

Skilled artisans create intricate "heirloom" reproductions.

Creative Use of Side Stones

Tiny channel-set stones lead eye to the center.

Class round wi tapered baguette

Interesting pavé work adds drama to the round center stone. From the Diana® Collection.

Three tapered baguettes on each side of oval.

Rare Fancy Vivid Yellow square emerald cut flanked by white trapezoid

Although gold was sometimes used, perhaps as a decoration upon silver, they worked mostly in inexpensive and less glamorous materials such as silver, beaten copper, and aluminum, and they used inexpensive cabochon-cut or uncut stones. Diamonds were never used, and faceted stones rarely. Opals and moonstones were especially popular, along with small, asymmetrical baroque pearls. There was little use of prong settings, the artists preferring bezel or collet settings, and connecting elements by wire or by slipping flaps through slits and bending the metal. Color was important, and many designs also incorporated bright enamel.

Leading figures in the Arts and Crafts movement include Arthur Gaskin, C.R. Ashbee, Fred Partridge, Edgar Simpson, Bernard Cuzner, Henry Wilson, John Paul Cooper, Alexander Fisher, Nelson Dawson, Archibald Knox, Edward Spencer, and Omar Ramsden.

Art Nouveau Period (Approximately 1890–1915)

A French jeweler named Oscar Massin set the tone and paved the way for the Art Nouveau period with his designs from 1860 to 1880. His work inspired designers at the end of the nineteenth century, looking toward a new era, to abandon the restraints of the day and start the new century with a fresh burst of creative energy. They took a bold new approach and were concerned more with the overall impression created by each jewel than with the use of valuable gemstones. Using free-flowing designs, they focused on detailing in the metalwork, using unusual stones, incorporating other materials, and using enamel to create works of art that were unique in every aspect.

This period was one of great experimentation. Designers were uninhibited and used new materials such as horn and ivory, unusual stones such as moonstone and natural "wing" pearls, and enamel in unusual combinations that had never before been done. The prevailing themes were taken from nature: flowers, insects, leaves, intertwined vines, and elusive, whimsical feminine figures. But their subjects were out of the ordinary; they used flowers such

Art Noveau *plique-a-jour* enamel and diamond choker by Lucien Gaillard

as large irises, and insects such as butterflies and dragonflies captured in flight. The softly flowing movement and the more abstract character of Art Nouveau jewelry created a feeling of peace and serenity, an almost dreamlike quality.

French designers moved to center stage during this period, the main stars being names such as René Lalique, Henri Vever, Georges Fouquet, Joe Descomps, Boucheron, Phillipe Wolfers, Plisson and Hartz, and Lucien Gaillard, but Peter Carl Fabergé was an Art Nouveau master as well. In America, Louis Comfort Tiffany created a sensation with jewelry in the Art Nouveau style. Other American names of the period include Theodore Dreicer; J.E. Caldwell; Shreve & Company; Peacock & Company; Bailey, Banks & Biddle; Black, Starr & Frost; Marcus & Company; Spaulding & Company; and T.B. Starr.

Edwardian and Belle Epoque Period (Approximately 1901–1914)

The Edwardian period coincides with the Belle Epoque (the French term that means "beautiful era"). During this period we find new styles of diamond cutting entering the scene, creating greater brilliance and sparkle and providing designers with new incentives to show them off to best advantage. While gold was still used, designers turned to platinum because its strength and malleability allowed for innovation in the design of settings, including ways to set diamonds in which the settings became virtually invisible. Platinum settings of this period, referred to as "marvels of engineering," are so delicate and lacelike that one wonders how they did it, and how the settings have survived generations of wear.

Jewelry from the Edwardian and Belle Epoque period is ornate but incredibly light, with a soft, feminine, romantic feel. It is characterized by very delicate lacelike open work, sometimes incorporating garlands and swags, and other times being somewhat more geometric. Natural pearls, seed pearls, and diamonds were the preferred gems of the period. Some of the most exceptional pieces were created by stringing small natural pearls on platinum and weaving them into delicate patterns for use in necklaces, bracelets, and even watch bands. Tassels, sautoirs—especially pearl sautoirs—"negligee" pendants (a necklace at the center of which were two drops of unequal length, suspended from a single stone, all on a slim chain), and pearl chokers were favorites of the Edwardian period as well.

Among the masters of this period you will find the names Tiffany, Cartier, Van Cleef & Arpels, LaCloche, Mauboussin, and Boucheron.

Art Deco Period (Approximately 1920–1935)

The jewelry of the Art Deco period reflects the new order of things after World War I—the Roaring Twenties—although some of the pieces that clearly show the Art Deco style were produced many years earlier. Some early Art Deco jewelry continued the "older" Art Nouveau style, characterized by highly ornamental floral designs in bright colors, but this gradually changed, moving away from flowing, curving lines toward stronger lines and geometrical patterns.

While platinum and diamonds were used extensively, we see much greater use of colored gemstones, including—in addition to ruby, emerald, and sapphire—citrine, peridot, aquamarine, and garnet, which were available in large sizes and typically cut in square and rectangular "emerald-cut" shapes. We also find widespread use of jade, coral, and black onyx. The Art Deco period featured geometic shapes for colored gemstones, and also introduced unusual geometric shapes for diamonds—trapezoid, square, triangle, and half-moon—to use as side-stones with larger diamonds or to incorporate into intricate geometric patterns.

Another innovation in the Art Deco period was the use of colored gemstones to create or augment geometric patterns. You will often see rows of black onyx, or small *calibré*-cut colored gemstones—square or rectangular step-cut stones—to create interesting patterns within the overall design. And it seemed to matter little whether they were natural or synthetic. Since it was often too difficult and time consuming to find rubies, sapphires, and emeralds that were perfectly matched in color, only the finest jewelers insisted on all natural gemstones; some of the manufacturers of less costly jewelry would substitute synthetics. Given their small size and inconsequential total weight, the gemstone component was an insignificant

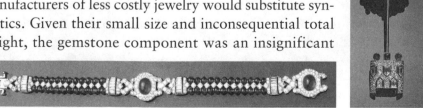

Above: Art Deco cabochon ruby and diamond bracelet by J.E. Caldwell
At right: Art Deco diamond, cabochon emerald, and black onyx tree jabot pin

factor in the overall value of the piece, but one must never assume they are natural, regardless of the genuineness of the diamonds and the use of platinum. The small *calibré*-cut stones found in many pieces of period Art Deco jewelry sold at auction as genuine have turned out to be synthetic.

The Art Deco period cannot be mentioned without the name of the House of Cartier because of the impact of Cartier's designers on the entire Art Deco period. Cartier's most important designer of the period, Charles Jacqueau, is considered one of the great pioneers of Art Deco style. His influence affected not only the work of Cartier but that of all the great jewelers of the period: his interest in Persia and China can be seen in the dominant "oriental" themes of the period; his intense interest in the Ballet Russes—and their dramatic use of color in their costume design—inspired his strong use of color; his love of India and the influence of the maharajahs, from whom Cartier acquired many fine gemstones, inspired the fruit basket style now known as Tutti Frutti; and his love of Egyptian history and art resulted in what came to be known as Egyptian Revival, which was perhaps the crowning glory of his contributions, and which received an enormous impetus after the discovery of the tomb of Tutankhamen in 1922.

Among the masters of the Art Deco period you will find the names of Cartier, Van Cleef & Arpels, Boucheron, Chaumet, Mauboussin, Boivin, Belperron, Mellerio, Georg Jensen, LaCloche, Templier, Tiffany, Marchak, J.E. Caldwell, and Fouquet.

Retro Period (Approximately 1940–1950)

Retro jewelry is a modern style that emerged after World War II. The style is very distinctive and recognizable, and you will quickly develop an eye for it. Gold was the preferred metal, and rose gold was very popular. You often see two-tone pieces combining yellow and rose gold. The goal was wearability. These pieces are not overly ornate or formal. The jewelry tends to be larger and architectural in feel, often set with large, affordable, colored gemstones such as citrine, aquamarine, topaz, and peridot. One can also find diamonds, sapphires, rubies, and emeralds, often set in a pavé style, in designs where the metal seems to fold over and meld into itself; you'll find horn shapes, paved inside and out with stones, and three-dimensional comet shapes.

Retro period jewelry is just coming into its own and offers excellent value and a very wearable, distinctive choice. All of the major jewelry houses, including Cartier, Bulgari, Tiffany, and Van Cleef & Arpels, made beautiful jewelry in this period, but so did other firms that are less well known, including American firms such as J.E. Caldwell and Black, Starr & Frost.

What's in a Name?

Signed pieces have added value. This is largely because artists want to sign their work when they create something beautiful, and they don't want to put their names to something that isn't fine, so a signature usually means high quality. While even the most prestigious jewelry houses have created some truly awful pieces, when a piece is signed by Cartier, Tiffany, Mauboussin, Van Cleef & Arpels, and so on, it reassures buyers that the piece is well designed, well made, and rarer than other jewelry because these houses don't mass-produce thousands of pieces. As a result, buyers will normally pay more for a signed piece.

Since signed pieces command higher prices, however, you must be on guard against inadvertently buying a fake. Be sure to buy only from reputable sources. *Never rely on a signature alone.* There have been numerous cases where pieces with signatures from houses such as Cartier or Winston were *not* made by these firms, or which had been altered to such an extent that they could no longer be attributed to the particular maker. In other cases, the pieces of jewelry were made by the firm to which they were attributed, but the original gemstone was replaced with one of much lower quality. Also keep in mind that sometimes, for whatever reason, a piece is not signed, or the signature is too worn to read. While it won't have the same value that it would if you could document the maker, it may still offer an exceptionally fine, beautiful piece of jewelry that you can get for a much lower price.

Contemporary jewelry designers and houses are also moving into the limelight. There are many books that provide extensive information on great jewelers and designers—information that can help you recognize their work, signatures, marks, and fakes.

PART FIVE

Important Advice Before You Buy

20

What to Ask
When Buying the Stone

Asking the right questions is the key to knowing what you're getting when it comes to buying gemstones. It is also the only way you can be sure about what you are comparing when considering gems from different jewelers. Be sure the jeweler can answer your questions or can get the answers for you. Then, be sure the jeweler is willing to put the answers *in writing* on your bill of sale. Finally, verify the facts—double-check that the stone is as represented—by having it examined by a qualified gemologist-appraiser. In this way you'll be able to make an informed choice about quality and value, you'll have no doubt about what you are getting, and you'll begin to develop a solid relationship with the jeweler from whom you make the purchase, based on confidence and trust. And, in the event the stone is not as represented, you'll know in time—and have the information you need—to get your money back.

Questions to Ask When Buying a Diamond

You should always have very specific information before purchasing a fine diamond weighing one carat or more. For smaller stones, the information may not be so readily available, since most jewelers don't take the time to grade them precisely. An experienced jeweler, however, should be able to provide information regarding quality for stones from a half carat and up, or offer to find it for you. Indeed, some laboratories are now providing grading reports for diamonds as small as half a carat or smaller.

Also keep in mind that since it is not possible to grade mounted diamonds accurately, we recommend that fine diamonds weighing one carat or more be purchased unmounted, or removed from the setting and then remounted. In jewelry containing numerous small diamonds, the stones are graded before they are set, and the information may be on the sales tag. If not, it is extremely difficult to know for sure what the true quality is, and much can be concealed by a setting. We recommend buying such pieces only from a knowledgeable jeweler with a good reputation.

Here are the basic questions to ask and the information that needs to be included on the bill of sale of your diamond:

1. *What is the exact carat weight?* Be sure the stone's *weight* is given, not its *spread* (see chapter 7).
2. *What is its color grade?* And what grading system was used (see chapter 5)? Is the color natural?
3. *What is its clarity (flaw) grade?* Again, ask what system was used (see chapter 6).
4. *What shape is it?* Round, pear, marquise (see chapter 4)?
5. *Is it well cut for its shape?* How would the make be graded: excellent, good, fair (see chapter 2)?
6. *What are the exact millimeter dimensions of the stone?*
7. *Is this stone accompanied by a diamond grading report or certificate?* Ask for the full report (see the book *Diamonds: The Antoinette Matlins Buying Guide* for more detailed information on how to read a diamond report).

Be sure to find out what system was used to grade the stone. If Gemological Institute of America (GIA) terms are used, ask if GIA standards and methods have been applied to grading the stone.

Be sure to get the *exact* millimeter dimensions of the stone; the dimensions can be approximated if the stone is mounted. For a round stone, be sure you are given *two* dimensions for the stone's diameter; since most are not round, you need the highest and lowest dimensions. For fancy shapes, get the dimensions of the length and width. Always get the dimension from the table to the culet as well, that is, the depth of the stone.

Be especially careful if the diamond is being taken out on consignment, on a jeweler's memorandum or sales slip, or on a contingency sale. Having the measurements in writing helps protect you from being accused of switching should you have to return the stone for any reason.

Always ask if the stone has a certificate or diamond grading report. If so, make sure it accompanies the stone; if you are taking the stone on approval, ask for a copy of the report. If there is no report or certificate, find out who determined the color and flaw grades, make sure the seller puts that information on the bill of sale, and insist that the sale be contingent on the stone's actually having the grades represented.

Additional Questions to Help You Make Your Selection

Is it large enough? This is a valid question and one you should be honest with yourself about. If you think the diamond is too small, you won't feel good about wearing it. Remember that such other factors as clarity and color can be juggled several grades with little visible difference, and this might enable you to get a larger diamond. And remember that the color and type of setting can also help you achieve a larger look.

Does this stone have a good make? Does this stone have good proportions? How do its proportions compare to the "ideal?" Remember, much variance can exist and a stone can still be a beautiful, desirable gem even if it does not conform to the ideal. Nonetheless, you won't want a stone with poor proportions, so if you have any question about the stone's brilliance and liveliness—if it looks lifeless or dull in spots—you should ask specifically about the proportioning of the cut. In addition, you should ask if there are any cutting faults that might make the stone more vulnerable to chipping or breaking, as, for example, an extremely thin girdle would.

Has this stone been clarity enhanced? Be sure to ask whether or not the diamond has been laser treated or fracture-filled (see chapter 6). If it is accompanied by a GIA report, the report will indicate lasering, if present. However, the GIA won't issue a report on a fracture-filled stone, and some jewelers don't know how to detect them. If there is no GIA report, be sure to ask explicitly, and get a statement in writing that the diamond is or is not clarity enhanced, whichever the case may be. Getting this fact in writing may save you a big headache should you learn later that the stone is enhanced.

Does this stone show any fluorescence? If a diamond fluoresces blue when viewed in daylight or under daylight-type fluorescent light, it will appear whiter than it really is. This can be a desirable quality so long as the stone has not been graded or classified incorrectly. A diamond may also fluoresce yellow, which means that in certain lights its color could appear worse than it actually is. If the stone has a diamond grading report, any fluorescence will be indicated there. If there is no report, and if the jeweler can't tell you whether or not the stone exhibits any fluorescence, the stone's color grade may be incorrect.

Special Tips When Buying a Diamond

Ask the Jeweler to Clean the Stone

Don't hesitate to ask to have the stone cleaned before you examine it. Cleaning will remove dirt, grease, or indelible purple ink. Cleaning is best done by steaming or in an ultrasonic cleaner. Cleaning also helps to ensure that you'll see the full beauty of the stone; diamonds can become very dirty just from customers handling them and, as a result, look less brilliant and sparkling than they really are.

View the Stone Against a Dead-White Background

When looking at unmounted stones, look at them only against a *dead-white background* such as white blotter paper or a white business card, or on a grading trough. Examine the stone against the white background so that you are looking at it through the side, not down through the table (see chapter 5). Tilt the stone toward a good light source; a daylight fluorescent lamp is best. If the stone shows any yellow body tint when viewed through the girdle, if it is not as colorless as an ice cube, then the diamond is not white or colorless.

Get the Facts on a Bill of Sale

Ask that all the facts concerning the stone be put on the bill of sale. These include the carat weight, the color and flaw grades, the cut, and the dimensions. Also, be sure you obtain the report on any certificated stone, as diamonds accompanied by laboratory reports are sometimes called.

Verify Facts with a Gemologist

If a stone is one carat or larger and is not accompanied by a respected laboratory report, make the sale contingent on verification of the facts by a qualified gemologist, gem-testing lab, or the GIA. While the GIA will not estimate dollar value, it will verify color, flaw grade, make, fluorescence, weight, and other physical characteristics.

Weigh the Facts

Decide what is important to you, and then weigh the facts. Most people think color and make are the most important considerations when buying a diamond, but if you want a larger stone, you may have to come down several grades in color, or choose a slightly spread stone, or select one of the new shapes that look much larger than traditional cuts. The most important thing is to know what you're getting, and get what you pay for.

What to Ask When Buying a Colored Gemstone

As with diamonds, it's very important to ask the right questions to help you understand the differences in gems you may be considering. Asking the following questions should help you to gain a greater understanding of the differences, determine what's right for you, and have greater confidence in your decision.

1. *Is this a genuine, natural stone, or a synthetic?* Synthetic stones are *genuine* but not *natural* (see chapter 12).
2. *Is the color natural?* Most colored gemstones are routinely color enhanced (see chapters 12 and 13). However, stones such as lapis should not be, and you must protect yourself from buying dyed material that will not retain its color permanently. See information on specific gems (chapters 15, 16) to determine whether or not this is an important question for you to ask.

   Be especially cautious when buying sapphires and rubies; make sure you ask whether or not the stone has been checked for diffusion treatment and oiling. Today, with diffused sapphire and ruby being mixed in to parcels of natural stones, unknowingly set into jewelry, it's possible that one may be sold inadvertently (see chapter 13).

   For especially fine and costly gems, ask not only whether or not the color has been treated, but if so, what type of treatment was used, and what is the *extent* of treatment.
3. *Clarify what the name means.* Be particularly careful of misleading names (see chapter 13). When a stone is described with any qualifier, such as Rio topaz (which is not topaz), ask specifically

whether or not the stone is genuine. Ask why the qualifier is being used.

4. *Is the clarity acceptable, or do too many inclusions detract from the beauty of the stone?* Are there any flaws, inclusions, or natural characteristics in this stone that might make it more vulnerable to breakage with normal wear? This is a particularly important question when you are considering a colored stone (see chapter 11). While visible inclusions are more common in colored gems than in diamonds, and their existence has much less impact on value than it has on diamond value, value is nonetheless reduced if the inclusions or blemishes affect the stone's durability, or are so numerous that they mar its beauty.

Be especially careful to ask whether or not any inclusion breaks the stone's surface, since this may weaken the stone, particularly if the imperfection is in a position normally exposed to wear, like the top of the stone or around the girdle. This would reduce the stone's value significantly. On the other hand, if the flaw is in a less vulnerable spot, where it can be protected by the setting, it may carry minimal risk and have little effect on value.

A large number of inclusions will usually detract noticeably from the beauty, especially in terms of liveliness, and will also generally weaken the stone and make it more susceptible to any blow or knock. Such stones should be avoided unless the price is right and you're willing to assume the risk.

Also, certain gems, as we've mentioned, are more brittle than others and may break or chip more easily, even without flaws. These stones include opal, zircon, and some of the new and increasingly popular gems, such as tanzanite. This does not mean you should avoid buying them, but it does mean you should give thought to how they will be worn and how they will be set. Rings and bracelets are particularly vulnerable, since they are more susceptible to blows or knocks. Brooches, pendants, and earrings are less vulnerable.

5. *Do you like the color? How close is the color to its pure spectral shade? Is it too light? Too dark? How does the color look in different types of light?* Learn to look at color critically. Become familiar with the rarest and most valuable color of the gem of your choice. But after you do this, decide what you yourself really like. You may prefer a color that might be less rare and there-

fore more affordable. Be sure the color pleases you—don't buy what you think you *should* buy unless you really like it.

6. *Is the color permanent?* This question should be asked in light of new treatments (such as diffusion) and also because color in some stones is prone to fading. Two examples are amethyst and kunzite (one of the new and increasingly popular gems). Just which ones will fade and which ones won't, and how long the process might take, no one can know. This phenomenon has never affected the popularity of amethyst, and we see no reason for it to affect kunzite's popularity, but we feel the consumer should be aware of it. There is evidence that too much exposure to strong sunlight or intense heat contributes to fading in these stones, so we suggest avoiding sun and heat. It may be wise to wear these gems primarily for evening or indoor activities.

7. *Does the stone need a protective setting?* The setting may be of special importance when you are considering stones like tanzanite, opal, or emerald. They require a setting that will offer some protection—for example, one in which the main stone is surrounded by diamonds. A design in which the stone is unusually exposed, such as in a high setting or one with open, unprotected sides, would be undesirable.

8. *Does the stone have a pleasing shape? Does it have a nice "personality?"* This will be determined by the cutting. Many colored gems are cut in fancy shapes, often by custom cutters. Fine cutting can enrich the color and personality, and increase the cost. However, with colored gems, brilliance and sparkle are less important than the color itself. The most critical considerations must focus on color, first and foremost. Sometimes a cutter must sacrifice brilliance in order to obtain the finest possible color. But if the color isn't rich enough or captivating enough to compensate for less brilliance, ask if the jeweler has something that is cut better and exhibits a little more sparkle. Keep in mind, however, that the more brilliant stone may not have the precise color you like, and that when you are buying a colored gem, *color* is the most crucial factor. Unless you find the stone's personality unappealing, don't sacrifice a beautiful color for a stone with a less appealing color just because it may sparkle more. Compare, and decide based on what you like and what you can afford.

When considering a pastel-colored gem, remember that if it is cut too shallow (flat), it can lose its appeal quickly (but only temporarily) with a slight buildup of greasy dirt on the back; the color will fade, and liveliness will practically disappear. This can be immediately remedied by a good cleaning.

9. *What are the colorless stones?* In a piece of jewelry where a colored stone is mounted with colorless stones to accentuate or highlight its color, ask, "What are the colorless stones?" Do not assume they are diamonds. They may be diamonds, zircons, artificial diamond imitations such as CZ or YAG, or synthetic white spinel (spinel is frequently used in the Orient).

Special Tips to Remember When Buying a Colored Stone

When looking at unmounted stones, view them through the side as well as from the top. Also, turn them upside down on a flat white surface so they are resting on the table facet and you can look straight down through the stone from the back. Look for evenness of color versus color zoning—shades of lighter or darker tones that create streaks or planes of differing color.

Remember that color is the most important consideration. If the color is fine, flaws or inclusions don't detract from the stone's value as significantly as with diamonds. If the overall color or beauty is not seriously affected, the presence of flaws should not deter a purchase. But, conversely, flawless stones may bring a disproportionately higher price per carat because of their rarity, and larger sizes will also command higher prices. In pastel-colored gems, or stones with less fine color, clarity may be more important.

Be sure to check the stone's color in several different types of light— a spotlight, sunlight, or fluorescent or lamplight—before making any decision. Many stones change color—some just slightly, others dramatically—depending on the light in which they are viewed. Be sure that the stone is a pleasing color in the type of light in which you expect to be wearing it most.

If you are considering a stone with rich, deep color—especially if it is for special occasions and likely to be worn mostly at night—be sure it doesn't turn black in evening light. Some stones, like sapphire, can look like black onyx in evening light.

Remember to give special attention to wearability. If you are considering one of the more fragile stones, think about how the piece will be worn, where, and how frequently. Also, pay special attention to the setting and whether the stone is mounted in a way that will add protection, or allow unnecessary, risky exposure to hazards.

Get the Facts on the Bill of Sale

If a colored stone is over one carat and is exceptionally fine and expensive, make the sale contingent on verification of the facts by a qualified gemologist, appraiser, or gem-testing lab such as the GIA or American Gemological Laboratories (AGL).

Always make sure that any item you purchase is clearly described in the bill of sale exactly as represented to you by the salesperson or jeweler. For diamonds, be sure each of the 4Cs is described in writing. For colored gems, essential information also includes the following:

- The identity of the stone or stones and whether or not they are genuine or synthetic, and not in any way a composite (doublet, triplet).
- A statement that the color is natural, if it has been so represented; or, in the case of sapphire, a statement that the stone has been diffusion treated or a statement that it has *not* been diffusion treated if that is what you were told.
- A statement describing the overall color (hue, tone, intensity).
- A statement describing the overall flaw picture. This is not always necessary with colored stones. In the case of a flawless or nearly flawless stone, it is wise to note the excellent clarity. In addition, note any unusual flaw that might prove useful for identification.
- A statement describing the cut or make. This is not always necessary, but it may be useful if the stone is especially well cut, or has an unusual or fancy cut.
- The carat weight of the main stone or stones, plus total weight if there is a combination of main and smaller stones.
- If the stone is to be taken on approval, make sure that the *exact* dimensions of the stone are included, as well as any other identifying characteristics. The terms and period of approval should also be clearly stated.

Other Information That Should Be Included for Jewelry

If the piece is being represented as being made by a famous designer or house (Van Cleef and Arpels, Tiffany, Caldwell, Cartier, etc.) and the price reflects this, the name of the designer or jewelry firm should be stated on the bill of sale.

- If the piece is represented as antique (technically, an antique must be at least a hundred years old) or as a period piece from a popular, collectible period like Art Deco, Art Nouveau, or Edwardian (especially if made by a premier artisan of the period), this information should be stated on the bill of sale, with the approximate age or date of manufacture and a statement describing the condition.

- If the piece is made by hand, or custom designed, this should be indicated on the bill of sale.

- If the piece is to be taken on approval, make sure millimeter dimensions—top to bottom, as well as length, width, or diameter—are provided, as well as a full description of the piece. Also, check that a time period is indicated, such as "two days." Before you sign anything, be sure that you are signing an approval form and not a binding contract for purchase.

21

How to Select
a Reputable Jeweler

It's very difficult to give advice on this matter, since there are so many exceptions to any rules we can suggest. Size and years in business are not always absolute indicators of the reliability of a firm. Some one-person jewelry firms are highly respected; others are not. Some well-established firms that have been in business for many years have built their trade on the highest standards of integrity and knowledge; others should have been put out of business years ago.

One point worth stressing is that for the average consumer, price alone is not a reliable indicator of the integrity or knowledge of the seller. Aside from variations in quality, which often are not readily discernible by the consumer, significant price differences can also result from differences in jewelry manufacturing processes. Many jewelry manufacturers sell mass-produced lines of good-quality jewelry to jewelers all across the country. Mass-produced items, many of which are beautiful, classic designs, are usually much less expensive than handmade, one-of-a-kind pieces, or those on which there is a limited production. The work of some designers may be available in only a few select establishments and may carry a premium because of skill, labor, reputation, and limited distribution. Handmade or one-of-a-kind pieces are always more expensive, since the initial cost of production is paid by one individual rather than shared by many, as in mass-produced pieces.

Furthermore, depending on the store, retail markups also vary based on numerous factors unique to each retailer, including differences in insurance coverage, security costs, credit risks, education and training costs, special services such as in-house design and custom jewelry production and repair, customer service policies, and more.

The best way to select wisely is by shopping around. Go to several fine jewelry firms in your area and compare the services they offer, how knowledgeable the salespeople seem, the quality of their products, and pricing for specific items. This will give you a sense of what is fair in your market area. As you do so, however, remember to ask the right questions to be sure the items are truly comparable, and pay attention to design and manufacturing differences as well. As part of this process, it may be helpful to consider these questions:

- *How long has the firm been in business?* A quick check with the Better Business Bureau may reveal whether or not there are significant consumer complaints.
- *What are the gemological credentials of the jeweler, manager, or owner?* Is there a gemologist on staff? Does the store have its own laboratory?
- *What special services are provided?* Are custom design services, rare or unusual gemstones, educational programs, Gemprint, or photographic services for your jewelry available?
- *How would you describe the store window?* Is the jewelry nicely displayed? Or is the window a mélange of incredible bargains and come-on advertising to lure you in?
- *How would you describe the overall atmosphere?* Is the sales staff's manner professional, helpful, tasteful? Or hustling, pushy, intimidating?
- *What is the store's policy regarding returns?* Full refund or only store credit? How many days? What basis for return?
- *What is the repair or replacement policy?*
- *Will the firm allow a piece to be taken "on approval"?* It won't hurt to ask. Some jewelers will. However, unless you know the jeweler personally this is not often permitted today, since too many jewelers have suffered from stolen, damaged, or switched merchandise.
- *To what extent will the firm guarantee its merchandise to be as represented?* Be careful here. Make sure you've asked the right questions, and get complete and accurate information on the bill of sale, or you may find yourself stuck because of a technicality.

If the jeweler can't or won't provide the necessary information, we recommend that you go to another store, no matter how much you've fallen in love with the piece. If you're making the purchase on a contingency basis, put the terms of the contingency on the bill of sale.

Never allow yourself to be intimidated into accepting anyone's claims. Beware of the person who says "Just trust me" or who tries to intimidate you with statements such as "Don't you trust me?" A trustworthy jeweler will not have to ask for your trust; he or she will earn it through knowledge, reliability, and a willingness to give you any information you request—in writing.

Again, in general, you will be in a stronger position to differentiate between a knowledgeable, reputable jeweler and one who isn't if you've shopped around first. Unless you are an expert, visit several firms, ask questions, examine merchandise carefully, and then you be the judge.

Using a Gemologist Consultant

Somewhat new to the gem and jewelry field is the arrival of the gemologist consultant. People interested in acquiring a very fine diamond, natural-colored gemstone, or fine piece of period or antique jewelry that may be difficult to find in traditional jewelry stores are now seeking the professional services of experienced gemologist consultants. A gemologist consultant can provide a variety of services, including general consulting to help you determine what you really want, what it will cost, and how to best acquire it; how to dispose of jewelry you already own, or from an estate; how to design or redesign a piece of jewelry and have it made. A gemologist consultant can also provide the expertise needed to help you safely purchase gems or jewelry at auction, or from private estate sales. An experienced gemologist consultant can expand your view of the possibilities in terms of gemstones and also suggest ways to make jewelry more personal and distinctive.

As with all else in the sparkling world of gems and jewelry, be sure to check the credentials of anyone offering services as a gemologist consultant. Do they have a gemological diploma? How long have they been working in the field of gems? Do they have a laboratory? Can they provide references within the field? Can they provide client references? If you have jewelry you wish to sell, arrange meetings at a safe place, such as a bank vault.

Fees vary, depending on the gemologist consultant's level of expertise and experience and the nature of the assignment. For example, for general consulting about how to buy or sell gems or jewelry, you should expect to pay about $125 to $200 per hour for someone with good credentials.

For assistance in the acquisition or sale of specific gems or pieces of jewelry, some gemologist consultants work on a fixed fee for the project, some on a percentage of the purchase or sale amount, and some at an hourly rate. When we are retained by clients, our work is done on one of the bases noted above, or even a combination of them, depending on the nature of the work to be done and what best meets the client's needs.

If You Want to File a Complaint

If you have a complaint about a firm's practices or policies, please contact the Better Business Bureau in your city. In addition, if any jeweler has misrepresented what was sold to you, please contact the Jeweler's Vigilance Committee (JVC), 25 West 45th Street, Suite 400, New York, NY 10036, (212) 997-2002. This group can provide invaluable assistance to you, investigate your complaint, and take action against firms believed to be guilty of fraudulent activity in the jewelry industry.

22

A Word about Gemstone Investment

Caution!

Caution is the only word we can apply to gem investment. If you have taken the time to read any of this book, you should now fully understand that the world of gems is very complex, that fraud and misrepresentation can be costly, and that the average consumer lacks the knowledge and experience to make sound judgments about the purchase of expensive gems without the assistance of a qualified gemologist-appraiser.

It is for this reason primarily that we recommend that gems and jewelry be purchased first and foremost for the pleasure they will bring to the purchaser/wearer, or as something to be handed down to future generations. The investment consideration, while it is certainly valid, in most cases should remain secondary.

Gemstones have been attracting investors by startling numbers since the late 1970s. While gems have a magical allure, and some investors have done well with them, few people outside the gem trade possess sufficient knowledge about the gems themselves—and their value—to make sound decisions in this arena. Fewer still have the means to liquidate such investments.

We have never recommended gems as investments for the average consumer. But since *investment* is a word the public continues to apply to gem and jewelry purchases, we think it important to discuss some of the pros and cons. Before we begin, however, let's take a look at what has occurred over the last two decades, including fraudulent investment scams to be on guard against.

During the late 1970s, gem prices were pushed to unprecedented levels. Numerous gemstone investment companies appeared, as did fraudulent investment schemes. Prices for diamonds began to plummet in 1981, followed shortly thereafter by price declines for other gems. Consumer losses were significant. Many gem investment companies went out of business.

The gem market stabilized and strengthened as people returned to buying jewelry to wear, to give as a token of love, or as a special gift or memento. People seemed to have learned that investing in gems is not a quick and easy way to make money.

In the mid-1980s and again in the mid-1990s, interest in gemstone speculation reappeared. Published figures began to give gems renewed investment allure, but the frequently simplistic presentation of rewards without full discussion of the risks was extremely misleading. Such claims created a fertile market for the proliferation of fraudulent gemstone investment companies between 1985 and 1993. The result is that once again gems have lost their sparkle for thousands of unsuspecting victims.

Fraudulent Gemstone Telemarketing: A Serious Problem

Today, prospective buyers must be especially careful not to fall victim to sophisticated telephone marketing schemes offering gemstones as investments. Americans have been the primary targets for several Canadian-based companies. The Toronto Fraud Squad estimates that the companies behind these schemes have already made over a billion dollars in net profit and are beginning to expand operations into Europe and Asia.

Normally, the scam begins with a telephone call offering an opportunity to buy gems at prices represented to be wholesale or below. Impressive, professional-looking documentation is provided. Gems are shipped in sealed plastic or lucite containers for security, accompanied by seemingly reliable reports from a gem-testing laboratory. The brokerage firm promises to resell the gems at the appropriate moment for handsome profits. Unfortunately, the stones are never sold, and the victims are left holding stones for which—they learn too late—they paid prices far in excess of full retail.

In most cases, victims are lucky to recover 10 percent of their investment. By the time they realize what has happened, there is usually nothing that can be done. The company is either no longer in business, or
hiding behind international boundaries. In the United States, activity is
handled from Canada; in the UK, from Antwerp or Amsterdam. The
complexity of international laws makes it virtually impossible for the
average person to bring legal action.

Gemstone Investment: Not for the Average Investor

Gemstone investment can be profitable, but in light of our concern
about the growing potential for renewed speculation, and a concomitant
increase in fraudulent schemes, we advise you to exercise extreme caution
and be especially alert to telemarketing and internet schemes, and make
no purchase without a laboratory report from a respected laboratory
(see appendix).

If one takes the time to become knowledgeable about the gem industry; is interested in a long-term investment (over five years); and is willing to locate, retain, and work with a knowledgeable, reputable gem
consultant, gems can offer an exciting, sparkling, and very enjoyable area
for speculation. But entered casually, without knowledge of the industry
and the risks, this investment may lose its sparkle quickly.

If you can't resist the temptation of gem investment, and if a con-
templated investment can be professionally evaluated before you close the
deal, it may have merit. There are certainly some strong facts to support
gem investment.

Gems can be used and enjoyed without adversely affecting value,
unlike most other beautiful things people buy and use (autos, furs, furni-
ture, etc.).

Historically, there has always been a market for gems. Good stones
are not trendy and don't go in and out of fashion, like some fine-art
investments, where an artist is popular today and never heard of in a
few years.

Gems have portability—they are easily moved and stored, so they
are readily available to the owner, easy to show when the need arises.

Some Facts That May Discourage Gem Investment

Extreme care must be taken to verify the authenticity of the gem being considered and to determine its precise quality and value. For this reason, we advise against consideration of sealed merchandise.

Gems are not a short-term investment. In most cases, depending on the price you have paid (the average consumer buys at retail, not at wholesale) and the rate of appreciation, there is a minimum five-year period simply to break even.

Liquidity can be a problem. Since you are not a jeweler, your own credibility will be suspect where the average consumer is concerned, so it may be very difficult to find a buyer for your gem.

Jewelers may be interested in buying "off the street," but the seller usually gets less than the current wholesale price in such transactions. This is not because the jeweler is trying to take advantage necessarily; rather, it is a matter of simple economics. When the jeweler has a customer for a specific piece, he can always go to his dealer to obtain what he needs. Not only does he not risk tying up his money until he actually has a customer, but also he may charge the cost to his account and carry his cost for an extra thirty days or more, earning that extra interest on the money in the bank. Therefore, the only incentive for him to tie his money up in a cash transaction off the street, for which he may or may not even have an immediate customer, is an attractive enough price—usually *half the wholesale cost.* Yet another consideration is his own protection—he has no way to determine whether merchandise bought off the street is stolen property, which could end up confiscated by the police (in which case he loses whatever he paid for the goods). There may be exceptions made if the piece is particularly fine or rare or unusual in some way, but the norm is as stated above.

Investment-house buy-back guarantees are *no* guarantee. Some of the new investment firms guarantee buy-back after a prescribed time period. Unfortunately, you have no way of knowing where they will be after the prescribed period of time.

23

Buying on the Internet:
E-Commerce & Online Auctions

E-commerce is the current buzzword, and gem and jewelry websites are springing up almost daily, along with online auction sites. The internet offers an endless array of merchandise from around the world—a virtual international flea market—and opens doors to more choices than ever imagined, at prices often represented to be much lower than what can be found in traditional jewelry stores. Buying on the internet can be fun, and there are some good opportunities for knowledgeable buyers, possibly even a real "treasure" at a bargain price. But e-commerce and online auctions are not for everyone, and the risk of buying something that is not properly represented is very high. Before flying off into cyberspace, take a few moments to consider some of the pros and cons.

For many, the major attraction of shopping on-line is convenience. It is fast and easy, enabling you to make decisions in private—but without the assistance of salespeople. For those who live in remote areas far from fine jewelry stores, it provides an opportunity to see what is available, see what's new and exciting, and keep current about everything from gemstones to the latest award-winning designers. Many online vendors also provide educational sites to help you understand more about what you are buying. And for people who leave important gifts to the last minute, the internet can bring the world of jewelry directly to the screen, in time to be a real lifesaver!

It is easy to see the allure of internet shopping, but in all too many cases it is not all that it appears to be. Where gems and jewelry are concerned, the disadvantages may quickly outweigh the advantages, especially on auction sites.

The first disadvantage is the inability to see and compare gems and jewelry firsthand. As we hope you've learned from previous chapters, this is a serious shortcoming, since it is impossible to accurately judge beauty and desirability from a static photo. Furthermore, you can't determine how well made a piece of jewelry might be or how it might compare with the alternatives. Be sure to ask about the vendor's return policy, and read the fine print. Find out how quickly merchandise must be returned and whether you will receive a refund. Be leery of vendors who will only give a credit toward future purchases.

Another serious problem is the absence of any screening mechanism to help you determine the reliability of information provided. Sales information pertaining to gems or jewelry being sold is often incomplete and inaccurate, and many "educational" sites are also filled with inaccurate, incomplete, or misleading information. It is also difficult to find reliable information about the competence or trustworthiness of many online vendors, and written representations may be meaningless unless you can work out a way to verify the facts before making payment to the vendor.

Auction sites have become a place where unscrupulous dealers sell jewelry at inflated prices, often with meaningless "laboratory reports" and appraisals that show outrageous values. I've seen cultured pearls offered on auction sites with appraisals describing them as "AA" quality (fine) and showing values exceeding $20,000; when received, they turned out to be "discard" quality. I've seen diamond jewelry appraised at $2,000, which the bidder succeeded in getting for under $150. Its true value: about $75!

In these cases, even if your bid is just a fraction of the "appraised value," the price you end up paying will actually be more than what you would have paid at a local jewelry store. In many cases, especially where diamonds and pearls are concerned, you won't even be able to find it in any jewelry store, at any price, because it is such low quality that it was not meant for jewelry use.

In general, everything we have warned about in previous chapters applies to purchases from an online vendor or auction. As we have stressed repeatedly, many of the factors affecting quality and value cannot be accurately judged without gemological training, experience, and proper equipment, and many online vendors are so deficient in requisite knowledge and skill that their representations may be unreliable.

We cannot emphasize too strongly the importance of taking every precaution to protect yourself and ensure you are getting what you think you are getting, at an appropriate price. Remember that many internet companies and individual vendors are unknown entities, without reliable track records or well-established reputations. This means that problems might be more difficult or impossible to resolve satisfactorily, regardless of "guarantees" made before purchase. You must also remember that it may be difficult or impossible to find the seller off-line, and you cannot rely on vendor ratings because they can be easily rigged by the unscrupulous.

Appraisals and Laboratory Reports Provide a False Sense of Security

Appraisals and gem-testing laboratory reports are being used increasingly by online sellers to increase confidence among prospective buyers. Unfortunately, they are also being used increasingly by the unscrupulous. We are seeing an increase in bogus appraisals and fraudulent lab reports that have duped unsuspecting buyers into purchasing something that has been misrepresented. We have also seen diamonds accompanied by reports from highly respected labs, where the quality of the stone does not match the description on the report. There have also been numerous cases where diamonds have been sold with counterfeit GIA reports. Be sure to get independent verification of any documentation provided by the seller (see chapter 8), before payment if possible.

Remember also that you cannot properly judge a gem on the basis of a lab report or appraisal alone. We've seen many diamonds with "great reports" that were not beautiful (and should sell for less than one might surmise based on the report alone), and others with "questionable" reports that were exceptionally beautiful (and should cost more than the report would indicate). In other words, you really must see the stone along with the report.

Other problems that are surfacing on the web include the following:

- *Failure to comply with Federal Trade Commission (FTC) guidelines.* The FTC has found extensive failure to comply with FTC guidelines. Most notably, descriptions provided by sellers often omit critical information pertaining to quality factors, exact weight, and treatments used on diamonds, colored gemstones, and pearls.

- *Prices are often higher than fair retail.* Don't assume you will pay a lower price, and beware of fictitious "comparative retail" prices that lead you to believe you are getting a bargain. Prices are often no lower than those at a local jewelry store, and many e-retailers sell jewelry at prices significantly higher than what you would pay for comparable quality from knowledgeable, independent jewelers. Before buying on-line, check prices from a variety of sources, including your local jeweler.
- *"Wholesale" claims may be misleading.* "Wholesale" online offerings present even greater risks to consumers than buying in any wholesale jewelry district (see chapter 8), because you do not see the actual gem or jewelry firsthand and have no guarantee you are buying from a bona fide wholesaler. Many people buying "wholesale" through online sources are not getting the bargains they believe they are getting, and many mistakes would have been avoided had the buyer seen the jewelry first or had an opportunity to compare it with alternatives.

  In some cases, arrangements can be made to allow you to view the stone before the vendor receives payment, using a local bank or gemological laboratory, for example, as an intermediary. We recommend this be done wherever possible.
- *Here today, gone tomorrow.* In numerous reported cases, buyers have never received the merchandise for which they paid, or received merchandise that was not as represented. Often there is no recourse because vendors cannot be located once the transaction is complete.

Online Auctions—Rewards and Rip-Offs

Fine auction houses are an important source of exquisite jewelry from bygone eras, often exhibiting elaborate workmanship that cannot be duplicated today. They are also an important source of some of the finest, rarest, and most magnificent natural gemstones—gems that surpass even the best material being mined today—which are no longer available in the jewelry trade. Such gems may fetch handsome prices—possibly even a new record—or some knowledgeable buyer may recognize a treasure that others have missed and pay very little. This, for many, is what makes the auction arena so fascinating.

Items offered at auction may also come to the auction block to settle estates, or as a means to dispose of unclaimed property, and usually must be sold at whatever the highest bid might be, regardless of value. While this is no guarantee that you'll get a bargain, because knowledgeable buyers know the value of pieces on which they are bidding, sometimes these pieces are sold at very low prices because no one obtained proper certification and they get overlooked, even by the pros!

Buying at auction can be a rewarding experience, but keep in mind that even at the best firms there is an element of risk. One must be very knowledgeable, or work with an expert consultant, to recognize opportunities and spot pitfalls. Over the years we've seen many pieces acquired from reputable auction firms that contained synthetic stones, fracture-filled diamonds, and diffusion-treated sapphires.

As we have stressed throughout this book, no one can properly judge any fine gem without seeing it firsthand and examining it with proper gem-testing equipment. Where auctions are concerned, proper examination is even more critical because the auction house has limited liability. We never bid on any item at auction without having personally viewed the piece and examined it with proper gem-testing equipment. Firms such as Antiquorum, Christie's, and Sotheby's provide opportunities to view the items at exhibitions held at various locations around the country before the auction, and bidding takes place both on-site and on-line, as a convenience to people who cannot be present. However, this is not the case with all online auction sites, and in many cases there is no opportunity to view the item before bidding on it. In such cases, more than anything else, success is dependent upon having incredible luck!

Protection May Be Illusion

Where some auction sites are concerned, you may be under the impression that you are protected against misrepresentation and have recourse should there be a problem, but this may be just an illusion. In reality, you may have no recourse at all. Never forget that in situations where proper examination is not possible, the risk is dramatically increased: you are bidding on a blind item from a blind source. Even among legitimate sources, not seeing the gem or jewelry before purchase can result in disappointment when you receive your purchase. Be sure to read the "terms and conditions" very carefully, especially the fine print pertaining to "representations, warranties, and limits of liability."

We were recently contacted by a woman regarding a diamond purchased from an individual through an online auction site. She had previously purchased a diamond through an internet auction, and arranged for us to confirm that the diamond was properly represented before she paid for it. She did very well, and obtained a very nice diamond at a price comparable to legitimate wholesale. In the second case, she thought she had arranged a similar transaction. She was very excited about the diamond, which she thought she had purchased at a "bargain" price. She expected to be able to confirm the quality, as she had in the earlier transaction, before paying for it. Here is where the problem began.

The diamond was described as having a certain color, clarity, and weight, but it was not accompanied by any lab report or appraisal. The buyer was aware of this when she bid, but she had been told by the seller that she could have it verified by a third party. She became alarmed and suspicious when the seller would not accept a credit card or agree to an escrow arrangement, especially since she, the buyer, was willing to pay all costs related to the escrow arrangement or credit card fee. The seller had agreed that the buyer could send the stone to a third party for verification, but what was never made clear before the bidding was that the seller would send the stone to a third party only *after* receiving full payment!

We tried to be helpful, but when we spoke with the owner, we also became very suspicious. We asked the owner how she was able to provide such a precise description of the diamond without any appraisal or lab report, and she responded that she knew "by looking." So I asked her if she was a gemologist or in the jewelry trade and was told no, but that she had looked at "hundreds of diamonds" and "knew what she was looking at." She then told me she was "a lawyer" and began her litany about the buyer having entered into a legally binding contract, and that the buyer knew before bidding that the description was only her "opinion," and so on. We quickly realized that this woman was an experienced "pro" who knew how to legally exploit the auction arena . . . and the unsuspecting.

To sum it all up, the seller used the "terms and conditions, warranty and limits of liability" clauses established by the auction site to construct a situation in which she was able to rip off the inexperienced. She knew that representations made in the auction arena without documentation are not guarantees and fall outside the legal constraints placed on other online vendors, and once payment had been received, she had no intention of ever refunding one penny, regardless of what any independent evaluation revealed.

Buying at auction can be an exciting and exhilarating experience with compelling financial incentives, but there are always risks for the unknowledgeable, and buying through online auction sites poses even greater risk. The FTC has warned that internet auction fraud has become a significant problem. According to the FTC, most consumer complaints center on these situations:

- Sellers who don't deliver goods
- Sellers who deliver something far less valuable than they described
- Sellers who don't deliver in a timely way
- Sellers who fail to disclose all the relevant information about the product or terms of sale.

Form of Payment May Provide Protection

There are several payment options that might provide some protection. Credit cards offer the most consumer protection, usually including the right to seek a credit through the credit card issuer if the product isn't as delivered. If the seller won't agree, other options include setting up an escrow arrangement (for which there is usually a nominal fee) or using a reliable third party for verification, such as a well-known gem-testing laboratory, before an exchange of products or money.

To sum up, whether you are buying or selling gems or jewelry on-line—from e-retailers, auction sites, or individuals—the rewards may be great, but the risks are much higher than buying from traditional sources. For additional information on how to reduce the risk in buying or selling on-line, or to file a complaint, write to the Federal Trade Commission, Consumer Response Center, 600 Pennsylvania Avenue, NW, Washington, DC 20580, or see their website: www.ftc.gov.

Online Sources of Information

There are many sources of online information but no screening mechanism to separate reliable from unreliable information. Consider the source and be wary of information provided by sellers of gems or jewelry. The following sites may provide helpful information:

1. www.ftc.gov (Federal Trade Commission)
2. www.jewelryinfo.org (Jewelry Information Center)
3. www.gia.edu (Gemological Institute of America educational site)
4. www.diamondregistry.com (diamond industry newsletter with consumer information)
5. www.ags.org (American Gem Society)
6. www.gem.net (colored gemstone information site)
7. www.pearlinfo.com (Cultured Pearl Information Center)

PART SIX

*Important Advice
After You Buy*

23

Choosing the Appraiser & Insurer

Why Is It Important to Get an Appraisal?

Whether you have bought diamond or colored gemstone jewelry, getting a professional appraisal and keeping it updated is critical. An appraisal is necessary for four reasons: (1) to verify the facts about the jewelry you have purchased (especially important with the abundance of new synthetic materials and treatments); (2) to obtain adequate insurance to protect against theft, loss, or damage; (3) to establish adequate information to legally claim jewelry recovered by the police; and (4) if items are lost or stolen, to provide sufficient information to make sure they are replaced with jewelry that actually is of comparable quality, if that is what your insurance policy provides.

The need for appraisal services has increased greatly because of the high incidence of theft and sharp increases in the prices of diamonds and colored gems. It has become necessary to have any fine gem properly appraised, particularly before a purchase decision, given today's costs and the potential for financial loss if the gem is not accurately represented.

It is also important, given recent rising prices, to update value estimations from old appraisals. This will ensure adequate coverage should gems that have been in your possession for several years or more be lost or stolen. In addition, current and accurate appraisals may be needed in connection with inheritance taxes, gifts, or the determination of your net worth.

How to Find a Reliable Appraiser

The appraisal business has been booming over the past few years, and many jewelry firms have begun to provide the service themselves. We must point out, however, that there are essentially no officially established guidelines for going into the gem-appraising business. Anyone can represent himself or herself as an appraiser. While many highly qualified professionals are in the business, some others lack the expertise to offer these services. So it is essential to select an appraiser with care and diligence. Further, if the purpose of the appraisal is to verify the identity or genuineness of a gem as well as its value, we recommend that you deal with someone who is in the business of gem identification and appraising and not primarily in the business of selling gems.

To find a reliable gem-testing laboratory, see page 282 for a selected list of laboratories that issue internationally recognized reports. To find a reliable gemologist-appraiser in your community, contact:

The American Society of Appraisers
P.O. Box 17265, Washington, DC 20041
(703) 478-2228   • Ask for a list of *Master Gemologist Appraisers.*

The American Gem Society (AGS)
8881 W. Sahara Ave., Las Vegas, NV 89117
(702) 255-6500   • Ask for a list of *Certified Gemologist Appraisers or Independent Certified Gemologist Appraisers.*

The Accredited Gemologists Association
17 Kercheval Ave., Grosse Point Farms, MI 48236
(800) 475-8898   • Ask for a list of *Certified Gem Laboratories or Certified Master Gemologists.*

The International Society of Appraisers
16040 Christensen Rd., Ste. 320, Seattle, WA 98188-2929
(206) 241-0359   • Ask for a list of *Certified Appraisers of Personal Property.*

National Association of Jewelry Appraisers
P.O. Box 18, Rego Park, NY 11374
(718) 896-1536   • Ask for a list of *Certified Master Appraisers or Certified Senior Members.*

In addition, when selecting a gemologist-appraiser, keep the following suggestions in mind:

- *Obtain the names of several appraisers and then compare their credentials.* To be a qualified gemologist-appraiser requires extensive formal training and experience. You can conduct a preliminary check by telephoning the appraisers and inquiring about their gemological credentials.
- *Look for specific credentials.* The Gemological Institute of America (GIA) and the Gemmological Association of Great Britain provide internationally recognized diplomas. The GIA's highest award is the G.G. (Graduate Gemologist) and the Gemmological Association of Great Britain awards the F.G.A.— Fellow of the Gemmological Association (F.G.A.A. in Australia; F.C.G.A., Canada). Some hold this honor "With Distinction." In Germany, the D.G.G. is awarded; in Asia, the A.G. Make sure the appraiser you select has one of these gemological diplomas. In addition, when seeking an *appraiser,* look for the title C.G.A. (Certified Gemologist Appraiser), which is awarded by the American Gem Society (AGS), or M.G.A. (Master Gemologist Appraiser), which is awarded by the American Society of Appraisers. Some fine gemologists and appraisers lack these titles because they do not belong to the organizations awarding them, but these titles currently represent the highest awards presented in the gemological appraisal field. Anyone holding these titles should have fine gemological credentials and adhere to high standards of professional conduct.
- *Check the appraiser's length of experience.* In addition to formal training, to be reliable a gemologist-appraiser needs extensive experience in the handling of gems, use of the equipment necessary for accurate identification and evaluation, and activity in the marketplace. The appraiser should have at least several years' experience in a well-equipped laboratory. If the gem being appraised is a colored gem, the complexities are much greater and require more extensive experience. In order to qualify for C.G.A. or M.G.A. titles, the appraiser must have at least several years' experience.
- *Ask where the appraisal will be conducted.* An appraisal should normally be done in the presence of the customer, if possible. This is important in order to ensure that the same stone is returned to you and to protect the appraiser against charges of "switching." Recently we appraised an old platinum engagement

ring that had over twenty years' filth compacted under the high, filigree-type box mounting typical of the early 1920s. After cleaning, which was difficult, the diamond showed a definite brown tint, easily seen by the client, which she had never noticed when the ring was dirty. She had just inherited the ring from her deceased mother-in-law, who had told her it had a blue-white color. If she had not been present when this ring was being cleaned and appraised, it might have resulted in a lawsuit, for she would certainly have suspected a switch. This particular situation does not present itself often, but appraisers and customers alike need to be diligent and watchful.

- If there are several pieces, the process can be very time-consuming. It normally takes about a half hour per item to get all of the specifications, and it can take much longer in some cases. Several appointments may be required for a proper job.

Appraisal Fees

This is a touchy and complex subject. As with any professional service, there should be a suitable charge. Fees should be conspicuously posted or offered readily on request so that the customer knows beforehand what to expect to pay for this service. Fees are essentially based on the expertise of appraisers and the time required of them, as well as the secretarial work required to put the appraisal in written form, since all appraisals should be done in writing. While it used to be standard practice to base appraisal fees on a percentage of the appraised value, this practice is no longer acceptable. Today, all recognized appraisal associations in the United States recommend that fees be based on a flat hourly rate, or on a per-carat charge for diamonds.

There is usually a minimum appraisal fee, regardless of value. The hourly rate charged by a professional, experienced gemologist-appraiser can range from $50 to $150, depending on the complexity of the work to be performed and the degree of expertise required. Find out beforehand what the hourly rate is and what the minimum fee will be.

For certification or special gemological consulting that requires special expertise, rates can easily be $125 to $150 per hour. Extra services such as photography, radiography, Gemprint, or spectroscopic examination of fancy-colored diamonds will require additional fees.

Be wary of appraisal services offering appraisals at very low rates and of appraisers who continue to base their fee on a percentage of the "appraised valuation." The Internal Revenue Service, for example, will not accept appraisals performed by appraisers who charge a percentage-based fee.

Some appraisers can photograph jewelry, which we suggest. On the photo, the appraiser should note the approximate magnification and the date, along with your name as the owner. This provides a means of identifying merchandise that may have been stolen or lost and subsequently recovered by police. The photo can also be useful with the U.S. Customs Service should you take your jewelry with you on a trip outside the United States and find yourself having to prove that the jewelry was not purchased abroad.

Protecting Your Diamond with Gemprint™

Gemprint is a unique service offered by many jewelers and appraisers. While not totally foolproof (recutting the diamond may affect Gemprint's reliability), it is playing an increasingly important role in the recovery and return of lost and stolen diamonds, and we recommend it where available.

Gemprint offers a fast and practical way to identify a diamond, even one already mounted, by capturing the image of the pattern of reflections created when the diamond is hit by a low-level laser beam. Depending upon the Gemprint system being used by the jeweler or appraiser, the image can be captured and stored on computer with digital imaging, or a photograph of the image may be taken. Each diamond produces a unique pattern, which is documented by this service. As with human fingerprints, no two gemprints are ever alike.

The process takes only a few minutes. The jeweler or appraiser will provide you with a certificate of registration that includes either a photograph or scanned image of the stone, along with other pertinent information about it. The information about your diamond is kept in the jeweler's or appraiser's file and is also transferred to Gemprint's international database, whereby interested law enforcement agencies can verify ownership of a diamond when recovered.

If your stone is ever lost or stolen, you or your insurer sends a notice-of-loss form to Gemprint, which will then notify appropriate law enforcement agencies. Police can then verify with the registry the identification of recovered diamonds, many of which are thereby returned to the rightful owners. As another safeguard, Gemprint also checks each new registration against its lost-and-stolen file before confirming and storing the registration. Gemprint can also be useful in checking a diamond that has been left for repair, cleaning, or resetting, to assure you that your stone has been returned.

Whether purchasing a diamond, or repairing, resizing, or remounting an heirloom, getting a Gemprint is another way to secure your investment. Increasingly, jewelers are offering Gemprint at no additional charge to customers making a diamond purchase. Whatever the case, the cost is nominal ($35 to $50) and may actually save you money in the long run since some insurance companies give 10 percent off the annual premium you pay if the diamond you are insuring has a Gemprint.

Gemprint is available in about 650 locations in the United States. For the location nearest you, contact Gemprint at 1-888-GEMPRINT.

Laser Inscriptions Add Protection As Well As Romance

Several gem-testing laboratories now offer laser inscription services whereby an inscription is lasered onto the girdle edge of the diamond. While not easily discernable without magnification, inscriptions can provide the number of your diamond grading report or a secret message. In addition to the romantic touch, laser inscriptions offer another means of identification in cases where lost or stolen diamonds are recovered. Check directly with the lab to learn whether or not this service is offered (see appendix).

Choosing an Insurer

Once you have a complete appraisal, the next step is to obtain adequate insurance. Most people do not realize that insurers differ widely in their coverage and reimbursement or replacement procedures. Many companies will not reimburse the "full value" provided in the policy, but instead exercise a "replacement" option by which they offer a *cash sum less than the amount for which the jewelry is insured,* or offer to replace it for you. Therefore, it is important to ask very specific questions to determine the precise coverage offered. We recommend asking at least the following:

- How do you satisfy claims? Do you reimburse the insured amount in cash? If not, how is the amount of the cash settlement determined? Or do you replace the jewelry?
- What involvement do I have in the replacement of an item? What assurance do I have that the replacement will be of comparable quality and value to the original?
- What is your coverage on articles that cannot be replaced?
- Exactly what risks docs my policy cover? All risks? Mysterious disappearance? At all times?
- Does the policy have any geographic restrictions?
- Are there any exemptions or exclusions? What if the loss involves negligence?
- What are the deductibles, if any?
- What documentation do you expect me to provide?

To help with insurance claims, keep a photo inventory of your jewelry. Take a photo and store it in a safe place (a bank safe-deposit box). In case of theft or fire, a photo will be useful in helping you describe your jewelry, and also in remembering other pieces that are missing, and in identifying them if recovered. A photo is also useful for insurance documentation. In addition, when planning a trip, whatever jewelry you will be taking should be photographed. Just put it on a table and take a snapshot.

Appendix

A Selected List of
Recognized Laboratories

American Gemological
  Laboratory (AGL)
580 Fifth Avenue, Suite 706
New York, NY 10036

American Gem Society Laboratory
  8881 W. Sahara Ave.
  Las Vegas, NV 89117

American Gem Trade Association
  (AGTA) Gemological Testing Center
18 East 48th St., Suite 1002
New York, NY 10017

Asian Institute of Gemological
  Sciences (AIGS)
Jewelry Trade Center, N. Tower, 6th Fl.
Silom Rd.
Bangrak, Bangkok 10500
Thailand

CISGEM-External Service for
  Precious Stones
Via Ansperto, 5
20123 Milano, Italy

European Gemological
  Laboratory (EGL)
30 W. 47th St., Suite 205
New York, NY 10036
and
United Kingdom Building
409 Granville St., #456
Vancouver, BC V6C1T2

Gemmological Association and Gem
  Testing Laboratory of Great Britain
27 Greville St.
London EC1N 8TN, England

Gemological Association of All Japan
Katsumi Bldg., 5F, 5-25-8
Ueno, Taito-ku
Tokyo 110, Japan

Gem Certification and Appraisal Lab
580 Fifth Avenue, Suite LL-05
New York, NY 10036

Gemological Institute of America (GIA)
  Gem Trade Laboratory (GTL)
580 Fifth Avenue
New York, NY 10036
and
5345 Armada Dr.
Carlsbad, CA 92008

GemWorld International
  Laboratories
576 Fifth Avenue, Suite 904
New York, NY 10036

German Gemmological Laboratory
  (DSEF)
Prof.-Schlossmacher-Str. 1
D-55743 Idar-Oberstein, Germany

Gübelin Gemmological Lab
Maihofstrasse 102
CH-6006 Lucerne, Switzerland

Hoge Raad voor Diamant (HRD)
Hoveniersstraat, 22
B-2018 Antwerp, Belgium

Professional Gem Sciences (PGS)
5 South Wabash, Suite 1905
Chicago, IL 60603

Swiss Gemmological Institute (SSEF)
Falknerstrasse 9
CH-4001 Basel, Switzerland

Selected Readings

Arem, Joel E. *Color Encyclopedia of Gemstones*. New York: Van Nostrand Reinhold, 1987. Excellent color photography makes this book interesting for anyone. An invaluable reference for the gemologist.

Becker, Vivienne. *Antique and Twentieth Century Jewellery*. London: N.A.G Press, 1987. A beautifully illustrated classic focusing on eighteenth-through twentieth-century collectible jewelry.

Blauer, Ettagale. *Contemporary American Jewelry Design*. New York: Van Nostrand Reinhold, 1991. Beautifully illustrated and informative book revealing the work of many of America's most talented jewelry designers.

Bronstein, Alan. *Forever Brilliant: The Aurora Collection of Colored Diamonds*. New York: Ashland Press, Inc., 2000. An excellent guide to the world of colored diamonds.

Bruton, E. *Diamonds*. 2nd ed. Radnor, Pa.: Chilton, 1978. An excellent, well-illustrated work for amateur and professional alike.

Desautels, Paul E. *The Jade Kingdom*. New York: Van Nostrand Reinhold, 1986. Important resource on world occurrences, history, uses, and identification.

Downing, Paul B. *Opal Identification and Value*. 2nd ed. Tallahassee, Fla.: Majestic Press, 2002. Excellent book on opals for the serious opal lover. Includes retail price guides.

Farn, Alexander E. *Pearls: Natural, Cultured and Imitation*. Oxford: Butterworth-Heinemann Ltd., 1991. The definitive volume, covering pearl evolution, biology, science, and trade.

Hofer, Stephen C. *Collecting and Classifying Colored Diamonds*. New York: Ashland Press, 1998. A lavish, comprehensive work essential for anyone with a serious interest in the subject. The book is a treasure of information on the world's rarest and most valuable gems: natural-color diamonds.

Hurlbut, Cornelius, and R.C. Kammerling. *Gemology*. New York: John Wiley & Sons, 1991. Excellent, well-organized textbook for beginning through advanced students.

Keller, Peter C. *Gemstones and Their Origins*. New York: Van Nostrand Reinhold, 1989. A very interesting, well-illustrated resource covering geological origins and mining of gems.

Keverne, Roger, ed. *Jade*. New York: Lorenz Books, 1996. Superb, encyclopedic work on jade with lavish illustrations. A must for anyone who loves jade; 450 lavish photos.

Liddicoat, R. T. *Handbook of Gem Identification*. 12th ed. Los Angeles: Gemological Institute of America, 1989. Textbook for the student of gemology.

Matlins, Antoinette. *Colored Gemstones: The Antoinette Matlins Buying Guide—How to Select, Buy, Care for & Enjoy Sapphires, Emeralds, Rubies and Other Colored Gems with Confidence and Knowledge*. 2nd ed. Woodstock, Vt.: GemStone Press, 2005. Covers every aspect of colored gemstones in detail, from their symbolic attributes to current frauds.

———. *Diamonds: The Antoinette Matlins Buying Guide—How to Select, Buy, Care for & Enjoy Diamonds with Confidence and Knowledge*. Woodstock, Vt.: GemStone Press, 2001. Covers every aspect of diamonds in detail, from how to read a diamond grading report to brilliant new cuts.

———. *Engagement & Wedding Rings: The Definitive Buying Guide for People in Love*. 3rd ed. Woodstock, Vt.: GemStone Press, 2003. Everything you need to know to select, design, buy, care for, and cherish your wedding or anniversary rings—his and hers. Beautiful photos of rings from fifteenth century to present.

———. *The Pearl Book: The Definitive Buying Guide—How to Select, Buy, Care for & Enjoy Pearls*. 3rd ed. Woodstock, Vt.: GemStone Press, 2002. Covers every aspect of pearls, from lore and history to complete buying advice. An indispensable guide for the pearl lover.

Matlins, Antoinette, and A. C. Bonanno. *Gem Identification Made Easy: A Hands-On Guide to More Confident Buying & Selling*. 3rd ed. Woodstock, Vt.: GemStone Press, 2003. A nontechnical book that makes gem identification possible for anyone—even without a science background. A "must" for beginners, and the experienced may pick up a few tips, too. Practical, easy to understand.

Miller, Anna M. *Cameos Old & New*. 3rd ed. Woodstock, Vt.: GemStone Press, 2002. A valuable resource for cameo lovers. Beautifully illustrated.

———. *Gems & Jewelry Appraising: Techniques of Professional Practice.* 2nd ed. Woodstock, Vt.: GemStone Press, 1999. Covers all the standards, procedures, and ethics of appraising gems, jewelry, and other valuables, with step-by-step instructions.

———. *Illustrated Guide to Jewelry Appraising: Antique, Period, and Modern.* 3rd ed. Woodstock, Vt.: GemStone Press, 2004. A comprehensive guide to antique, period, and contemporary jewelry identification and appraisal.

Nassau, Kurt. *Gemstone Enhancement.* 2nd ed. Woburn, Mass.: Butterworth's, 1994. Possibly the most comprehensive and understandable book available on gem enhancement.

Pagel-Theisen, V. *Diamond Grading ABC.* 10th ed. New York: Rubin & Son, 1990. Highly recommended for anyone in diamond sales.

Pardey, Greg. *Black Opal, The Book: A Comprehensive Guide to Cutting and Orientating.* Australia: Quality Opals Australia, 1999. Includes step-by-step instructional video.

Pough, F. H. *The Story of Gems and Semiprecious Stones.* New York: Harvey House, 2000. Good for beginning and amateur gemologists.

Read, Peter G. *Gemmology: A Textbook for Students.* 2nd ed. Oxford: Butterworth-Heinemann Ltd., 1999. One of the best books for the student of gemology.

Rygle, Kathy J., and Stephen F. Pedersen. *The Treasure Hunter's Gem and Mineral Guide: Where and How to Dig, Pan and Mine Your Own Gems and Minerals.* 2nd ed. Woodstock, Vt.: GemStone Press, 2003. Offers state-by-state details on more than 250 gems and minerals that the United States has to offer, and the very affordable "fee dig" sites where they can be found.

Sauer, Jules. *Emeralds Around the World.* Rio de Janeiro: Amsterdam Sauer, 1992. A new, exciting approach to an intriguing subject, for layman and specialist alike.

Schumann, W. *Gemstones of the World.* Translated by E. Stern. New York: Sterling Publishing Co., 2000. This book has superior color plates of all of the gem families and their different varieties and for this reason would be valuable to anyone interested in gems.

Sofianides, Anna S., and George E. Harlow. *Gems and Crystals.* New York: Simon & Schuster, 1991. Features 150 stunning full-color photos of 400 different gems and crystals from the collection of the American Museum of Natural History.

Webster, R. Revised by B. W. Anderson. *Gems*. 4th ed. London: Butterworth & Co., 1990.

————. *Practical Gemology*. 6th ed. Colchester, Essex: N.A.G. Press Ltd., 1987. Both Webster books are highly recommended for the serious student of gemology, especially *Gems*.

Zeitner, June C. *Gem and Lapidary Materials: For Cutters, Collectors, and Jewelers*. Tucson: Geoscience Press, 1996. A beautifully illustrated book with a wealth of information about gemstones and the variety of forms in which gemstones are fashioned into works of art. Includes many works from the finest contemporary gemstone cutters, as well as examples throughout history.

Zucker, Benjamin. *Gems and Jewels: A Connoisseur's Guide*. Woodstock, NY: Overlook Press, 2003. Lavishly illustrated book on principal gems and "great" gemstones of the world, with fascinating historical facts, mythological tidbits, and examples of the jeweler's art from widely differing cultures.

Color Plates and Exhibits

Charts

All the charts and the tables that appear here were especially designed and executed for use in this book; however, some from other publications were used as inspiration and reference. Grateful acknowledgment is given to the following for use of their charts as references:

The chart on page 60, "Sizes and Weights of Various Diamond Cuts," with permission of the Gemological Institute of America, from its book, *The Jewelers' Manual*.

The chart on page 62, "Diameters and Corresponding Weights of Round Brilliant-Cut Diamonds," with permission of the Gemological Institute of America, from its book *The Jewelers' Manual*.

The chart on page 85, "Comparison of Diamonds and Diamond Look-Alikes," with permission of the Gemological Institute of America, from its publication *Diamond Assignment No. 36*, page 27.

Black-and-White Photographs and Illustrations

Illustrations by Kathleen Robinson.

Page 25: EightStar® from EightStar Diamond Company (photo/Richard von Sternberg)

Page 32: Radiant and princess from Eugene Biro Corp.; Crisscut® from Christopher Designs (photo/Christony Inc.); Quadrillion™ from Ambar Diamonds; Trilliant from MEFCO Inc. (photo/Sky Hall); Lily Cut® designed by Siman-Tov Bros., courtesy of LiliDiamonds; Gabrielle® from Suberi Brothers (photo/Peter Hurst); Spirit Sun® and Context® from Freiesleben; Lucida™ from Tiffany and Company (photo/Monica Stevenson).

Page 35: Royal Asscher® from Royal Asscher Diamond Company Ltd. (photo/ Donald Barry Woodrow).

Page 54: Courtesy of Suberi Brothers.

Page 111: Cabochon emerald ring by Jack Abraham for Precious Gem Resources.

Page 116: Courtesy of AGL.

Page 117: Courtesy of AGTA.

Page 224: Titanium men's collection by Ed Mirell; stainless steel cufflinks by William Richey.

Page 225: Tungsten rings by Trent West.

Pages 227–229: Bezel-set rings by Robin Garin from Kwiat Couture; partial bezel-set ring from George Sawyer Design; five-stone bands from Lazare Kaplan, Inc.; heart-shaped diamond ring from Suberi Brothers; rings in gypsy and collet settings from Circle Round the Moon; channel-set baguette wedding band from JFA Designs; bar-set band (left) from Kwiat Couture; bar-set band (right) from J.B. International (photo/Peter Hurst); pavé rings from Barnett Robinson; micro-pavé ring from J.B. International.

Pages 235–239: Georgian brooch courtesy of Christie's Images, NY. Lucien Gaillard choker from Christie's. J.E. Caldwell bracelet from Weschler's. Art Deco pin courtesy of Christie's Images, NY.

Color Photographs

We wish to thank the following persons and companies for the color photographs appearing in this new edition:

Gemstones

Page 1   Fancy diamond "peacock," blue and pink diamonds, green diamonds, courtesy of Robert Haack Diamonds. Photos/Sky Hall. Fancy-color diamond floral brooch, courtesy of Sotheby's, NY. Assorted natural-color diamond suite (top left) courtesy of Aurora Gems Inc., NY. Photo/Tino Hammid.

Page 2   Star ruby, courtesy of International Colored Gemstone Association (ICA). Photo/Bart Curran.
Selection of red and pink gemstones and rhodochrosites, courtesy of Pala International, Inc.; Red beryl, courtesy of Rex Harris. Photo/Sky Hall. Rubellite tourmaline and diamond pendant by Stephen Webster.

Page 3   Star sapphire and moonstones, courtesy of International Colored Gemstone Association (ICA). Photos/Bart Curran.
Selection of blue gemstones, courtesy of Pala International, Inc.; Chrysocolla, courtesy of American Gem Trade Association (AGTA), cut by Glenn Lehrer, AGTA *Cutting Edge* competition winner. Photo/Sky Hall.
Blue Paraiba tourmaline, courtesy of Cynthia Renee Co. Photo/ Robert Weldon.
Blue sapphire ring by James Breski.

Page 4   Selection of yellow and orange gemstones, courtesy of Pala International, Inc. Photo/Sky Hall.
Topaz, courtesy of American Gem Trade Association (AGTA). Photo/Natural Arts, Inc.

Sunstone, courtesy of Ponderosa Mine, Inc. Photo/Bart Curran. Sapphire, andalusite, and cat's-eye chrysoberyl, courtesy of Krementz Gemstones; fancy-cut citrine with concave facets, courtesy of American Gem Trade Association (AGTA), cut by *Cutting Edge* winner Richard Homer, American Lapidary Artists; yellow beryl, courtesy of AGTA, cut by *Cutting Edge* winner Karl Egan Wilde. Photos/Sky Hall.
Yellow sapphire ring courtesy Richard Krementz Gemstones.

Page 5   Selection of green gemstones and tsavorite garnet, courtesy of Pala International, Inc. Photos/Sky Hall.
Emerald-cut emerald, courtesy of International Colored Gemstone Association (ICA). Photo/Sky Hall.
Paraiba tourmaline, courtesy of Cynthia Renee Co., CA. Photo/Robert Weldon.
Laboratory-grown synthetic stones, courtesy of Chatham Created Gemstones.
Period Art Deco jadeite brooch, courtesy of Christie's, NY.

Page 6   Andamooka crystal opal, Andamooka matrix opal beads, and two free-form black opals, courtesy of Western Opal. Photos/Sky Hall.
Mexican opals and oval cabochon black opal, courtesy of International Colored Gemstone Association (ICA). Photos/Bart Curran.
Boulder opal ring by Gaia Pelikan. Photo/Gaia Pelikan.

Page 7   Lapis sculpture by Michael Dyber. Photo courtesy of Ledge Studio.
Belt buckles, courtesy of Elizabeth Rand Studio.
Intarsia box by Nicolai Medvedev, courtesy of E. F. Watermelon Co. Photo/Sky Hall.
Stone cabochons and beads: Photo/Sky Hall.
Sedona Landscape agate from the collection of Rare Earth Mining Co., Trumbull, Connecticut.

Page 8   Diamonds cut in classic shapes, courtesy of MEFCO Inc. Photo/Sky Hall.
Trapezoid and half-moon diamonds, courtesy of Doron Isaak.
Crisscut®, courtesy of Christopher Designs. Photo/Christony Inc.
Tiana™, courtesy of Brite Star Diamond Co., Ltd.
Lucida™, courtesy of Tiffany and Company. Photo/Monica Stevenson.
Royal Asscher®, courtesy of Royal Asscher Diamond Company Ltd. Photo/Donald Barry Woodrow.
Lily Cut®, courtesy of Lili Diamonds (designed by Siman-Tov Bros.).

Quadrillion™ diamond courtesy of Ambar Diamonds.
Shield, Tapered Bullet, and Epaulette courtesy New Diamond Connection Corp.
Diana® Classic enngagement ring courtesy Frederick Goldman.
Spirit Sun®, courtesy of Freiesleben.
Context®, courtesy of Freiesleben.
EightStar®, courtesy of EightStar Diamond Company. Photo/ Richard von Sternberg.

Jewelry

Page 1   Platinum and diamond Tension ring by Steven Kretchmer. Design copyrighted. Ring patented, U.S. patent no. 5,084,108. Photo/ Weldon Photography.
Platinum micro-pavé ring courtesy of Claude Thibaudeau, Montreal.
Platinum and tanzanite ring courtesy of Mark Schneider. Photo/ John Parrish.
Collection of Edwardian jewelry: Photo/Sky Hall.
Rings by Scott Keating.
Platinum and diamond "ball" jewelry by Etienne Perret.

Page 2   Antique gold jewelry from the collection of the British Museum. Photo reprinted with permission of the British Museum, London.
24 karat necklace courtesy of Gurhan.
Brooch courtesy of Barbara Berk Designs. Photo/Dana Davis.
Brown and black gold jewelry courtesy of Yvel.
Black and blue gold jewelry courtesy of Jarretiere.

Page 3   Necklace (top left), courtesy of Wilhelm Buchert. Photo/Heinz Teufel.
Round curb-link necklace courtesy of Abel & Zimmermann.
Selection of popular chains: Photo/Sky Hall.
Makume Gane bands, courtesy of George Sawyer Designs.
Rings courtesy of Maria Kiernik. Photo/Dana Davis.
Enameled rings courtesy of Lemoz.
Sundial, courtesy of John David Cooney.

Page 4   Gold and pearl earrings by Eric Russell.
Selection of pearls pictured at bottom of page courtesy of King Partners and A&Z pearls. Photos/Sky Hall.
Gold pearl ring courtesy of US Abalone.
Platinum pearl ring courtesy of Mark Schneider. Photo/John Parrish.

All other photos courtesy of the Cultured Pearl Association of America.

Page 5   Natural black-color cultured-pearl necklace, courtesy of Robert Adams. Photo/Sky Hall.
Natural black-colored cultured pearl, ruby, and diamond pendant/enhancer, courtesy of Sultan Company. Photo/Sky Hall.
American freshwater natural pearls from the collection of John Latendresse.
American freshwater cultured pearls, courtesy of American Pearl Company. Photos/Rich Mays.
Pearl rings courtesy of Alishan.

Page 6   All jewelry, courtesy of the designers pictured. Falcher Fusager brooch courtesy of Magick. Photo/Jael Fusager. Photographs of Jeffrey Dunningham and Virginia Anderson pieces courtesy of Geoffrey Kudlick for Jewelers of America. Michael Good neck piece, photo by Ted Pobiner Studio. William Richey photo courtesy of the American Gem Trade Association (AGTA) and the *Spectrum* awards committee. Photos/Sky Hall.

Page 7   All jewelry, courtesy of the designers pictured. Photograph of Karen Feldman and Russ Copping pieces courtesy of Geoffrey Kudlick for Jewelers of America. Photograph of Gaia Pelikan rings by Gaia Pelikan.

Page 8   Three-stone rings: top, from private collection of David and Agnes Sarns (design/Carvin French and Antoinette Matlins; photo/Tibor Ardai); middle right and left, from Jonathan Birnbach for J. B. International; bottom, from Fullcut. Classic solitaires: left and right, from Lazare Kaplan International; Diamond Floater® courtesy of Paul Klecka; Tiffany-style from the Diamond Information Service. Ring with tiny channel-set stones from a private collector (design/Carvin French and Antoinette Matlins; photo/Tibor Ardai). Classic round (with tapered baguettes), and oval (with tapered baguettes) rings from Jonathan Birnbach for J. B. International. Heirloom reproductions: left, from Mark Silverstein for Varna; right, from Richard Kimball. Rare vivid yellow emerald-cut ring from Antiquorum Auctioneers. Micro-pavé ring from J. B. International. 18K gold rings from Alishan. Pavé ring from Diana® collection courtesy of Frederick Goldman.

Index

Notes

Notes

Notes

Notes

Notes

Notes

Notes

DIAMONDS: THE ANTOINETTE MATLINS BUYING GUIDE
How to Select, Buy, Care for & Enjoy Diamonds with Confidence and Knowledge
by Antoinette Matlins, P.G.

Practical, comprehensive, and easy to understand, this book includes price guides for old and new cuts and for fancy-color, treated, and synthetic diamonds. **Explains in detail** how to read diamond grading reports and offers important advice for after buying a diamond. **The "unofficial bible" for all diamond buyers who want to get the most for their money.**

6" x 9", 220 pp., 12 full-color pages & many b/w illustrations and photos; index
Quality Paperback Original, ISBN 0-943763-32-0 **$16.95**

Antiques Roadshow™ Book Club Selection

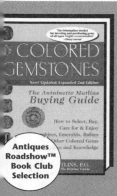

COLORED GEMSTONES, 2ND EDITION:
THE ANTOINETTE MATLINS BUYING GUIDE
How to Select, Buy, Care for & Enjoy Sapphires, Emeralds, Rubies and Other Colored Gems with Confidence and Knowledge
by Antoinette Matlins, P.G.

This practical, comprehensive, easy-to-understand guide **provides in depth** all the information you need to buy colored gems with confidence. Includes price guides for popular gems, opals, and synthetic stones. Provides examples of gemstone grading reports and offers important advice for after buying a gemstone. **Shows anyone shopping for colored gemstones how to get the most for their money.**

6" x 9", 224 pp., 24 full-color pages & many b/w illustrations and photos; index
Quality Paperback Original, ISBN 0-943763-45-2 **$18.99**

Antiques Roadshow™ Book Club Selection

THE PEARL BOOK, 3RD EDITION:
THE DEFINITIVE BUYING GUIDE
How to Select, Buy, Care for & Enjoy Pearls
by Antoinette Matlins, P.G.
COMPREHENSIVE • EASY TO READ • PRACTICAL

This comprehensive, authoritative guide tells readers everything they need to know about pearls to fully understand and appreciate them, and avoid any unexpected—and costly—disappointments, now and in future generations.

Antiques Roadshow™ Book Club Selection

- A journey into the rich history and romance surrounding pearls.
- The five factors that determine pearl value & judging pearl quality.
- What to look for, what to look out for: How to spot fakes. Treatments.
- Differences between natural, cultured and imitation pearls, and ways to separate them.
- Comparisons of all types of pearls, in every size and color, from every pearl-producing country.

6" x 9", 232 pp., 16 full-color pages & over 250 color and b/w illustrations and photos; index
Quality Paperback, ISBN 0-943763-35-5 **$19.99**

OR CREDIT CARD ORDERS CALL 800-962-4544 (8:30AM–5:30PM ET Monday–Friday)
Available from your bookstore or directly from the publisher. TRY YOUR BOOKSTORE FIRST.

Do You Really Know What You're Buying?
Is It Fake or Is It Real?

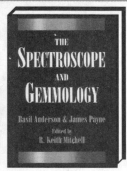

Buy Your *"Tools of the Trade"*...

Gem Identification Instruments directly from *GemStone Press*

Whatever instrument you need, GemStone Press can help.
Use our convenient order form, or contact us directly for assistance.

Complete Pocket Instrument Set
SPECIAL SAVINGS!
BUY THIS ESSENTIAL TRIO AND SAVE 12%
Used together, you can identify 85% of all gems with these three
portable, pocket-sized instruments—the essential trio.
10X Triplet Loupe • Calcite Dichroscope • Chelsea Filter

Pocket Instrument Set:
Premium: With Bausch & Lomb 10X Loupe • RosGem Dichroscope • Chelsea Filter **only $197.95**
Deluxe: With Bausch & Lomb 10X Loupe • EZview Dichroscope • Chelsea Filter **only $179.95**

ITEM / QUANTITY	PRICE EA.*	TOTAL $
Pocket Instrument Sets		
_____ **Premium:** With Bausch & Lomb 10X Loupe • RosGem Dichroscope • Chelsea Filter	$197.95	$ _____
_____ **Deluxe:** With Bausch & Lomb 10X Loupe • EZview Dichroscope • Chelsea Filter	$179.95	_____
Loupes—Professional Jeweler's 10X Triplet Loupes		
_____ Bausch & Lomb 10X Triplet Loupe	$44.00	_____
_____ Standard 10X Triplet Loupe	$29.00	_____
_____ Darkfield Loupe	$58.95	_____
• Spot filled diamonds, identify inclusions in colored gemstones. Operates with mini maglite (optional).		
Analyzer		
_____ Gem Analyzer (RosGem)	$299.00	_____
• Combines Darkfield Loupe, Polariscope, and Immersion Cell. Operates with mini maglite (optional).		
Calcite Dichroscopes		
_____ Dichroscope (RosGem)	$135.00	_____
_____ Dichroscope (EZview)	$115.00	_____
Color Filters		
_____ Chelsea Filter	$44.95	_____
_____ Synthetic Emerald Filter Set (Hanneman)	$32.00	_____
_____ Tanzanite Filter (Hanneman)	$28.00	_____
_____ Bead Buyer's & Parcel Picker's Filter Set (Hanneman)	$24.00	_____
Diamond Testers and Tweezers		
_____ SSEF Diamond-Type Spotter	$150.00	_____
_____ Diamondnite Dual Tester	$269.00	_____
_____ Diamond Tweezers/Locking	$10.65	_____
_____ Diamond Tweezers/Non-Locking	$7.80	_____
Jewelry Cleaners		
_____ Ionic Cleaner—Home size model	$69.95	_____
_____ Ionic Solution—16 oz. bottle	$20.00	_____

Buy Your *"Tools of the Trade..."*
Gem Identification Instruments directly from *GemStone Press*
Whatever instrument you need, GemStone Press can help.
Use our convenient order form, or contact us directly for assistance.

ITEM / QUANTITY	PRICE EA.*	TOTAL $
Lamps—Ultraviolet & High Intensity		
_____ Small Longwave/Shortwave (UVP)	$72.00	_____
_____ Large Longwave/Shortwave (UVP)	$199.95	_____
_____ Viewing Cabinet for Large Lamp (UVP)	$175.00	_____
_____ **Purchase Large Lamp & Cabinet together**	$339.95	_____
and save $35.00		
_____ SSEF High-Intensity Shortwave Illuminator	$499.00	
• For Use with the SSEF Diamond-Type Spotter		
Other Light Sources		
_____ Solitaire Maglite	$11.00	_____
_____ Mini Maglite	$15.00	_____
_____ Flex Light	$29.95	_____
Refractometers		
_____ Precision Pocket Refractometer (RosGem RFA 322)	$625.00	_____
• operates with solitaire maglite (additional—see above)		
_____ Refractive Index Liquid 1.81—10 gram	$59.95	_____
Spectroscopes		
_____ Spectroscope—Pocket-sized model (OPL)	$98.00	_____
_____ Spectroscope—Desk model w/stand (OPL)	$235.00	_____
Scale		
_____ GemPro50 Carat Scale	$174.95	_____

Shipping/Insurance per order in the U.S.: $7.95 first item, SHIPPING/INS. $_____
$3.00 each add'l item; $10.95 total for pocket instrument set.
Outside the U.S.: Please specify *insured* shipping method you prefer
and provide a credit card number for payment. **TOTAL $ _____** **

Check enclosed for $ _____ (Payable to: GEMSTONE PRESS)
Charge my credit card: ❏ Visa ❏ MasterCard
Name on Card _____ Phone (_____)_____
Cardholder Address: Street _____
City/State/Zip _____ E-mail _____
Credit Card #_____ Exp. Date _____
Signature _____ CID # _____
Please send to: ❏ Same as Above ❏ Address Below
Name _____
Street _____
City/State/Zip _____ Phone (_____)_____
Phone, mail, fax, or e-mail orders to:

GEMSTONE PRESS, P.O. Box 237, Woodstock, VT 05091
Tel: (802) 457-4000 • *Fax:* (802) 457-4004
Credit Card Orders: (800) 962-4544 (8:30AM–5:30PM ET Monday–Friday)
sales@gemstonepress.com • www.gemstonepress.com
Generous Discounts on Quantity Orders

TOTAL SATISFACTION GUARANTEE
If for any reason you're not completely delighted
with your purchase, return it in resellable condition
within 30 days for a full refund.

*Prices, manufacturing specifications, and terms subject to change
without notice. Orders accepted subject to availability.
**All orders must be prepaid by credit card, money order or check
in U.S. funds drawn on a U.S. bank.

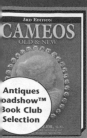
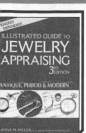
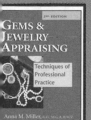

Please send me:

CAMEOS OLD & NEW, 3RD EDITION
_____ copies at $19.95 (Quality Paperback) *plus s/h**

COLORED GEMSTONES: THE ANTOINETTE MATLINS BUYING GUIDE, 2ND EDITION
_____ copies at $18.99 (Quality Paperback) *plus s/h**

DIAMONDS: THE ANTOINETTE MATLINS BUYING GUIDE
_____ copies at $16.95 (Quality Paperback) *plus s/h**

ENGAGEMENT & WEDDING RINGS: THE DEFINITIVE BUYING GUIDE, 3RD EDITION
_____ copies at $18.95 (Quality Paperback) *plus s/h**

GEM IDENTIFICATION MADE EASY, 3RD EDITION:
A HANDS-ON GUIDE TO MORE CONFIDENT BUYING & SELLING
_____ copies at $36.95 (Hardcover) *plus s/h**

GEMS & JEWELRY APPRAISING, 2ND EDITION
_____ copies at $39.95 (Hardcover) *plus s/h**

ILLUSTRATED GUIDE TO JEWELRY APPRAISING, 3RD EDITION
_____ copies at $39.99 (Hardcover) *plus s/h**

JEWELRY & GEMS AT AUCTION: THE DEFINITIVE GUIDE TO BUYING & SELLING
AT THE AUCTION HOUSE & ON INTERNET AUCTION SITES
_____ copies at $19.95 (Quality Paperback) *plus s/h**

JEWELRY & GEMS: THE BUYING GUIDE, 6TH EDITION
_____ copies at $19.99 (Quality Paperback) *plus s/h**
_____ copies at $24.99 (Hardcover) *plus s/h**

THE PEARL BOOK, 3RD EDITION: THE DEFINITIVE BUYING GUIDE
_____ copies at $19.99 (Quality Paperback) *plus s/h**

THE SPECTROSCOPE AND GEMMOLOGY
_____ copies at $69.95 (Hardcover) *plus s/h**

TREASURE HUNTER'S GEM & MINERAL GUIDES TO THE U.S.A., 2ND EDITIONS:
WHERE & HOW TO DIG, PAN AND MINE YOUR OWN GEMS & MINERALS—
IN 4 REGIONAL VOLUMES $14.95 per copy (Quality Paperback) *plus s/h**
_____ copies of NE States _____ copies of SE States _____ copies of NW States _____ copies of SW States

* In U.S.: Shipping/Handling: $3.95 for 1st book, $2.00 each additional book.
  Outside U.S.: Specify shipping method (insured) and provide a credit card number for payment.

Check enclosed for $_____ (Payable to: GEMSTONE Press)
Charge my credit card: ❑ Visa ❑ MasterCard
Name on Card (PRINT) _____ Phone (____)_____
Cardholder Address: Street _____
City/State/Zip _____ E-mail _____
Credit Card # _____ Exp. Date _____
Signature _____ CID# _____
Please send to: ❑ Same as Above ❑ Address Below
Name (PRINT) _____
Street _____
City/State/Zip _____ Phone (____)_____

TOTAL SATISFACTION GUARANTEE If for any reason you're not completely delighted with your purchase, return it in resellable condition within 30 days for a full refund.	*Phone, mail, fax, or e-mail orders to:* **GEMSTONE PRESS,** Sunset Farm Offices, Rte. 4, P.O. Box 237, Woodstock, VT 05091 *Tel:* (802) 457-4000 • *Fax:* (802) 457-4004 *Credit Card Orders:* (800) 962-4544 (8:30AM–5:30PM ET Monday–Friday) sales@gemstonepress.com • www.gemstonepress.com **Generous Discounts on Quantity Orders**

Prices subject to change

Try Your Bookstore First